To Dave,

A wonderful colleague, whose
continuous 'partnership' and friendship
over the years have made a huge
difference to our joint aspirations to
move BL's reputation and relationships
forward – With tons of thanks and
very best wishes, yours ever –

London, 19 December 2013 –

STRATEGIC PARTNERING

STRATEGIC PARTNERING

REMOVE CHANCE AND DELIVER CONSISTENT SUCCESS

LUC BARDIN, RAPHAËL BARDIN AND GUILLAUME BARDIN

KoganPage

Publisher's note

Every possible effort has been made to ensure that the information contained in this book is accurate at the time of going to press, and the publishers and authors cannot accept responsibility for any errors or omissions, however caused. No responsibility for loss or damage occasioned to any person acting, or refraining from action, as a result of the material in this publication can be accepted by the editor, the publisher or any of the authors.

First published in Great Britain and the United States in 2014 by Kogan Page Limited.

2nd Floor, 45 Gee Street	1518 Walnut Street, Suite 1100	4737/23 Ansari Road
London EC1V 3RS	Philadelphia PA 19102	Daryaganj
United Kingdom	USA	New Delhi 110002
www.koganpage.com		India

© Luc Bardin, Raphaël Bardin and Guillaume Bardin, 2014

ISBN   978 0 7494 6880 4
E-ISBN   978 0 7494 6881 1

British Library Cataloguing-in-Publication Data

A CIP record for this book is available from the British Library.

Library of Congress Cataloging-in-Publication Data

Bardin, Luc.
    Strategic partnering : remove chance and deliver consistent success / Luc Bardin, Raphaël Bardin, and Guillaume Bardin.
        pages cm
        ISBN 978-0-7494-6880-4 (hardback) – ISBN 978-0-7494-6881-1 (ebook)   1. Strategic alliances (Business)   I. Bardin, Raphaël.   II. Bardin, Guillaume.   III. Title.
        HD69.S8B372 2013
        658'.044–dc23
                                                                                      2013032121

Typeset by Graphicraft Limited, Hong Kong
Print production managed by Jellyfish
Printed and bound in Malta by Gutenberg Press.

THANKS

Without you, this book of a lifetime would never have existed.

Thank you to BP and Kogan Page for supporting the project; to Iain Conn for his great leadership over the years; to Andrea Abrahams, Verna Stewart, Paul Page and Marc Leppard for their essential contribution; to Kevin Murray and Matthew Smith for their guiding encouragement; to John Seifert for his precious advice.

Thank you to the BP Strategic Co-operations teams, past and present, for their deep expertise, dedication and our complicity over many years.

Thank you to the 30 leading global executives who have provided their invaluable insights to *Strategic Partnering* with considerable impact and generosity.

Thank you to the extraordinary leaders across multiple organizations who, over the last 35 years, have 'gifted' me with their partnership. We have reached mutual 'transformational' value together often and this has happened only through deep personal trust and care. Wherever you are in the world, you have inspired this book and are friends forever.

Thank you to my cherished co-authors, Raphaël and Guillaume, and to Françoise, Clara and Elsa for their infinite love and patience.

Thank you!

ABOUT THE AUTHORS

Luc Bardin

 Throughout his 35-year career, Luc Bardin has been a passionate proponent of strategic thinking and flawless execution across the many relationships and businesses he has led. He has deep experience in the three connected areas of corporate branding, strategic partnering and transforming business value through ground-breaking offers.

A Group Vice President for more than 10 years, Luc has been Group Chief Sales and Marketing Officer of BP plc since 2007. Prior to this, he was a member of BP's Refining and Marketing Executive Team and Chief Executive of various major marketing businesses, of Castrol Europe and of Procurement. He started his career running global businesses in the Burmah Castrol, Hoechst and Pechiney Groups.

Ten years ago, he founded BP's 'Strategic Accounts' division and has been its CEO ever since, building and growing strategic partnerships with passenger and commercial vehicle OEMs, mining, retail, logistics, technology and other leading global institutions. In the last five years, this has included BP's first tier partnership with the London 2012 Olympic and Paralympic Games.

Before BP, Luc headed various strategic co-operations with governments, major corporations, universities and NGOs. Twenty years ago, he also founded a partnership between two cities in France and Germany.

Building deep value-generating partnerships has been at the heart of Luc's career. He is committed to helping organizations and people break through the limitations of vertical silos and, by operating more horizontally and entering alliances, to build different, transformational, strategic value opportunities.

Raphaël Bardin

Raphaël studies Business Administration at École Sainte-Geneviève, France. His exposure to partnerships comes from various work experiences, for example with Ford. He has travelled around the world and spent more than three quarters of his life living in foreign countries. He has also learned about 'One Team' through playing competitive rugby since the age of five, being captain and founding a new team with his brother. Raphaël places partnerships at the heart of his business leadership approach.

Guillaume Bardin

Guillaume studies Medicine at the University of Reims, France. His practice of partnership started very early in life, as he and Raphaël are twins. His work experiences, notably with Hertz, guided him towards partnerships. He has spent most of his life outside France and has been exposed to multiple countries and cultures. He continues to strengthen his partnering practice by playing national level rugby, and is regularly recognized as a players' player. Guillaume wants to specialize in sport medicine, developing deep relationships with his athlete patients.

CONTENTS

FOREWORD

BP has always considered partnerships of critical importance to what we do and who we are.

Our company's mission is to deliver energy to the world. We find, develop and produce essential sources of energy. We turn these into products that people need everywhere. We could not do this without strong co-operations with many other parties around the world.

Central to what we stand for is that we care deeply about 'how' we deliver energy to the world. Above everything, that starts with safety and excellence in our operations. Our approach is built on respect, being consistent and having the courage to do the right thing. We believe success comes from the energy of our people. We have a determination to learn and to do things better. We depend on developing and deploying the best of technology and building long-lasting relationships.

Working well together with others is a defining attribute. By the nature of our operations, be it exploration and production of oil and gas, refining, business to business marketing or retailing, we invest for the long-run in our people, countries, assets and capabilities. This is why, all around the world and throughout our operations, we strive to develop enduring high quality relationships. This includes our dealings with governments, communities, partners, customers and suppliers. We are not perfect but we try continuously to improve in all these areas.

We believe in mutual advantage, where shared gains help to build trust and reward deeper and more valuable relationships. We believe in long-term. We believe in commitments. We believe that partnerships are better able to provide competitive global solutions than through trying to shape the future alone.

Over the last 20 years and as part of this intent, we have looked at how to improve the ways we manage our relationships with some of the world's largest and most influential commercial organizations.

There have been a number of attempts to crystallize the concept of an integrated marketing organization that would have the authority and resource to 'think big' and manage our global customers and suppliers on a joined-up basis. We were not yet thinking in terms of partnerships, just how we could better transact with customers in multiple locations, with multiple product needs.

An approach to bring a more powerful, leveraged and integrated offer to BP's biggest customers started in the late 90s, in an attempt to break down the business unit silos that existed then and clearly left mutual value 'on the table'. There is never a perfect answer to this, and business unit accountability is of huge importance, but we felt we could do better.

Following this and more than ten years ago, we set up an organization known internally within BP as Strategic Accounts. Today, many of our most important commercial strategic relationships are managed through this business function. These co-operations are sophisticated, with an unprecedented focus on close partnering, and bringing innovative, mutually beneficial technology and offers to market.

Several big barriers existed at the start: resources; uncertainty in how to host such a business; identifying the most likely customer segments; and resistance from some quarters. Three big successive mergers were transformational to BP but they did not help an Integrated Marketing approach in the short term.

In 2002, a team was tasked with identifying the global organizations with the most strategic existing and potential commercial links across the new larger BP Group. The initial focus was on customers and certain global suppliers. This was groundbreaking. By early 2003, there was enough proof that additional value from an integrated approach to the best, but not always most obvious, blue-chip organizations was sufficiently material to pursue.

The concept of a Strategic Accounts organization was born and pursued, an operating framework developed and a great team assembled. Partners were selected, internal co-operations established and BP people and businesses were progressively rallied around the concept and practice of strategic account management. The BP Strategic Accounts business and operating models naturally share many common points with those presented in *Strategic Partnering*.

This organization celebrates its 10th anniversary in 2013. It has been a great 10-year journey. Firstly, it has required all involved to epitomize BP's values, today expressed as safety, respect, courage, excellence and One Team. BP's values are deeply in sync with how a strategic partnership organization can best operate.

Second, it has delivered strong results to BP and its partners in multiple forms: enabling better strategic collaboration and prioritization; delivering bottom line growth; and providing a number of industry-firsts, new technology and powerful joint customer offers. The development of extensive and high-quality relationships, in truth, has helped us to contribute to the resolution of some of our partners' challenges and weather some of our own most difficult times.

If I was to describe this partnership model beyond the performance it delivers, I would emphasize the following:

- It works. It requires persistence and discipline but it really works and is positively transformational to the relationships themselves.

- It recognizes and internalizes our own complexity and that of our partners, making access to each other's organizations simpler and more efficient, and therefore making new solutions and approaches possible.

- It leads to remarkably strong relationships, able to withstand challenging times.

- The people involved grow into strong human assets for the organization, from both leadership and functional expertise standpoints and in relationship management.

Being successful at strategic partnership management across a number of dimensions and offers requires deep relationship building. To do so demands acting with a very high degree of internal discipline, a very considered offer development approach, and a more sophisticated set of behaviours as contrasted with key account and other relationship management paradigms.

But embedding a winning strategic partnership model across complex organizations takes time and courage and anybody considering a similar approach should be ready for internal highs and lows, notably in the early days.

In my view, our Strategic Accounts approach has an important role to play in the Group's future. The world has changed over the last ten years and continues to do so. More relationships are international, frequently global, and multi-disciplinary. We will continue to use the capability we have developed to the advantage of both our strategic partners and of BP.

Luc Bardin, BP's Group Chief Sales and Marketing Officer and co-author of *Strategic Partnering*, has been instrumental in setting up BP's Strategic Accounts organization and has led the business continuously from its inception till now, 10 years later. He brings the combination of deep understanding of strategy and relationships and practical experience to this fascinating and value-generating discipline.

I have been privileged to oversee BP's Strategic Accounts at Board level for over six years now and am proud of our strategic partnering practice. It provides real strategic advantage and results in some of the best, strongest and most productive relationships we have globally.

As you might expect, many methods employed and successes enjoyed by BP in the area of partnering are of a similar nature to those in this book content. I very much hope that *Strategic Partnering* is successful and plays its part in helping other organizations to significantly improve their approaches in this important dimension.

Iain Conn
BP Group Managing Director and
Chief Executive Refining & Marketing

01
Introduction: Strategic partnering as a system

No matter how much creativity goes into it, cooking is an art. Or perhaps I should say a craft. It abides by absolute rules, physics, chemistry, etc., and that means that unless you understand the science you cannot reach the art. We're not talking about painting here. Cooking's more like engineering. I happen to think that there is great beauty in great engineering.

ALTON BROWN

This is a cook book! And a recipe for success

How many times in business have you heard an 'interesting' conversation similar to this one?

'Hey Henry, this business is so big and complex we're going to need a strategic partner, and fast!'

'Agreed John, this will be the best way to kill off the competition – but we need to act now: speed will be our key advantage.'

'Okay, I know just the company to talk to and the CEO is a personal friend – should be a walk in the park. He owes me some big favours.'

'Yes, and I've got Phil to lead the deal. He has a self-confidence the size of a planet – no partner will get one over on him.'

'Better include our corporate lawyers in the initial discussions. They'll ensure that the partnership is built on solid ground. Make sure our good friends have no place to hide!'

Strategic partnerships have always been a critical source of business value and are becoming ever more essential in today's connected economy, as organizations and companies become increasingly inter-dependent. This practice is simply massive: commonly available statistics refer to an average of 10,000 alliances formed each year worldwide.

Yet strategic partnering today is a 'hit and miss' process that fails far more times than it succeeds. Actually, studies report that over 70 per cent of business relationships fail over time and less than 10 per cent deliver to or above original expectations. Isn't it time to build on the existing abundant learning, do things differently ... and avoid Henry and John's fatal errors and assumptions? *Strategic Partnering* is designed to help you do just that in a practical, step-by-step way.

We will argue that failure originates primarily when strategic partnering is approached as an art rather than a science, driven by a focus on short-term versus longer-term goals, and treated as 'intuition' rather than a process: the sources of many vain attempts. We present a system, a tried and tested plan of rules and practices, that takes the chance out of the process and can deliver the fabled '100 per cent success' rate in your strategic partnerships.

A great deal has already been written on strategic partnering, but interestingly most of the existing literature is largely centred on 'why' partnerships are so important. Occasionally, organizations and companies, directly or through academia, share actual cases and show us the 'what'. Even more rarely do we find extensive comprehensive and practical analysis of the 'how' of strategic partnering, the practicalities behind the strategy and the methods and techniques required to achieve high rates of success from this essential practice.

A book on the 'how' of strategic partnering

Hence, *Strategic Partnering* is driven by a unique focus on the 'how' of this vital business practice.

It introduces a comprehensive and practical new model of demonstrated methodologies as observed and practised by the authors over 35 years of building and growing successful strategic partnerships. Used in a systematic way, this system will be an essential aid to your own strategic partnering success.

It also provides valuable insights into why 'good management judgement' alone continues to fail in this space. The methods described are applicable to and achievable across a wide range of institutions and businesses, and open up opportunities for further entrepreneurial exploitation. They are enlightened by a number of senior executives from some of the world's leading global organizations in a series of incisive and ground-breaking interviews included throughout the book.

We hope you will find it bold and original, that you will enjoy it and take some benefits from the unique set of partnering techniques presented. As with the greatest recipes, strategic partnering is not just about finding the right ingredients: it is about combining them to greatest effect. Flair and intuition alone are not enough. Success requires discipline and method – so, combine all the elements to fully enjoy our strategic partnering cook book!

Why this book is for you

Strategic partnerships are no longer a 'nice to have'. Entire industries now depend on them to operate, improve performance, accelerate innovation and reduce costs; they are integral to government or business success.

If you are a board member, CEO, senior executive, account or procurement leader, government official, or a manager involved in value-added relationships within your organization, then this book could prove vital to the development of your strategic partnering strategy:

- In many organizations, the board is likely to oversee such deep partnerships – and be ready to judge success or failure. As studies show, strategic alliances formed by companies that have experience in the discipline produce a higher return on equity than any other single activity. The value of these techniques will therefore be a strong asset to any Fortune 1000 board.

- For the CEO and senior executives, it will remove the uncertainty surrounding decisions on their strategic partnering approach, its focus, organization, people and performance management. It will provide a method and a guide upon which to build their organization's own partnering model.

- For the account manager, the relationship holder, the sales person and the procurement leader, the ability to progress beyond a transactional arrangement will make the difference between talking value rather than price, between acceptable and exceptional performance, between average and great remuneration, and between incremental and breakthrough career prospects.

- For leaders and officials of government departments and agencies, as well as local authorities, the ability to work long term across multiple public organizations, internationally or closely with the private sector, is often defining to their performance.

- And it will be useful for business students attending executive education and MBA courses, as the careers of skilled value builders through strategic relationships are often the most exciting, rewarding and fast-growing ones.

The book has a global reach. Our experience is that there is equal and considerable interest across all geographies and cultures around the world, as the language of 'co-operating for success' simply has no borders.

What are strategic partnerships?

The phrase 'strategic partnership' is heavily used (and in many cases over-used), especially in modern business circles. In our personal lives, often the person closest to us is our 'partner'. Language tells us that our most valuable relationships are frequently referred to as partnerships. Ian Davis shares with us the relevance of the concept and how often it is misrepresented.

Ian Davis, former Worldwide Managing Director, McKinsey & Company

"Strategic partnering is a much abused concept. People talk about it a lot, but a lot of what people call 'strategic partners' are neither partners nor strategic; they are relationships of convenience. The taxonomy is confused and it is a big and deep topic. So, point one, when is a partnership a partnership, and then, when is it truly strategic as opposed to opportunistic? At times, people talk about and start believing in a partnership and then it all stops, which can create antagonism. And they say, 'I thought we were partners', but people respond, 'We never were, really'.

So, what are true strategic partnerships, why are they important and why are they very rare? They are rare, because the definition of partnership is when you care about the interests and outcomes of your partners as much as you do yours. In the end, partners have to share objectives, outcomes and mutual gains. Most so-called partnerships don't meet that test of genuinely sharing, genuinely worrying about the interests of the other. You have to think about people in a partnership as an extension of yourself basically!

Defining strategic partnering

So, what are we talking about in reality? Wikipedia, often the first port of call for a definition, defines a strategic partnership as 'a formal alliance between two commercial enterprises, usually formalized by one or more business contracts, but falling short of forming a legal partnership, or agency, or corporate affiliate relationship. Typically two companies or two organizations form a strategic partnership when each possesses one or more business assets that will help the other, but that each respective other can't or does not wish to develop internally'.

In this book, we will use an ambitious perspective of this definition. As suggested by Ian Davis, we believe 'strategic partnering' covers complete enterprise strategies, as opposed to individual projects. Such alliances aim at creating material and even 'transformational' value for the partners across the breadth of their portfolio. They want to position the associates in such a way that a wide array of strategically important opportunities stem from their unique relationship. Hence our main purpose will be to explore how organizations taking advantage of a deliberate strategic partnering approach can utilize other organizations' strengths to make both stronger in the long run.

The critical importance of strategic partnering in today's world

Why are such relationships so central and becoming increasingly more so? At the most basic level, the complexities of the global economy now call for the sharing of competencies and capabilities between an ever growing number of parties. Few if any corporations can exist purely on their own account. Each must cultivate its customers, suppliers, shareholders and trading partners, as well as appreciate the essential role of national interests and local communities.

Accenture analysis reports that when asked in 2011 which operational imperatives became more important during the recent downturn, an impressive proportion of almost 90 per cent of electronics and high-tech executives surveyed said 'developing and enhancing alliances and partnerships'. This was their top priority by a long way!

But only the most successful corporations are able to maintain and strengthen the relationships they absolutely need over time. Arguably, Toyota's success has been grounded in its loyalty and commitment to long-term supply partners. As shared with us by Dr Toyoda, it is no surprise that the whole company regards external partnerships as core to its global success.

Dr Shoichiro Toyoda, Honorary Chairman, Toyota Motor Corporation

I have always believed that both co-operation and competition are essential for ensuring the development of the global economy. It is beyond question that competition drives innovation and economic development. But through deep collaboration and complementing one another, we should pursue the harmonious coexistence of all involved parties and the sustainable development of society as a whole.

We can never achieve sustainable development without addressing the environmental challenges as well. It is the mission of Toyota to supply safe and clean products, thereby helping to create a comfortable living environment and an affluent society. But we can't do this alone.

Internal combustion engines are expected to remain the mainstream of power-train operations for a long time ahead and reducing both energy consumption and CO_2 emissions is crucial. In this regard, we must fully co-operate with fuel companies and material component companies.

Toyota sincerely hopes that it can continue to learn from working closely with these companies, that's my aim.

It could be argued that we have passed an inflection point in the structure of the modern firm. Those companies that have chosen to share and even 'virtualize' into networks of strategic relationships and are doing it well, are out-performing the monoliths at every level of operating and financial performance, from operational metrics to free cash flow to stock market valuations – and notably on ROCE. 'Small and focused' is increasingly more beautiful in the mind of the shareholder, because firms can concentrate on what they need to do uniquely well, optimize the use of their capital, and be more adaptable to market changes. Business today is increasingly about 'access rather than ownership'.

But the practice of sharing or virtualization is fundamentally at odds with the core background, deep capability, experience and often intuitive drivers of leaders, who find it easier and more secure to exercise direct control rather than to rely on co-leadership. Frankly, this is very understandable, given the poor track record of alliances and the different mindset and skills it takes to succeed through sharing. So, how can businesses tackle this dilemma positively and improve performance accordingly?

Why strategic partnering? Beyond 'instant' relationships and benefits

As we know in our domestic lives, real value often lies in achieving positive long-term relationships. In the same way, business relationships must run through a complex set of challenges to achieve longevity or 'strategic partnering'. Real business value arises only when such relationships progress through stages, which we describe as: 'improvement', 'enhancement' and finally, 'transformation'.

Let's get the views of a number of the world's business leaders on the 'what' issue, ie 'What does strategic partnering mean for them, personally and for their organizations?'

Lord John Browne, former Group Chief Executive, BP

To me, it means mutual advantage. It is providing something which is of mutual benefit to both parties, which they couldn't do otherwise and separately. And normally, it is for the long term.

Ian Robertson, member of the Board of Management, BMW AG, Sales and Marketing

Successful partnerships work best between organizations of similar strength, which each have something to gain from working together. The strongest companies in the world are always looking for ways to get even stronger.

John Seifert, Chairman and CEO, Ogilvy & Mather North America

"It starts with an absolute commitment to sharing the most strategic perspective of an organization's objectives, beliefs and priorities from the highest level. Then, the relationship is not simply about buying or selling something. It is about what we ultimately want to accomplish together.

Andrew Mackenzie, Chief Executive Officer, BHP Billiton

"Strategic partnering has considerable potential to improve the returns on both sides. It is an over-used term and I don't think it has actually added anything like the value that it could. For me, a strategic relationship has to be more than balancing out supply and demand through the cycle; it has to be there at all points in the cycle because it helps out our own volatility.

Viren Doshi, Senior Partner at Booz & Company

"It's a commitment to create a win–win situation – to make sure that both partners are more successful together than if on their own. It is technology sharing, it is knowledge sharing – always with a view that you only win if your partner wins. And as Cesare Mainardi, our CEO says: 'Our clients expect exceptional results from us, and we succeed by being integral to their success.'

So what are these strategic, material, unique and long-term mutual benefits and where are they to be found? Actually, there are an ever-increasing number of reasons why organizations and businesses engage in partnerships and their related value networks in order to be successful. As Ian Davis tells us, it is all about access, and more precisely, access to those crucial capabilities that otherwise could not be reached as powerfully, or even at all.

Ian Davis

"When you are truly partnering, you get something that you cannot get through some other form, something unique within your given space. Usually, people partner because they can't get that skill, that access or that relationship through a simpler buy, hire or source approach. So when you are partnering, there needs to be an absolute dependence, or better, a co-dependence.

Arguably, most strategically important 'accesses' fall into one of four main categories (see Figure 1.1):

FIGURE 1.1   Key motives for strategic partnering

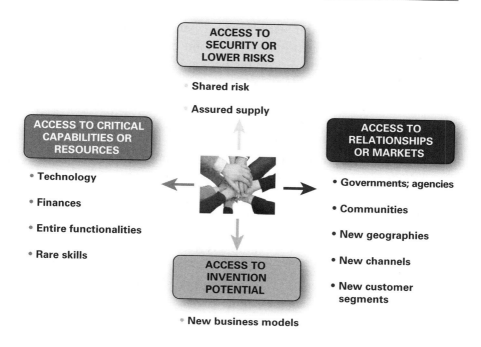

- **Access to critical capabilities or resources,** be it technology, finance, entire functionalities or rare skills.
- **Access to crucial relationships or markets,** be it with governmental organizations, communities, developing countries, channels or customers.
- **Access to higher security or lower risk solutions,** in sharing risks between partners or agreeing long-term irrevocable, progressive supply relationships.
- **Access to invention potential,** to create new business models which organizations could not contemplate or progress on their own.

Later in the book, we will look at the individual components of each of these key motives (Chapter 8) and how accessing these through partnerships can generate extraordinary value for the partners (Chapters 2 and 11).

Partnering examples

For now, let us mention just a few types of partnerships:

- **Provision of public services and infrastructures at scale**, resulting from government–private partnerships. There is a growing demand for more and better strategic partnerships between government and the private sector. Some established and material examples include those with the banking system or infrastructure companies, or those involving cross-departmental partnerships, such as the recent UK NHS healthcare reforms, which encourage integrated working across different sectors, such as health, social care and local government.

- **'Hand-in-glove' combinations of product and service packages**, which take advantage of different companies' competencies. Modern customers and consumers need solutions, not piecemeal answers. The telecommunications sector has spawned a multitude of partnerships such as Sony Ericsson and Nokia Siemens Networks. Another such example is Accenture (which claims 150 alliances) and SAP, which jointly offer integrated solutions to their clients. Or Cisco and its multiple alliance networks, to deliver its commitments to connectivity.

- **'Hand-in-glove' integration of expertise and products**, such as in the aerospace industry, where engine manufacturers and air framers are on the same platforms for clear reasons. Boeing says 'we don't do engines' and GE 'we don't do aircraft', but together 'we create extraordinary flying machines'. Similarly, Microsoft and Nokia co-design advanced smartphones.

- **Complex innovation and supply networks.** In the automotive sector, key technologies result from co-operative joint engineering. Over 75 per cent of the value of the modern Ford car is generated by parties external to the corporation – compared to a mere 5 per cent in the 1930s. The 'made in world' sticker is replacing the 'made in country' variety, with at least 10 companies in 3 different countries directly involved in the manufacturing of an iPhone 5.

- **Virtual supply chains,** such as those that are increasingly common in the IT and fashion sectors. Just look at the way Cisco, Dell, Nike and Benetton run their operations, each employing external manufacturers, distributors and resellers who respond directly to each customer order.

- **Going to market and servicing differently.** Since 1925, Caterpillar has made a commitment to its approximately 220 dealers worldwide, putting them at the heart of its distribution strategy and its primary route to market. Some of these dealer businesses, even though on three months' notice contracts, achieve multi-billion dollar sales annually. Another example is Acer which builds and develops innovative channel partnerships to expand its global reach at pace.

- **Marketing differently**, with companies associating their brands, leveraging each other's channels or cross-fertilizing their customer base. Alliances such as SkyTeam or Star Alliance offer major long-term benefits to their airline members. Hertz's strategic partnerships with Ryanair, Air France and Relais & Chateaux are other examples of going to market differently as is the Nike–Apple co-operation in digital marketing, designed to boost direct sales of iPods in the 'running' segment.

- **Providing differently**, to continuously improve security of supply, product quality, integrated supply chain efficiency and to allow better management of price cycles together. The strategic alliance between leading consumer marketer Nestlé and leading cereals manufacturer General Mills now spans over 20 years. Japanese steel manufacturers have enjoyed 30–35 years of deep relationships with their iron ore supply partners, such as Rio Tinto. Major fuel users such as FedEx or international airlines develop sophisticated long-term integrated supply plans with global fuel suppliers.

- **Inventing differently.** Small biotech or software companies lead the research into breakthrough solutions or products with the support of, or for, bigger firms such as Pfizer, Novartis, Schering-Plough or Dupont. These major multinational firms then take these breakthroughs to the global market.

- **Simplifying complex corporate structures** through aggressive outsourcing and out-tasking of non-core activities. Oil companies such as ExxonMobil and Shell directly employ a mere 25 per cent of all staff associated with their complex global operations, respectively around 77,000 and 87,000 people. The rest are employed by contractors and outsourcing partners. And this percentage is continually increasing, as companies purpose themselves ever more on their core role and competencies.

These are just a few examples of using a partnering approach to do things differently and in fundamentally better, more impactful and efficient ways. As government missions, business services and consumer offers become more sophisticated all the time – encouraged by the power of personal aspiration and the multiplication of channels such as the internet – the need for more varied and complex partnerships is escalating rapidly.

But are these existing or desirable partnerships taken as far as they can go? Are organizations determined and fit to make partnerships a systematic source of success, differentiated capability and competitive advantage? Is every government leader or business professional today well equipped to engage and excel in this relatively unrecognized management competency? The answer is largely no – but our practical experience and analytical tools may prove instrumental to reverse this reality and help organizations and individuals tackle the opportunities and challenges presented by strategic partnering.

Why do strategic partnerships so often fail to deliver their full potential?

If a strategic partnership at work or home is key to our well-being and success, why do we so often fail to create such enduring and successful relationships? Well, as is the case with most things that are important in life, only a few people ever receive a formal education in how to avoid the many pitfalls involved in building deep interrelations. Having gained some 35 years' experience studying, implementing and rationalizing strategic business partnerships, we would suggest that adopting a 'common sense' approach is not enough in itself to guarantee success.

There is considerable consistency in the views expressed on why strategic partnerships often do not work, or if they start well, why they do not continue successfully, or remain constrained to one 'source of value' (SoV). These limitations are reflected with remarkable clarity by our world leader interviewees in Figure 1.2.

FIGURE 1.2   Critical impediments to success with strategic partnering

Not transcending individuals and letting the partnership depend on a CEO, a CFO	Ian Davis
Making decisions for short-term gains rather than long-term prosperity	John Seifert
Not making the effort to align the different levels in the company	Tom Albanese
Not preparing hard enough to understand what the other is	Viren Doshi
Not standardizing around a model as a way to do it for large opportunities	Mike Glenn
Not enough trust to truly release and share knowledge or disclose data	Takeshi Uchiyamada
Putting self-interests too much in the front and not help the other at all times	Frank Williams
Selecting partners who are not culturally able or deeply trustworthy	Shelly Lazarus
Missing a really fantastic account manager and truly delegate	John Browne
Letting conflicts or issues get overlooked, letting the relationship be put at risk	Jeff Immelt
Not agreeing and planning the route to get to the shared goal	Ian Robertson
We live in a suspicious world, so the risk is to lack transparency	Andrew Mackenzie
Lacking one of a same vision, mutual respect, loyalty or commitment	Martin Sorrell
Not identifying the right topic, or too small a one, to lead to a win-win	Wolfgang Reitzle
Not positioning trust- and confidence-based relationships as the most important	Shoichiro Toyoda
Not getting the right people: senior, confident, deep listener, asking questions	Peter Foss
Selecting a partner lacking competence, judgement or integrity	Kevin Murray
Start partnering without clarity on common goals or mutual benefits	Michael Johnson

Let's attempt to group these impediments to success into a few thematic threads. Unsuccessful partnerships:

- fail to develop a clear enterprise partnering strategy intertwined with the broader organization's strategy;

- neither have nor develop a true partnering culture, and partners notably remain self-centred and lack a long-term view;
- lack a comprehensive model and a disciplined set of processes, both strategic and operational;
- do not develop the right organization, leadership practices and people;
- simply do not work at it hard, deeply and long enough;
- fail to make the right partner selection;
- ill-define partnering value and 'performance', or make the measures of success self-centred.

Do any of the above look familiar? If so, please continue reading!

How does a strategic partnership work and succeed?

Creating a successful relationship will require the removal of these impediments. But simply avoiding the pitfalls will not necessarily guarantee success. There are a number of critical requirements to ensure good fortune, as suggested in Figure 1.3.

Building on these invaluable insights, and bearing in mind the learning gleaned from strategic partnering practices in many organizations and companies, success seems dependent on ensuring the following fundamentals:

- partnering is a fully integrated part of the culture;
- it is central to strategy and partnership design is an important facet of strategic planning;
- it has become an integral way of operating;
- practices are codified, widely available, and underpinned with learning experiences;
- partnership assessments are integral components of the performance cycle;
- the organization's public narrative has clear examples of 'heroes' and symbols of successful strategic partnerships.

FIGURE 1.3 Critical requirements for success with strategic partnering

Care as much about the interests of your partner as you do about yours	Ian Davis
Be ready to share the most strategic perspective of your organization	John Seifert
Act and build it on the ground, at commercial level, at strategic level	Tom Albanese
Considerable preparedness and a deep understanding of the other	Viren Doshi
Use executive sponsorship and don't let a set-back undermine the whole	Mike Glenn
Support people willing to take a risk and to develop something new	Takeshi Uchiyamada
Ensure partners buy into the same vision and a clear common purpose	Sebastian Coe
Start with trust and ensure it is never violated	Shelly Lazarus
Provide something of mutual benefit and which can't be done otherwise	John Browne
Share risk and reward. If times are tough for the other, do the extraordinary	Jeff Immelt
Like in a marriage, maybe there is more tension in a good partnership	Ian Robertson
You need an ethos of that sort of relationship in your organization	Andrew Mackenzie
Think and operate more horizontally, to bring the whole organization to it	Martin Sorrell
Greater advantage for one partner is OK, provided the other's is also deemed adequate	Wolfgang Reitzle
Develop trust-based, confidence-based long-term relationships	Shoichiro Toyoda
You need the right people: senior, confident, deep listener, asking questions	Peter Foss
Ask yourself about the need for contracts and negotiations in lieu of trust	Kevin Murray
It is certainly a process, needing consistency, a plan and monitoring	Michael Johnson

Does this look like a demanding set of requirements? Actually, and as we will discuss later in this book, success in strategic partnering does not demand perfection in every aspect of the 'system' from day one, but rather the achievement of some minimum threshold in each. Instead, it requires a model and the application of processes that will leverage the organization's strengths and mitigate its weaknesses in the partnering arena.

How to approach strategic partnering

Many of us will advocate that successful relationships are based largely on personality or 'personal chemistry'. A sort of 'personal magic', which might not work for others but does in our own case … after all, most of us select our life partner on a highly intuitive basis. Can this 'intuition' alone be the right basis for a successful 50-year relationship?

A comprehensive process

Contrary to our best human endeavours, we advocate that successful business partnerships are not built on intuition or 'gut feel'. In fact, looking at the impediments to and then the key requirements for success (see Figures 1.2 and 1.3), it all comes down to applying disciplined, clear and enduring methodologies. Indeed, we would assert that successful partnerships are the product of meticulous planning and execution and require deep analysis and the application of relevant expert techniques. Nothing should be left to chance!

In an interview given by Jeff Immelt, Chairman and CEO of General Electric, to the *Harvard Business Review* in June 2006, he draws us in this direction. In the article titled 'Growth as a process', Immelt argued for a set of new management techniques to reliably generate high levels of sustained organic growth. The article depicted a six-part process for growth, which is used by GE's managers to strategically and practically support accelerated growth. Interestingly, the six parts are: customers, innovation, technology, commercial excellence, globalization and growth leaders, with a critical role for 'One GE', enterprise selling and brand across all six. Immelt noted that each part was valuable in its own right but they were mutually reinforcing and it was the six parts together as a system that made the process truly powerful. As for setting up the model, Immelt argued that it is iterated until the point when, even if not perfect, it is adopted as 'the' process and used consistently across the organization.

A thorough and disciplined 'strategic partnering' system

This is precisely what we advocate in order to succeed with strategic partnering. Indeed, the partners need to ensure they have compatible backgrounds and aspirations. Enduring business relationships are based on carefully orchestrated steps where rigour and consistency are crucial. Friendly conversations on the golf course can never achieve the same outcomes as a formal and disciplined approach; they are only one ingredient in the whole recipe.

These methodologies are not all intuitive or straightforward though. Even more crucially, putting them into practice across the breadth of complex organizations is the true challenge. That is what this book aims to do: define good and best practice and demonstrate how to apply it effectively.

So, let's get into the system. You've got the key ingredients. It's time to cook!

Key areas of the strategic partnering system

We believe that successful partnering requires the development and use of thorough planning techniques, and an engagement and execution model supported by rigorous analysis. As such, our strategic partnering system entails a number of key components, as shown on Figure 1.4, with 'clarity' the golden rule at all stages.

FIGURE 1.4   Core components of the strategic partnering system

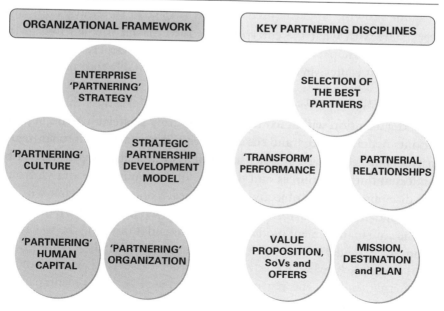

Reflecting the 'must have' and 'must avoid' issues raised by our interviewees in Figures 1.2 and 1.3, the 10 core areas of the system come under two main pillars:

- **A supporting organizational framework:** ie what the enterprise needs to possess or develop to be successful with strategic partnering (see left-hand side of Figure 1.4). This entails: an enterprise partnering strategy; a partnering model and associated processes; a partnering organization; carefully selected partnering people; and above all, a partnering culture.

- **A focus on a few core strategic partnering disciplines:** ie what the people involved need to concentrate on doing very well, to make the organization successful with strategic partnering (see right-hand side of Figure 1.4). This includes: selecting the right partners; building extraordinary relationships; forming a clear mission, 'destination' and plan for the partnerships; developing compelling value propositions and 'sources of value' (SoVs); and using a best-in-class 'performance' management model.

Let's consider these areas with more granularity, and use the analysis to introduce the chapters of the book.

A strongly supporting enterprise organizational framework

Let's start with what the enterprise needs to master if it is to perform well at strategic partnering, which we believe rests largely with the five components represented on Figure 1.5.

Setting up an enterprise partnering strategy: Chapter 2

Any organization will need to be clear on how strategic partnering fits into its overall strategy and the importance it wants to give to strategic partnerships compared to other forms of association. This will start with understanding the sources and the scale of the value to be drawn from the discipline, the real objective being to reach and achieve what we call and will define as 'transformational' value. It will also require a decision on the core management model, our recommendation being the so-called 'leadership model'. Chapter 2 deals extensively with these enterprise-level concerns.

FIGURE 1.5   Strategic partnering system: Organizational framework

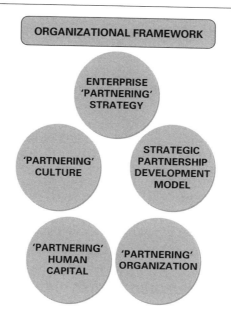

Designing a '100 per cent success' strategic partnership development model: Chapter 3

'Strategy is implementation' here and practical mechanisms are at the heart of turning ideas and aspirations into reality. As noted earlier, we do not believe enduring success can be achieved from partnering without a comprehensive, clear, well-defined and supported development model! Specifically, Chapter 3 will present a gated 5-stage/15-step model to develop strategic partnerships with a '100 per cent success' objective.

Establishing a winning strategic partnering organization: Chapter 5

We believe that a successful strategic partnering approach requires a clear organizational philosophy with an associated set of principles. In Chapter 5, we will propose some critical organizational guidelines, and how not to get them wrong from the very start. We will also reflect on the steps for establishing a 'leadership model' type organization.

Developing world-class strategic partnering human capital: Chapter 6

Who do you need on your team? Like most things in life, partnering is about people, and nothing could be more important when you are seeking long-term business relationships. The road to success demands exceptional individuals: those who can articulate the partnership mission and plan, and both lead and participate in its thorough execution. In Chapter 6, we will examine who should be in the team and the conditions required to assemble truly extraordinary partnering human capital.

Epitomizing culture to drive strategic partnering success: Chapter 12

Our world leader interviewees refer extensively to culture, as they consider the obstacles to and key requirements for successful partnering. We will reflect on culture in the final chapter of the book, integrating every element required for success into the organization's DNA.

The key strategic partnering disciplines

Now moving from the total enterprise down to its teams and individuals, we would argue that success with strategic partnering is predicated on mastering the five core disciplines shown on Figure 1.6:

FIGURE 1.6 Strategic partnering system: Key partnering disciplines

Selecting the best strategic partners: Chapter 4

As you would expect, selecting the right partners is imperative. They are often chosen because of their scale, reputation, existing links or business, even social relationships between leaders. These need to be complemented with or replaced by a thorough examination of the high-level objectives and goals, culture, attributes and capabilities of any potential partner. In Chapter 4, we will cover processes, criteria and learning required to make the right choice of partners.

Building extraordinary partnerial relationships: Chapter 7

Extraordinary relationships do not guarantee the success of strategic partnerships but they do act as essential and powerful enablers. As individuals, we tend to be confident in our ability to build great relationships – but do we really have this skill? And of course, building and sustaining high quality relationships between complex organizations is a very different kind of challenge to creating individual social ones.

Experience suggests that extraordinary relationships, at both organizational and personal levels, require careful planning so that they are based on clear and mutually beneficial outcomes, structures, mechanisms and processes. They need close nurturing and constant monitoring of their evolution over time. This set of key practices will be discussed in Chapter 7, providing the firm foundations for successful partnerships.

Forming a clear strategic partnership mission, 'destination' and plan: Chapter 8

Establishing the 'Why this strategic partnership?' with ultimate clarity is critical, from both partners' perspective. By 'destination' we mean the ultimate aim and range of 'transformational' outcomes of a strategic partnership. As such, the 'destination' towards which a partnership should progress needs careful and deliberate thought. Because humans are by nature impulsive, we need to be highly objective about what we want to achieve with the partner and why they are able to fulfil these objectives now, mid- and long-term by bringing their own distinctive capabilities. This clarity is central to the idea of strategic partnering, as the modern organization is ever more ruthlessly zeroing in on the few key competencies that define its competitive success, and relying on others to provide non-core though absolutely necessary functionalities.

Moreover, our potential partner has multiple departments and hundreds or thousands of influencers. They are of course successful, otherwise why bother considering them. In designing our 'destination' for the partnership, we need to identify the right 'hooks' or 'bait' to be as attractive to them as they are to us. This is how we firm up the 'why' and 'what' of the partnership, the sources of real and enduring substance and value to be generated from the association.

Developing compelling partnership 'value propositions', 'sources of value' and 'offers': Chapter 9

In designing the partnership's 'destination', we will need to 'cut the elephant into slices', ie not rush headlong into a general, complex and all-encompassing approach. Instead, preparation involves breaking down and then progressing in turn the foundations on which the strategic partnership is based (eg technology, new business model, etc) into individual value drivers and SoVs for the interested parties.

As we are dealing with large and complex organizations, we will establish a hierarchy and explore the relative importance of these SoVs. Every engagement will have a carefully defined 'value' and 'offer' associated with it that will be acknowledged by the recipient audience. One size does not fit all in this respect, except for two main principles:

- work as hard as necessary upfront to develop clarity on the SoVs;
- consider everything through the eyes of the partner, not simply your own.

'Navigating' towards a successful strategic partnership: Chapter 10

With a clear 'destination', a set of tangible 'hooks' and 'offers', and the right partnering team, we are ready to develop a rigorous campaign of carefully designed steps, to win over our target, on terms that will mature into a solid and enduring relationship. The emphasis here is on assembling a comprehensive map of the partner's organization and navigating in an orderly and skilful manner through its people.

Partnering is a lengthy journey and the key is to avoid becoming bogged down in process or distracting relationships. We will reflect on how to approach the right people first, those who will truly know, inform, influence and decide on the targeted partnership. A comprehensive approach to 'navigating' the partnership will be the focus of Chapter 10.

Boosting 'performance' with strategic partnerships: Chapter 11

As a strategic relationship may take many years to fully mature, signs of success are progressive and require time to develop. The foundation of any strategic partnership should be grounded in the delivery of deep and material 'value', in whatever legitimate form best represents the 'destination' that is being pursued. The partnership team is best placed to define and own the targets for enterprise success, as well as to develop the adequate tools to measure this success.

It is only by applying some clear and sometimes untypical principles to 'performance' management that 'performance' delivery itself becomes a strong strategic enabler to success – and we cover this best practice in Chapter 11. One of these principles is to allow the benefits of partnering to be retained in the organization's business areas and verticals who participate in the alliance, thus ensuring their full buy-in and active participation.

Counter-intuitive but vital!

Of course, the 'formal' approach taken in presenting the system goes hand-in-hand with sharing a set of empirical 'rules' and 'little' secrets that we see as vital for partnerships to be successful. Here are a few examples, some of which may feel somewhat counter-intuitive:

- **Don't talk to your partner ... at first:** Initially, don't talk to or visit your potential partner or, in a broader sense, even your customer. The priority is to develop clarity about your own objectives for the partnership, and study the intended partner in great depth but in isolation from them. It is important to ensure that this is a one-way exercise and as comprehensive as necessary at the start, so that you only engage when ready and when you have a clear 'destination' and plan.

- **Don't run, but rather walk to extraordinary value:** Once you engage in the relationship, do not declare your long-term intentions too quickly. Keep these unstated until both partners are in a position to clearly see and agree to the aspirational 'destination', or you may risk damaging your prospects from the word 'go'.

- **Be 'thoughtful' about your CEO's role:** As a CEO or a senior executive yourself, or as a leader in the partnering team, be deliberate about how you do or do not involve yourself, the organization's CEO or senior executives in the development of a strategic partnership. As the respected public face of your organization, CEOs are the best trump cards you have. But they have little time available and will need to take a rapid view of the proposition; they may be eager to announce a 'brilliant' deal fast; almost all will approach it at a high level and 'strategically', as opposed to focusing on the deeper and less visible 'make or break' details of the alliance.

- **Avoid negotiations at all costs:** Strategic relationships are built on progressive, continuous and day-after-day interactions and discussions held across multiple levels or 'silos'. Negotiations where one partner deliberately tries to 'win over' the other need to be replaced by a process that builds familiarity and creates a sense of mutual progress.

- **Let's not bundle:** Often strategic partnerships will span multiple SoVs and business silos. None of these will become stronger, better or more legitimate because another SoV elsewhere is perceived as big and successful! So other mechanisms need to be used to put the full weight of the organization behind each desired SoV, rather than bundling them together and carrying the risk of cross-subsidizing.

- **When it comes to 'affairs of the heart', make sure you manage communication carefully:** Big public announcements will not only inform your competitors: they could lead to your partner being courted aggressively by others. Better to keep communications discreet and on a need-to-know basis, as 'strong facts will speak louder than words'.

It may sometimes feel counter-intuitive to follow these suggestions; but they are based on the experimental evidence of many successful partnerships. You should expect to come across many others in this book, presented with the intention of replacing established practice with disciplined and fit-for-purpose methods capable of driving success.

Shall we get ready to succeed with strategic partnering?

If any or all the above questions appear to be sensible and worthy of application within your own organization, please continue reading this book ... and start winning today. As you read ahead, keep the basic tenets to hand. And in summary of this introductory chapter, here is a synopsis of the core approaches to consider to secure success with strategic partnering:

Summary: Strategic partnering as a system

- Articulate a clear enterprise partnering strategy, and a considered operating model and related processes. Only rigour and logic can build a truly sustainable basis for long-term strategic partnerships.

- Apply the system in its entirety, from the selection of the best partner to forming a clear plan, before you even think of engaging in discussions with the target partner. You alone need to be the chess player, the guardian and owner of the 'end game'.

- Articulate and codify the SoVs across and for each of the organization's vertical silos, as well as the underpinning 'offers' required to deliver value to both parties. Assess if and how they meet the broader set of stakeholder interests.

- Map and navigate your campaign carefully, so that you win over each relevant layer or vertical silo of the partner's organization, using 'hooks' or 'offers' that have relevance there.

- Keep egos out of the picture. Choose team members very carefully, who bring specific capabilities, demonstrate deep humility and exude unlimited resilience. There are no quick wins in this game.

- Value delivery from the strategic partnerships will become increasingly material year by year. Don't skim over any of the deep and disciplined methods to develop the co-operations. It is depth of understanding and rigorous execution over time that will get you and your team to the finish line, to 'transformational' value.

Let's leave the final introductory words to Lord Browne:

John Browne

In the end, making it work well is about consistent application. So, having set out the framework well, it is consistently applying it and then building the trust. Sometimes, you will have to say (and as a leader you can say this for a big company), 'Well look, it is only a couple of million and we just have to swallow that'. People will then say, 'Well, two million is a lot of money'. The answer to that is, 'Well, yes it is, but actually I am dealing with a long-term analysis of the problem'. So I think that it is consistency, it is remembering you have to take the rough with the smooth, it is actually looking to the long term.

You also need a really strong partnership manager who looks after the relationship and is there and talking the whole time. The leader will at best focus in and focus out on one of the many things that are happening every day and if you are lucky, you might get 10 minutes of their attention. Or, you will get their attention for a particular problem or an initiative. But between times, quite correctly, the partnership has to be delegated to someone to run, and they need to be run, they really need to be run.

So this is strategic partnering as a system with its complete set of processes – not simply as intuition or an art! And as with cooking, it is through the careful blending of the right ingredients and processes that you will achieve a five-star dish.

02
Setting up an enterprise partnering strategy

Good is the enemy of the great.

JIM COLLINS

Say what you do; do what you say.

ISO 9001

This is a cook book ... so let's start cooking!

We are clear on just one goal: we want to produce an outstanding meal to share with friends. But we have no kitchen, no menu and are not organized for it.

As mentioned in Chapter 1, the provision of public services and business offerings is changing dramatically as the world becomes infinitely more connected. Both complex and smaller public and private organizations need to focus and specialize on core disciplines of excellence. They cannot afford to chase success down a countless number of avenues, and increasingly need to rely on their 'ecosystem', notably partnerships and (arguably) strategic partnerships, to develop high performance value networks.

As shown in Figure 2.1, even in the heartland of marketing, the famous '4 Ps' – product, price, place, promotion – are outdated and are being progressively replaced with four new Ps – purpose, presence, proximity, partnership. And these new '4 Ps' are deeply connected with, and relevant to, strategic partnering!

FIGURE 2.1 Marketing's '4 Ps' move towards partnering

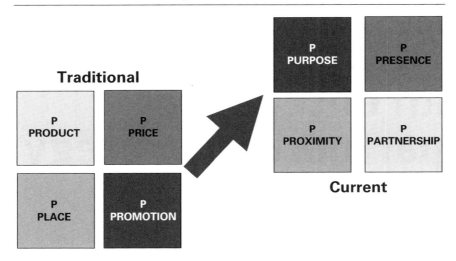

Consequently, enterprises increasingly need to form a clear and deliberate partnering strategy, as a prerequisite for developing specific co-operations. This chapter focuses on the three pillars that form the basis of an enterprise partnering strategy:

- **The enterprise's 'destination' and the level of value** we are aiming to achieve from strategic partnering. Drawing on our cooking analogy, how exceptional can and should the meal be?

- **The examination of alternative options to strategic partnering,** to access and provide the skills, assets or resources the organization lacks. Should the business acquire and merge, procure ... or partner? Back to our meal, should we cook it all ourselves or ask each of our guests to prepare and bring one element of a course?

- **The consideration of alternative management options** for developing a successful enterprise partnering strategy. Will we be cooking alone or creating and coordinating a kitchen team?

If we were to compare an enterprise partnering strategy with a journey, these three pillars would represent, respectively: Where are we going to? Which is the best way to reach our destination? Which vehicle will get us there most effectively?

Aiming for 'transformational' value

In Chapter 1 (see Figure 1.1), we discussed key motives for strategic partnering, which fall into four main categories: access to critical capabilities or resources; access to crucial relationships or markets; access to higher security or lower risk levels; and access to an unparalleled invention potential. Within each of these areas of motivation for partnering, different types of relationships, partnerships or strategic alliances can yield very different levels of reward, referred to as 'partnership value'.

'Improve', 'enhance' and 'transform' partnership value

Figure 2.2 illustrates the hierarchy of partnership value at three main levels: 'improve', 'enhance' and 'transform', each with their own dynamics, requirements and outcomes.

FIGURE 2.2   Strategic partnering aims at 'transformational' value

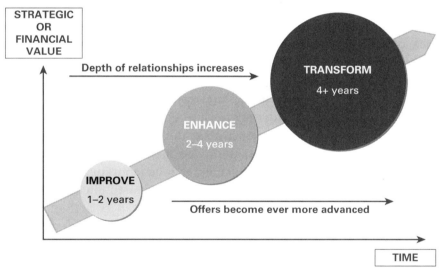

'Improve'

At the lowest end of the scale, many organizations focus on 'improving' relationships with their stakeholders. This translates into more sales to their customers, higher service levels from their suppliers, more efficient transactions with both more stable licence to operate from their hosting communities, and so forth. It is a valuable and rewarding effort, to be systematically encouraged to deliver low-hanging fruit fast. This is the 'improve' value, with a typical delivery cycle of one to two years.

'Enhance'

With a more integrated approach and longer-term efforts, organizations can access 'enhanced' value. Relationships evolve into partnerships and the involved parties are deliberate about their deeper and wider intent. Customers become global accounts, suppliers become first tier, hosting communities become guides and advisors, value chains are studied thoroughly and jointly, and systematically enhanced. The benefits of 'enhance' can be up to five times more than with the 'improve' approach, and the usual delivery cycle is two to four years.

'Transform'

This is the purpose of this book: how to access 'transform' value. As we will see in Chapter 11, Figure 11.3, 'transform' brings 10 or more times the value of an 'improve' strategy.

The difference between 'improve', 'enhance' and 'transform' lies essentially in the extent to which we change the paradigm and practice of building relationships and interfaces between the involved parties. What characterizes most interfaces between people and organizations is the lack of deep understanding of the other's drivers and business model. But in 'transform', the partners take a fully integrated view of the joint space they are considering, as if they were one single organization. Each partner works hard to understand the other parties' business model and drivers, so that they not only manage the interface more effectively but 'transform' the way they operate at this interface to deliver much greater value. These deep, mutual 'transformations' revolutionize their way of selling, procuring, operating and collaborating, unleashing massive 'transform' value at and from the transfigured interface.

An example of 'Improve', 'Enhance' or 'Transform'

Let's use the example of an interface between an automaker (OEM) and an energy provider. We will continue to use this illustrative case later in the book. Evidently they need each other, as engines use fuels and fuels will only sell if vehicles burn them. This said, the historical relationship between the two sectors has been at best transactional and quite often at arm's length, not to say challenging at times. There were deep-seated reasons for this friction, most notably the attempt by each industry to avoid some of the considerable and occasionally unproductive commitments on hardware and infrastructure arising from constantly changing regulations, by pushing parts of the task to the other party.

At the same time, essential joint technical work and close customer/supplier relationships occur between them, which continue to motivate the development of partnerships. The area of product technology illustrates 'improve', 'enhance' or 'transform' value options from their joint activity:

- 'Improve' arises from the need to clarify product standards. In this case, the OEM develops a precise product specification, which the energy supplier is tasked to match in every technical and commercial respect, hopefully to deliver 'improved' assurance and savings.

- Some OEMs and energy companies build on this base work and move up to 'enhance'. In this approach, the partners develop product specifications jointly, optimizing the potential of both the engine and the energy source, which now operate as one system. Clearly, this delivers material 'enhance' improvements and 'performance' at the engine–energy interface.

- They seldom reach 'transform'. In this approach and with the ambition to progress to 'transform', both parties would engage in co-engineering. The OEM would share its intended engine design at a very early stage, and the energy company their product options. The parties would then optimize their respective product design and compatibility, using each other's considerable knowledge and resources. The value to each would be immeasurable, reaching new levels of energy efficiency and product differentiation with the final solution.

Aiming for portfolio-wide 'transform' value

The example above illustrates what the majority of the most successful partnerships and alliances are about and what they manage to achieve, which is to change their approach to their partner, interface with them in one area of their portfolio and integrate their activities to achieve better results in this particular area. This activity may be important, but it is just one part of the overall opportunity.

So, could the combination of strategic intent, encouragement from earlier successes, great relationships, trust and confidence spur organizations on to further collaboration? In the example above, partners could have coordinated the marketing of their new jointly designed products, hence 'transforming' another of their interfaces (marketing) for mutual benefit and advantage to their respective customers. They could also have jointly talked to regulators about how to bring these innovations to market more quickly, hence 'transforming' a third interface (advocacy).

This portfolio-wide 'transform' value is what strategic partnering is all about. And it is clearly associated with considerable reward.

Ian Robertson

"We have to keep raising the bar. Our customers' expectations increase constantly, but they are not always ready or able to pay extra for the latest technology. Therefore, our challenge is constantly to search for innovative technologies which can meet our customers' needs and desires, but without increasing costs – or even at lower costs. We live in a competitive world and targets are constantly moving ever higher. It's like the old adage that when you finally attain the summit of the most challenging mountain, the view is of an even higher peak. So, we have to challenge ourselves constantly and also challenge the partner companies we work with, because otherwise, we won't be successful.

Accessing 'transformational' value is extremely hard to achieve. It requires a long-term joint aspiration and relationship based on trust. It needs enterprise-wide thinking and a bold innovative approach from the parties involved. It requires partners to make choices and accept risks, if only on sharing secret developments and changing long-held business models. It involves intimate joint working between multiple parties in each organization. None of this would happen or repeat consistently across organizations without a determined and disciplined process. It is this partnering approach and its mechanisms designed to deliver success that we are exploring in this book, and here are some insights from Ian Davis:

Ian Davis

"It takes time, and money, and patience, all these things. And you have always got to ask the commercial question: 'Is it worth it?' And that is about the purpose. If the purpose is big enough and the 'destination' is attractive enough, then you have got to spend the time, you have got to spend the money, you have got to manage the tough years with the good. Otherwise, this is not a strategic partnership. If you can't validate these questions, the partnership may not be worth it. And that's when you shouldn't develop a strategic partnership type of relationship. But at other times, if you say, 'we're in trouble if that relationship breaks down', then it's worth it!

Six main sources of 'transform' value

As presented in Chapter 1 (see Figure 1.1) and discussed above, the key motives for strategic partnering are to access skills, resources or decisions which could not otherwise be obtained. Gaining such access can lead to strategic and material 'transform' value. We will now focus on and describe some of the most frequent and important sources of 'transformational' value. They are presented in Figure 2.3 and introduced below in increasing order of complexity and reward for the partnering organizations.

FIGURE 2.3   Six main sources of 'transformational' value

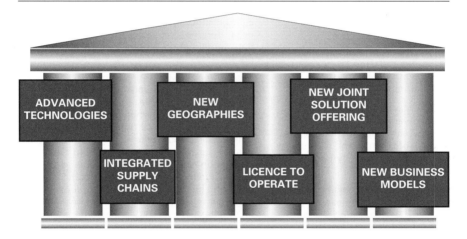

1. Advanced technologies

Together with customer and supplier management, advanced technologies is the one area where the greatest number of co-operative projects between different parties are being developed. In fact, studies report that over 50 per cent of all partnerships are driven by technology and innovation.

These partnerships may have multiple purposes, from gaining access to new technology, working together on connected and converging technologies, integrating hardware and application know-how, or developing new products requiring multi-sector expertise. There are countless examples covering all sectors: the automotive, railway and aerospace industries with their component manufacturers; equipment and engineering companies with their client sectors; the whole digital, IT and communications industry, as in the EMC example below. They can be private–private, as well as public–public and, very often, public–private technology partnerships.

FIGURE 2.4   Success through building a technology eco-system

EMC: Collaborating in the cloud

One of the hottest stocks in the 1990s – EMC Corp, the world's largest provider of enterprise data storage platforms – fell from grace when the dot-com bubble burst. Today, however, EMC is back, reaching for the stars.

Thanks to the company's 2001 decision to abandon its go-it-alone approach in favour of collaboration and partnership, EMC has not only dramatically broadened its product portfolio. It has also become a leader in the provision of cloud computing technologies – what CEO Joe Tucci calls 'the biggest wave in the history of information technology.'

Since 2002, EMC has bought more than 40 software, hardware and IT services companies, at the same time expanding its business network of channel and technology partnerships – and leveraging synergies between the two.

One of the company's key acquisitions was an 80 per cent stake in California-based VMware, which specializes in virtualization software that offers flexibility and cost savings by running multiple computer systems on one physical machine.

Meanwhile, a joint venture with Cisco, dubbed VCE, bundles EMC storage gear, VMware management tools, and Cisco networking and computing products with dedicated Internet hosting services. Yet another partnership, this one with Dell, helps provide the data center servers to support EMC's Atmos cloud platform. EMC has also developed its own cloud technology, VPLEX, which allows organizations to combine storage within their data centers into a single, virtualized storage pool.

The company owes much of its success in cloud computing to work carried out by RSA Laboratories, which became part of the EMC Innovation Network when EMC acquired RSA Security in 2006. Since then, EMC Research China, which also works on cloud technologies, has been established. And in keeping with the Innovation Network's motto – 'Expand knowledge locally; transfer it globally' – the company ensures that the work of local researchers, who are often located near leading universities, is shared (via teleconferencing and social media) with colleagues globally, and especially with those responsible for product development.

SOURCE: Accenture, *Outlook*, 2011 no 1

These co-operations are usually among the most natural and productive ones: engineers like engineers and they talk and work quite genuinely with each other. The parties involved usually exchange resources and knowledge to achieve valuable outcomes. As reflected in our earlier example involving automotive and energy companies, the main question lies with the true strategic nature, depth and repeatability of these collaborations. In most cases, technology co-operations are limited by how ready the parties are to share their data and knowledge. Organizations can also be reluctant to restrict themselves (some would say lock themselves in) to working with specific partners and risk losing some access to the rest of the industry, to IP ownership and exploitation, etc. There are, therefore, many more joint technology projects than true technology-led strategic partnerships, so many more cases of 'improve' or 'enhance' rather than 'transform' relationships. There is an opportunity here!

2. Integrated supply chains

Together with advanced technology, supply chain integration is the area of greatest frequency of partnerships. As organizations and firms constantly drive towards focusing on core activities where they can truly differentiate themselves, and also aspire to the highest levels of efficiency, they simultaneously attempt to reduce their direct involvement in non-core activities, particularly where they do not have superior capabilities. Business process outsourcing (BPO) and IT are major examples of this common reality.

There are tens of thousands of such supply chain-led partnerships around the world. With suppliers, they manifest themselves most frequently in the form of extensive outsourcing agreements. With customers, it is about providing services, solutions and functions that fulfil integral components of their own offering and supply chains. With channels, it is about putting sales, supply or servicing in the hands of customer- and consumer-facing partners.

The main issues and challenges lie in how profoundly and thoroughly this supply chain integration is approached. The following questions highlight the key success factors:

- How far does one go with true outsourcing or even full integration? Doing this well requires deep trust and transparency, developing joint external benchmarking systems, etc, a practice casually referred to as 'opening the kimono'.

- How deeply would the partners share and integrate their business models? The exercise is not only about immediate cost savings, but gets them to act 'as one' over a very long period of time.

- How much capability is retained and constantly developed within the outsourcer, in order to lead a continuous joint cycle of improvement with the provider? It is very common to find that bringing in entire parts of the supply chain from outside leads companies to lose most of their capabilities in the outsourced domain. This is imprudent and bad business and a true partnership should hold to and develop a strong 'demand' capability.

Research shows that the simple and fundamental disciplines meant by these questions are seldom applied, leading to disappointing mid- to long-term outcomes, high levels of risk and limited enduring value generation, most times restricted to 'improve' and only occasionally reaching 'enhance'.

3. Rapid entry and large-scale expansion into new geographies

As the world continues its fast and furious transformation, with China's GDP projected to surpass the euro area and India's GDP to surpass Japan's in a year or two (OECD, *Looking to 2060: Long-term global growth prospects*, 2012) the race is on for companies to create a strong and competitive presence in the new economies, both to follow their global customers and also serve the fast-growing local leaders and consumers.

This often requires the creation of capability, supply chains and physical assets at pace and scale. Strategic partnering uniquely enables this quality and rapidity, whilst critical mass is quickly built through risk sharing. Examples include car and truck manufacturers, who 'localize' their network of component manufacturers; mass retailers, who expect their key category captains to play their full role in support of their developing networks; resource companies who require their engineering partners to replicate their service consistently across all geographies, etc.

Entering and establishing a strong presence in a country very often requires local, knowledgeable partners with extensive and high-quality access into the country's decisional ecosystem. They will know who to talk to, how to set up and run operations in the country's regulatory context, where and how to mobilize resources and knowledge. There is a profusion of such arrangements across all sectors.

A strategic partnering approach can offer the required pace and scale, as it uniquely provides the risk and reward sharing and a long-term perspective. For example, by committing to a critical mass of business and openly agreeing the related business terms, the party seeking market entry offers sufficient incentives to ensure their partner accepts the risk in return for the reward. A less strategic, non-partnership-led approach would risk resulting in arms-length and self-centred decisions and provide neither momentum, nor the critical mid- to long-term approach.

Dr Francisco Garcia Sanz, Member of the Board of Management, Volkswagen AG

Sharing an example of great strategic partnering, in 1991 Volkswagen started working with a supplier of small metal stamping parts. Nowadays, we work very closely with this supplier and its 40 production sites in more than 15 countries. Over that period of time this supplier developed into one of the world's leaders in hot-forming technology.

The mutual trust in the developing relationship was fostered by Volkswagen continuously awarding business on the one hand and this particular supplier making high levels of investment on the other hand. Moreover, this supplier aligned his global strategy with Volkswagen perfectly, following us into new and challenging markets such as India and Russia. This supplier also turned a problem of two bankrupt companies, with the associated high risks of supply shortages, into an opportunity to expand business with Volkswagen. To sum up the relationship in two words: this supplier is a true 'global champion'!

4. Enabling or enhancing licence to operate

Increasingly, federal governments, local authorities and communities play a defining role in the ability of businesses to develop strategies and significant projects. In the mining and energy industries, long-term trustful partnerships are key to mutual success. Companies such as BHP Billiton, Rio Tinto, Anglo American, BP or Shell partner with local authorities on comprehensive community and infrastructure development plans, rather than dealing with industrial operations only. The construction industry and companies such as the Berkeley Group in London pride themselves on developing 'decade-long partnerships with local authorities, from the Mayor or Chief Executive down'.

Licence to operate can be deeply enabled or limited by regulatory standards. Experience suggests that businesses do not always have a great sense of politics, while governments and agencies do not have detailed expertise of the business areas for which they create frameworks and rules. Developing trusted relationships over long periods of time, setting up a structured dialogue, sharing mutual information and underpinning these interactions with science and facts, can go a long way to improving both the regulatory environment and the outcome of actions taken. Industries as diverse as the pharmaceutical, communications, energy, defence, gambling and other sectors rely fundamentally on their partnering ability with states and agencies. In the United States, the OSHA Cooperative Program is an interesting and untypical example of such an approach.

FIGURE 2.5   Example: US Department of Labor – OHSA Strategic Partnership program

UNITED STATES
DEPARTMENT OF LABOR

SEARCH

A to Z Index | En español | Contact Us | FAQs | About OSHA

OSHA   OSHA QuickTakes Newsletter   RSS Feeds   Print This Page   Text Size   ≡ **Was this page helpful?**

Occupational Safety & Health Administration   We Can Help   What's New | Offices

Home   Workers   Regulations   Enforcement   Data & Statistics   Training   Publications   Newsroom   Small Business   OSHA

OSPP Tips

The OSHA Strategic Partnership Program (OSPP) provides the opportunity for OSHA to partner with employers, workers, professional or trade associations, labor organizations, and/or other interested stakeholders. OSHA Strategic Partnerships are formalized through unique agreements designed to encourage, assist, and recognize partner efforts to eliminate serious hazards and achieve model workplace safety and health practices. Each OSHA Strategic Partnership establishes specific goals, strategies, and performance measures to improve worker safety and health. OSHA Strategic Partnership models include those focused on improving safety and health in major corporations/government agencies, at large construction projects, and for entire industries. The OSPP is available to private sector industries and government agencies in locales where OSHA has jurisdiction. Visit OSHA's Cooperative Programs Page for more information on OSHA's other cooperative programs.

Winter Storms
Quick Links

 Program Information   **Partner Information**

- What is an OSHA Partnership?   - Current Partnerships
- How to Propose A Partnership   - National Partnerships
- Frequently Asked Questions   - Regional Partnerships
                                             - By Industry/Emphasis
 Policy and Guidance   - Partnership Signings
                                        - Partnership Closures
- OSHA Strategic Partnership Program for Worker Safety   - Partnerships in the News
  and Health Directive (CSP 03-02-002)
- Clarification of Verification and Exemption Policies for   **Success Stories**
  Construction Participants
- Policy Memorandum #1 - Clarification of OSHA Strategic   - Success Stories
  Partnership Enforcement Incentives - July 27, 2012   - Template [DOC - 75 KB]

- Complete Listing of Partnerships
- Frequently Asked Questions
- OSHA's Strategic Partnership Program Fact Sheet [PDF* - 22 KB]
- Partnership Brochure [PDF - 81 KB]
- Regional Partnership Coordinators
- Use of OSPP Logo
- Preventing Fatal Falls in Construction
- OSHA Compliance Assistance
- OSHA We Can Help Worker Resources

Search All Strategic Partnerships

 Partnership Program Impact

Search   Clear
[Search Tips]

Current Active Partnerships as of December 31, 2012

Since Partnership Program Inception as of December 31, 2012

Accessibility Assistance: Contact the OSHA Directorate of Cooperative and State Programs at 202-693-2200 for assistance accessing DOC and PDF materials.

*These files are provided for downloading.

Freedom of Information Act | Privacy & Security Statement | Disclaimers | Customer Survey | Important Web Site Notices | International | Contact Us

U.S. Department of Labor | Occupational Safety & Health Administration | 200 Constitution Ave., NW, Washington, DC 20210
Telephone: 800-321-OSHA (6742) | TTY: 877-889-5627

www.OSHA.gov

United States Department of Labor, https://www.ohsa.gov

5. New joint solution offerings

The opportunities for new business development and differentiated solution offerings are the greatest and also the least developed outcomes of strategic partnering. Because without deep process and a long-term view, organizations find this hard to do!

Look at smart grids, the 'energy internet'. Here, the name of the game is to bring integrated products and solutions to market, while continuously innovating around new technologies. There are multiple components and parties to the solution, including utilities, providers of automation software and intelligent electronic hardware systems to control transmission and distribution grids, expert testing companies, etc. Reaching the finish line is a team game and no organization will do it alone, hence the need for partnerships. IBM, Microsoft and SAP build multiple alliances. Cisco alone has entered into dozens of partnerships to help with its ambition to be a leader in smart grid networking, including those with Itron, Elster, Alstom, Eaton and OSloft to name just a few.

Smart grids are of course not the only advanced solution or product which require partnerships to come alive. Interestingly, collaborations between effective but cash-strapped governments and the private sector continue to grow rapidly, to deliver essential services in face of the current funding crisis. As we meet with public institutions at conferences or speaking engagements, we remain impressed with their considerable interest in strategic partnering, its mechanisms and best practices ... and the considerable opportunity for improvement going forward.

6. New business models

The world is changing quickly and so are business and individual aspirations. Professionals and consumers increasingly want 'all-in-one' solutions, which can only come from multiple parties joining up their respective areas of excellence. By deploying the best of their technology, logistics and routes to market in an integrated way, they can quickly transform the traditional ways of offering or using products or services.

Books and music shops are being replaced by Amazon and its supply and logistics ecosystem; and so are multiple categories of commerce. TVs are being replaced by tablets and smartphones, with hardware manufacturers, network operators, search engine firms and content developers integrating their expertise and assets to provide infinite and flexible offers.

These business breakthroughs or new solution offerings need to be developed co-operatively and require true partnering, intimacy and trust, co-creation, integration, and multiple forms of joint risk taking. These are all part of the strategic partnering business model, which when applied well, will achieve the Holy Grail of top-line growth at 'transform' levels.

Strategic partnering should combine all 'transformational' opportunities

And what if some organizations decide to fundamentally shift their business model, to make strategic partnering their primary axis for participating and winning? Together with others, and creating mutual dependency, they would develop advanced technologies; take these advanced solutions or new offers to market; achieve industry-leading cost efficiency and service performance through integrated supply chains; join forces to develop leadership positions in new territories or market segments; and finally provide integrated science-based inputs and points of view to their regulatory partners. They would not look at the world as an individual organization any more, but as an ecosystem and as a team.

Figure 2.6 represents how a systematic and best-in-class strategic partnering approach, providing new and high-quality access to the four

FIGURE 2.6 Key motives for partnering and main sources of 'transformational' value

ACCESS TO / TRANSFORMATIONAL VALUE	CRITICAL CAPABILITIES OR RESOURCES	RELATIONSHIPS OR MARKETS	SECURITY OR LOWER RISKS	INVENTION POTENTIAL
ADVANCED TECHNOLOGIES	✓		✓	✓
INTEGRATED SUPPLY CHAINS	✓		✓	
NEW GEOGRAPHY ENTRIES	✓	✓		
ENHANCING LICENSE TO OPERATE	✓	✓	✓	
NEW JOINT SOLUTION OFFERING	✓			✓
NEW BUSINESS MODELS	✓	✓	✓	✓

categories of partnering resource (horizontal axis) can yield deep 'transformational' value across all six critical areas of partnering importance (vertical axis). It also shows that combinations of multiple partnering resources and capabilities are required to deliver any of the areas of 'transformational' value. This simple diagram illustrates how a deliberate, comprehensive and systematic partnering approach with third parties might be able to fulfil most of the key needs of a modern organization powerfully and efficiently.

By exploiting this strategic partnering methodology, organizations can get this magic to happen. As trust, knowledge, mutual understanding and joint 'performance' improves and expands, the ability and readiness of partners to broaden the partnership and explore unchartered territories grows further. These dynamics should motivate and reward an enterprise's portfolio-wide partnering approach, yielding extraordinary 'transform performance' outcomes.

When to adopt strategic partnering over other forms of association

Strategic co-operations are of course not the only form of possible association between organizations that can deliver a value-added combination of capabilities. As Ian Davis shares with us, there are many other relationship-based options and practices, which we briefly consider and assess here.

Ian Davis

You need to be very analytical, very purposeful and structured about what you mean by a partnership and what you are partnering for? And of course, why choose partnership over other options? Because the other options are important and there are a lot of them – joint ventures, alliances, buying arm's length, vendor, rent, hiring, consultants, agency. And what are the pros and cons of each methodology? Partnerships and strategic partnerships become much more meaningful when you look at them in the context of other forms of relationship. Relationship is a key word here in terms of other forms of co-operations. So why is it a better one?

Relationship-based association options

These relationship-based associations fall into various categories, each representing a different level of integration. They are presented here from the highest to the lowest degree of control:

- **Equity-based control:** an organization can take full control of another through merger or acquisition. It can also acquire a majority or minority equity stake. In these cases, it frequently happens that the equity owner will coordinate the use of capabilities and actions of the other party, reflecting a full or very high level of control. This scenario is considered to be 'high command' and permanent.

- **Cross- or shared equity:** two or more organizations can take cross-participations by purchasing a level of each other's stocks. They can also invest in and share ownership of a joint venture, which is a jointly-owned legal entity to deliver a focused objective for the benefit of its parent organizations. Alternatively, companies may enter into co-operatives, a coalition of organizations with joint management of their resources. These approaches are 'high mutual control' and very valid forms of strategic partnering.

- **Strategic partnerships, alliances or cartels:** two or more organizations share a connected or complementary mission and manage significant natural interfaces. They agree a meaningful value 'destination' and each has access to and uses some of the others' resources, capabilities and knowledge in accepting a certain level of dependency. Funding, resources, and information are shared, whilst strong linkages are built and formal or informal commitments are made for at least several years. The level of control is predicated on the strength of the partnering model, the processes being used and the mutual interdependency created.

- **Franchising, licensing:** a party grants rights to others in its areas of strength – brand, offer, technology, know-how, etc – in return for benefits, usually royalties or fees. The relationship can be quite hierarchical, with most of the control exercised by one party over the others. In some cases, there is greater mutuality and the relationship can become a true partnership, occasionally a strategic partnership.

- **Market-driven relations:** most commercial relationships are essentially arms-length transactions between organizations, such as sourcing, service arrangements, selling, consulting, distributing, etc. Nowadays, even transactional interactions usually include some level of collaboration, in an attempt to optimize quality, costs, time responsiveness, etc for the involved parties. These are modest but useful relationships, usually delivering 'improve' levels of value. They can be short or medium term, as the know-how associated with the 'improve' value is fully owned by the parties, gets quickly commoditized and is therefore easily transferable to any similar but alternative relationship.

Carefully selecting your optimal relationship approach

These relationship-based association options are all appropriate and each applies best to particular cases. Hence, as Ian Davis suggests, it is advisable and even required to consider other relationship options before electing for strategic partnering, as organizations should always go for the simplest and most productive model for their circumstances. In Figure 2.7, we can see how DaimlerChrysler used to represent their perspective of the options and hierarchy of relationships.

FIGURE 2.7   The hierarchy of relationship stages at DaimlerChrysler

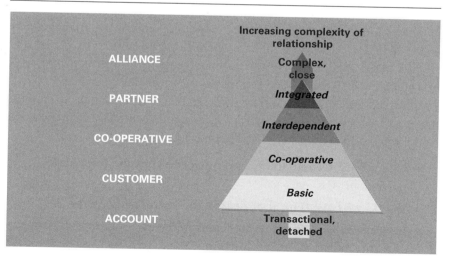

With these options in mind, it would appear that strategic partnerships are most appropriate when the following criteria apply to potential associates:

- same or connected scope and mission;
- existing complementary resources and capabilities;
- a mutual voluntary basis;
- distinctively able and successful organizations;
- a similar status (thus eliminating the acquisition option);
- a relationship-based culture and experience.

Hence, in many instances, partnerships – and arguably their most advanced and successful form, strategic partnerships – are the best and even the only real option for building truly value-added relationships. Interestingly, a lot of these criteria apply to competitors and some of the most successful alliances are indeed created between rivals, eg in the automobile, energy, IT, communications and airline sectors.

Management options for strategic partnering

There is considerable strategic and financial reward potential in succeeding with strategic partnering. But it does not seem easy to partner well with many organizations, who constantly fail to access the partnership value. We would argue that the root cause for this failure is the absence of a disciplined and precise partnering model, based on simple and powerful principles and related processes.

These fundamentals include an adequate enterprise management framework for partnering and its related operational routines. In this chapter, we consider the enterprise management options available and will come back to the related organizational guidelines in Chapter 5.

When setting up or developing their strategic partnering programmes, the most frequent questions which CEOs and executives ask themselves – and which often elicit very wrong answers – gravitate around:

- where does accountability and power lie for our strategic partnerships?
- should we have central or distributed partnership teams?
- how should we structure the teams in terms of number of people, seniority, location and so forth?
- what is their role and activity in relation to the organizational verticals, such as departments or business units?
- what is their role and activity relative to other horizontals, such as functions or regional/national organizations?

In essence, these and other questions centre around the balance between global integration (the horizontal) and business/local autonomy (the vertical).

Sir Martin Sorrell, Chief Executive Officer, WPP

"We are still very vertical. Our budgeting systems and our incentive systems, for example, are still mainly vertical. But about 30 top clients represent a third of our business and they are critical. We need client leaders to represent and grow them, working across different WPP agencies. Similarly, we can't approach every country from London or New York. We may need a country head to be there 24/7, instead of people from the verticals coming every four weeks. So working horizontally is going to become more important, which can be controversial as you can imagine. The essential idea is that clients can be exposed to all 165,000 of WPP's people instead of 1,000 or even 20,000.

There are as many variations of strategic partnering management set-ups as there are institutions or firms. But they almost inevitably fall into one of the three broad frameworks shown on Figure 2.8 and designated respectively as the 'coordination', 'integration' and 'leadership' models.

FIGURE 2.8   Three management options for strategic partnering

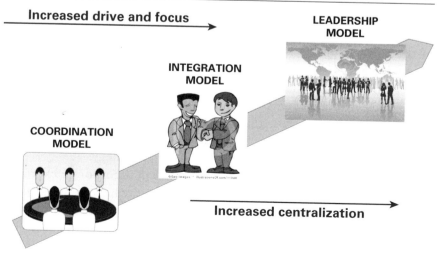

Increased drive and focus

LEADERSHIP MODEL

INTEGRATION MODEL

COORDINATION MODEL

Increased centralization

The 'coordination' model

The thrust of this approach is primarily to ensure a central point of contact and to show a consistent face and approach to the partner. The main objective is to create a favourable context in which the organization's vertical units can operate, facilitating their access to the partner so they can develop their individual relationships and business, mainly silo to silo. The main partnering activities are about enabling relationships, notably with the partner's central management and functional operations, and facilitating best practice sharing, both with the partner and within one's own organization. This approach only requires limited 'central' human resource and triggers little or no change in structure, as the coordinator(s) of the partnership is/are often part of the leading vertical business or functional area between the parties.

This model is often used when the need and value from centralization is limited compared to the value from incremental distributed activities. It leaves most of the power to the verticals – business units and regional organizations – and gives limited influence to the individual(s) assigned to coordinate the partnership. It is used extensively for the management of regional accounts, important suppliers and local governments. The typical business cycle is one to two years, within which tangible mutual value should be noticeable and delivered. Its outcome is generally 'improve' value.

The 'integration' model

This is a hybrid, a pure matrix model, where a combination of central and deployed resources leads the set-up, development and management of the partnerships. It is made clear to the partner's organization and internally that the central team holds the authority for the co-operation's strategy, the central functional joint initiatives and the corporate relationships. Their main activity is to ensure momentum and support progress of the joint projects across the partners' involved organizational silos. They have veto rights on verticals, business units or national initiatives in case they conflict with the overall partnership strategy.

In the majority of 'integration' models, a senior corporate executive has accountability for a dedicated partnering unit, which includes all the central individual partnership teams. In this model, each such partnership team is small, and the majority of the partnership's human capital is deployed 'locally' in the verticals, business units or regions. Ideally, the distributed partnership managers have a dotted reporting line into the partnership's central leader.

This model is mainly used when SoVs are well known and do not require strong innovation, but when central leadership provides consistency, scale and efficiency in rolling out best practice, technologies, products or solutions across multiple geographies or businesses, all at scale and pace. It remains the critical task of the vertical entities to tailor the offering and delivery to the local context – although as little as required – and leverage the central coordination to create mutual value 'locally'.

This framework is used extensively by complex and usually global institutions and businesses, which co-operate with partners to achieve targets in supply or client positions. They want to define solutions centrally with their partners and ensure flawless execution across their complex operations, without much reinvention 'in every village'. Examples include mass retailers and their category captains, the auto industry and their first-tier component providers, the downstream energy businesses with their air, marine, defence customers, the healthcare industry and their agency partners, etc. The typical business cycle is two to four years, within which material mutual value should be delivered, generally at 'enhance' levels.

The 'leadership' model

Here, extensive and ultimate accountability for the partnerships is held by a central team. It does not mean that the matrix disappears, as the verticals, business units and country organizations retain accountability for the physical 'local' delivery, and central functions such as research and development, public affairs and manufacturing remain controlled elsewhere.

But the central team has formal authority over what defines partnering: the co-operation strategy, the core value propositions, the governance and relationship management, the main deals, the standards of execution and the active monitoring of 'performance'. It also has the authority to mobilize resources and chair joint workstreams, ensuring that strategic goals are being progressed and momentum is being maintained.

The central team reports to a senior corporate executive accountable for the enterprise's strategic partnering programme and includes both central high profile and deployed resources. Interfaces with the business units and regional organizations are well codified and processed, with verticals operating within the parameters set out by the partnership central team.

This is the model for excellence and far-reaching 'transform' value objectives. Its typical business cycle is over four years, with the first years of the partnership delivering 'improve' and 'enhance' value, on the way to achieving 'transform' ambitions.

Typically, global service providers such as IBM, Accenture and Booz & Co use this model extensively and successfully, as they need to 'transform' their clients' practices all the time across very complex multi-business, multi-geography structures.

The 'coordination', 'integration' and 'leadership' models compared

Figure 2.9 below summarizes and compares the key attributes and some of the respective merits of each of these frameworks. This will hopefully be of some help when you design your own enterprise partnering system and decide on its management approach.

FIGURE 2.9   Partnering management models and their impact

MANAGEMENT MODEL IMPACTS	COORDINATION	INTEGRATION	LEADERSHIP
VALUE DELIVERY	IMPROVED	ENHANCED	TRANSFORMATIONAL
IMPORTANCE	LOCAL	HYBRID	CORPORATE
ROLE TO PARTNER	RELATIONSHIP	DRIVING	DECISION
IMPACT ON ORGANIZATION	LOW	MEDIUM	HIGH
COST	LOW	MEDIUM	MEDIUM HIGH
TEAM SET UP	DEPLOYED	SHARED	CENTRAL
CENTRAL TEAM AUTHORITY	INFLUENCE	VETO	DECISION
BUSINESS CYCLE	1–2 YEARS	2–4 YEARS	> 4 YEARS

Conclusion: 'transformational' value goes with the 'leadership' model

This chapter has made a start at defining our enterprise's strategic partnering value 'destination' and management framework. The organization and operating frameworks and their underlying principles will be defined in greater depth in Chapter 5, which will also outline the respective roles of the central partnering teams relative to the vertical business units and countries. Chapter 11 will describe value and 'performance' management in more detail.

Clearly, all of these management models are adequate in their own way, each being suited to particular types of enterprises, partnering objectives and circumstances. Any can be used, as long as they are codified and practised as a coherent, well-defined and disciplined approach.

> **Peter Foss**, former President, Corporate Accounts, General Electric
>
> "So it is really about an organization that is willing to reinvent itself and will let some people cause that to happen by building a different way of interfacing with large partnerships and opportunities. You need a vision for what the partnership wants to accomplish. Then it might need to break down some functional barriers and get through some separate agendas. Because the people running the individual businesses, and they are doing a nice job, have their own agendas and it is sometimes very difficult to work your way across. So in this world to try and work as a boundary-less organization, knocking down functional barriers and getting rid of separate agendas, I think you have to drive towards very clearly defined goals, use clear measurements that are mutually agreed upon and, in the end, deliver tangible results.

But each of these models will distinctively underpin a different partnering strategy and lead to very varied outcomes. 'Good is the enemy of great' here and we say this in the belief that success with strategic partnering aims at 'transformational' value, which in turn goes with the 'leadership' management approach. Extraordinary 'performance' could be attained so much more frequently, if this magic combination were applied with clear vision and with the right determination and discipline!

Let us summarize the conclusions to be drawn from this chapter.

Summary: Setting up an enterprise partnering strategy

- Set your enterprise partnering 'destination' as 'portfolio-wide transformational value'.
- Aim for a 'destination' that combines advanced technologies, integrated supply chains, new geographies, enhanced licence to operate, new solution offering and new business models.
- Select strategic partnering over other forms of association, eg equity-based or arms-length relationships, when it is the best fit.
- Reach 'transformational' value through a 'leadership' management model.
- Define and apply your own but clear 'leadership' model to manage partnerships.

Continuing with our cooking analogy, we have now determined the quality we are aiming for in our outstanding meal; we have a kitchen and an infrastructure; and we are organized enough to begin cooking. Clearly these are important steps and, like our two friends below, we are making progress on getting closer to our grand meal.

FIGURE 2.10 'Transformational' value from strategic partnering

In the next chapter, we move from enterprise portfolio-wide partnering to individual strategic partnerships. Our purpose will be to offer a systematic model on how to develop strategic co-operations consistently and step by step, and as we do so, move value from low to extraordinary levels!

03
Designing a '100 per cent success' strategic partnership development model

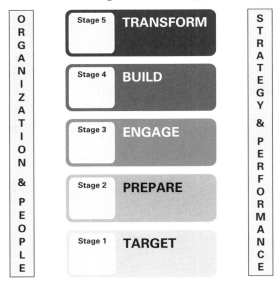

The Strategic Partnership Model

ORGANIZATION & PEOPLE

Stage 5	**TRANSFORM**
Stage 4	**BUILD**
Stage 3	**ENGAGE**
Stage 2	**PREPARE**
Stage 1	**TARGET**

STRATEGY & PERFORMANCE

Life is a road, not a destination. You reach your destination by walking in that road.

LAO TZU

S etting up and growing the strategic partnerships necessary to succeed in our global, complex and multi-competency world should be based on scientific method and analysis, rather than intuition and 'gut feel'. Here is Jeff Immelt on the importance of a process:

Jeff Immelt, Chairman of the Board and Chief Executive Officer, General Electric

If you run a multi-business company like GE and you are trying to lead transformative change, that objective has to be linked to hitting levers across all of the businesses – and it must keep that up over time. So you have got to have a process. That is true from an internal standpoint, but it is also the only way you get paid in the marketplace. Investors also have to see it is repeatable. I knew if I could define a process and set the right metrics, this company could go 100 miles an hour in the right direction.

In Chapter 2, we established that, at enterprise level, winning with partnering requires us to develop a collective strategic intent and a consistent management approach. We now want to address the individual strategic partnerships within the partnering portfolio and how to develop them in a consistent manner, usually starting from a small base to reach material 'transform' value. There are no short cuts, and meticulous planning and execution are needed.

In our experience of building dozens of such partnerships, diligently applying a stage-gate model invariably leads to one outcome: success. Relying on a more random, intuitive approach leads to an equally likely result: disappointment or failure.

Ian Davis

The idea of bringing a process, some sort of science, some systematic thinking, whatever you want to call it, to strategic partnerships is very valuable. It is even a big idea, as it extends to all sorts of external relationships, including for example supplier/vendor relationships, which are often not well managed.

The mindset of system, discipline and process, the principles of clarity of purpose and alignment, the build-up of respect and mutual dependence are all true and relevant to many sorts of relationships, of which strategic partnerships are one form.

It is our objective in this chapter to lay out an individual strategic partnership development model in its entirety, and invite leaders, practitioners and readers to use it and test its validity. The following chapters will explain the successive critical components of this approach.

Our model of strategic partnership building consists of a set of distinct and well-defined stages and steps that are infinitely repeatable across many types of organization and sector. The process incorporates rules and sequences that should be applied consistently at all times. It is the disciplined application of each of these steps in sequence that enables a prospective relationship to develop into a fully established strategic collaboration and deliver extraordinary mutual value, with an extremely high probability of success.

Winning through the five key stages model

Our strategic partnership development model can be broken down into five main stages, which are schematized in Figure 3.1.

FIGURE 3.1 Strategic partnership model: 5 key stages

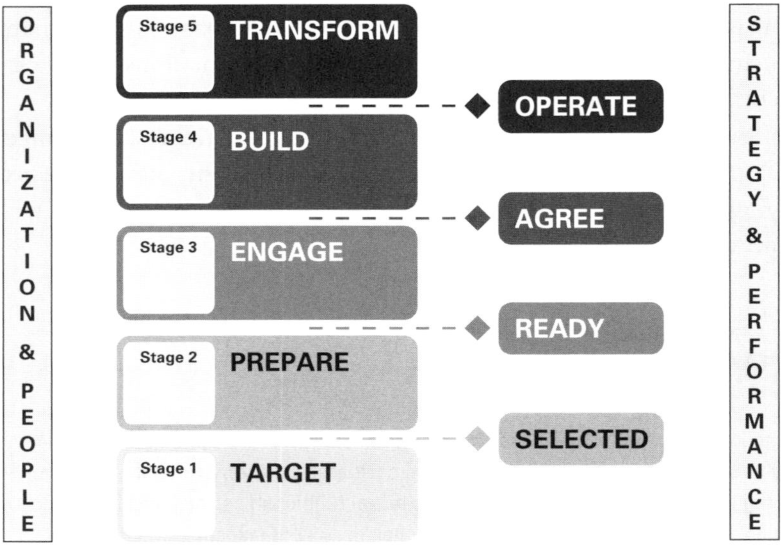

Stage 1: Target

The journey starts with considering and assessing an organization, a government, an agency, an account or a supplier as a potential strategic partner, through a coherent set of 'lenses'. This approach includes scoping the attainable value from the envisaged collaboration. This initial and critical stage can last up to 18 months, given the rigour and number of iterations required. It results in the selection of strongly qualified target strategic partners.

Stage 2: Prepare

The accountability to manage the relationship with the prospective target at enterprise level moves to the organization's strategic partnering central unit. And the first level of dedicated human resources is recruited into this team. This stage includes building tactical experience and 'performance' credentials through a number of 'demonstration' activities run with the partner, designed to deliver 'improve' value. It culminates in a well-defined and tested 'destination' for the potential partnership, an internal strategic co-operation framework (SCF) and a co-operation plan. This stage can last three to six months.

Stage 3: Engage

This is the time for deliberate engagements held for the first time with a strategic intent. The hypotheses developed during the previous 'prepare' stage are now tested with the target partner's organizations, based on hard-value 'offers'. The earlier 'improve' credentials are leveraged as evidence of the potential value and, when brought together, already create a powerful reality and a compelling case for further development. Successful completion of this third stage signals the start of the strategic partnership, when an aligned definition of a formal SCF is jointly agreed. This stage can be completed within two to six months, although longer might be needed in some cases.

Stage 4: Build

This stage is when the 'rubber hits the road'. It is about operationalizing the jointly agreed SCF, deploying the partnership strategy systematically across both organizations, setting up governance systems, implementation workstreams and getting joint teams to work together. It requires focus and intensity: some people in both organizations may still have strategic doubts, whilst others may have high expectations and be impatient for results. This stage should be run dynamically – over a few weeks or months – so the impetus and momentum are maintained.

Stage 5: Transform

This final but never-ending phase is about delivering material benefits from the execution of the SCF, achieving 'enhance'-level results and ultimately reaching 'transform' value. It requires the right mechanisms to be in place to deliver all workstreams of the SCF. Ongoing 'offer' development will move the partnership from early successes to long-term, strategic benefits across the partners' organizations. Hopefully, this phase will be continually renewed and expanded in years to come.

The five-stage partnership development model takes place within the context of the enterprise partnering strategy and management approach as defined in Chapter 2. It necessitates the formation of organizational, human capital and strategic performance frameworks for the individual partnership, as represented by the two vertical side-bars in Figure 3.1.

Let's hear Hertz's key steps for developing strategic partnerships from Michel Taride.

Michel Taride, Group President, Hertz International

"Partnerships can develop into strategic partnerships. We always start the partnership journey with strategy, by understanding each other's strategic goals. We assess if the other organization's drivers converge with ours. If so, we engage and move into developing a select number of initiatives and drive execution.

We then develop joint offers and a full commercialization package behind the set of products and services. Success leads to deeper relationships and often in our case, to exclusivity. In turn, exclusivity enables freer and deeper strategy discussions between the organizations, more openness, and a more long-term approach. That is what moves the partnership to a strategic alliance that can become 'transformational'. For example, the competitive position of Air Inter versus high-speed trains was truly enhanced by devising our joint innovative integrated offer.

Ensure success through a 15-step model

There is considerable detailed practice and know-how to be developed and actioned in each of the five stages. Their full effect and impact can be further defined in 15 individual steps, each of them providing its own critical contribution.

The 15 steps (see Figure 3.2) must be run sequentially, avoiding the temptation to jump straight to the next step, or directly to 'execution' when still in the 'planning' stages. You should define your own version of the model and once fixed, practice it as a strictly gated process, moving through your own 15 steps one by one.

FIGURE 3.2   Strategic partnership model: 15 fundamental steps

Let us explore the 'dos and don'ts' of each step:

FIGURE 3.3   Target stage: Steps 1–3

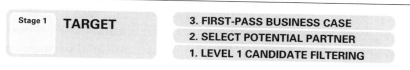

Step 1: Level 1 candidate filtering

This step starts with analysing and leveraging a 'third-party' segmentation, which usually already exists in good enterprises and identifies the general pool of organizations we want to work with and allocate resources to. We then apply a series of 'lenses' to the potential candidates, using factors such as existing relationships, size, strategic relevance, complexity, etc.

At the end of Step 1, we will have pre-selected a government, a firm, an organization – or a few of them – as potential target partners. Equally importantly, we will have made firm choices as to who we will not partner with: perhaps some of our competitors' targets, and organizations and companies with whom we have good relationships, but who do not appear fit for partnering with us.

Step 2: Select a potential partner

Failing to select the right target partner will almost inevitably mean loss of time, resource and possibly reputation in the future, both externally and internally.

A thorough approach will be used again in this next filtering step, to assess additional 'hard' substance and 'soft' culture areas, ie the potential strategic value to be derived from a partnership and its deliverability, the emotional and cultural fit between the organizations, etc. This step will be worked through intensively with the objective of turning 10 targets into 10 strategic partners later, rather than developing just one strategic partner from 10 targets. A very important measure of success!

Step 3: Define a first-pass business case

From Steps 1 and 2, we can determine which candidates pass a significant number of critically important 'lenses' and therefore represent very valuable prospects. Strategic partnering being all about value, and hopefully value at 'transform' levels, it is therefore worth testing the reality and accessibility of the potential benefits, in the form of a first-pass business case. We will do this by involving selected leaders in the organization.

At the completion of Steps 1, 2 and 3, we will be confident enough to declare the successful candidate(s) as our 'target strategic partner(s)'. Failing to make a good choice at this stage is not irreversible, although internal commitment is ramping up and other potential partners could in the meantime disappear into collaborations of their own.

Now, let's move the target strategic partner(s) from the 'target' phase to the next major stage of the process: 'prepare'.

FIGURE 3.4 Prepare stage: Steps 4–6

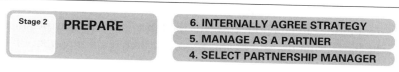

Stage 2	PREPARE	6. INTERNALLY AGREE STRATEGY
		5. MANAGE AS A PARTNER
		4. SELECT PARTNERSHIP MANAGER

Step 4: Select and install a dedicated Strategic Partnership Manager (SPM)

From now on, the focus narrows considerably, moving the potential partnership towards reality. Consistent with the 'leadership' management approach defined in Chapter 2, we advocate an organizational model whereby a small, high-profile, dedicated and specialized unit is set up to lead each strategic partnership. We will describe the principles and components of this unit (the partnering group) in Chapter 5.

This group materializes for the first time in Step 4. Doing this earlier would have been risky, as the individual partnership opportunity might not have been assessed clearly enough. Leaving it until later would put the opportunity at risk altogether, as a lack of attention from dedicated leadership and resources would prevent it being pursued with enough determination, depth and intensity.

The specific activity of Step 4 will be to design and shape the team required for the partnership. In general, we advise a small, but high-quality team of people, especially in the initial phases of a partnership. Most important at this stage is to provide the partnership possibility with a leader, in our terminology a Strategic Partnership Manager (SPM). He or she will have a defining role and be the person to whom the entire organization turns when the target partner is under discussion or in play.

Sooner or later, one or more other individuals, whom we call Value & Offer Managers (VOMs), will be required to deepen the partnership core value propositions and 'offers'. They may even be appointed as early as Step 4, if material strategic value streams between the partners have already been identified.

The critical outcome of Step 4 is to provide leadership to the nascent partnership and a main point of contact both internally and to the target organization.

Step 5: Manage as a strategic partner

A likely and desired potential strategic partner has now been identified and we have already developed a good sense of a clear joint mission, where mutual value will arise, and where there is demonstrated compatibility with our own enterprise. The whole organization now needs to adopt a consistent mode of behaviour towards the target strategic partner, in sync with the partnering objective. This requires three main interventions:

- Many touch points may already exist between two equally complex organizations, probably without any consistency of intent, tone or integrated approach. It is very common for 'the left hand not to know what the right hand is doing'. These interactions are usually of a disparate nature and quality: partly supply, partly procurement; partly deep and friendly, partly difficult and conflicting. It is therefore important to create early internal visibility for the possibility of the partnership, to establish greater consistency and positive tone across all organizational silos in their interactions with the target partner.

- The organization's verticals and departments need to be informed that a central team will now be coordinating the relationship, meaning all interactions with the target should be sanctioned by the partnership team.

- Equally important at this stage is to fully engage the enterprise areas likely to be involved in a deeper and more valuable relationship with the target. This early syndication throughout the organization will draw positive outcomes, such as the awareness of the relationship by the involved verticals and their consequent engagement to work on the opportunity with the central team.

Step 6: Define and agree the SCF internally

This is probably the most intriguing, challenging and counter-intuitive step of the entire model: not for its outcome, but in its practice.

When Step 6 is complete, a 'destination' and a strategic framework for the potential co-operation will have been designed and codified internally. It will encompass:

- a simple and powerful mission, and strategy 'story' on why the organizations should partner and of their collaboration's 'destination'. In other words, what excellent looks like and where they should aim for;

- the core potential 'enhance' and 'transform' value threads to be drawn from the upcoming alliance;
- a co-operation plan, including a contact map, as defined in Chapter 7;
- and an intended 'navigation' process, as described in Chapter 10.

From this point, we will be ready for the first institutional engagements with the 'prospect', with a robust understanding of the other party, clear objectives, a strong 'story' and well-defined 'navigation' steps to follow.

You are probably wondering what makes this step unusual. The key lies in the depth of the preparation and its process. In our model and as we will detail in Chapters 8, 9 and 10, this step typically lasts some months, far longer than would usually be the case with other, similar processes. During this time, and contrary to the received wisdom of 'go and talk with them to better understand their needs', the partnership team will not be permitted to engage formally with the target, despite the considerable temptation to do so. The SPM will need to go through a long, rigorous, quiet and behind-the-scenes process of discovery. At the end of Step 6, the partnership 'destination' will have to be crystal clear, powerful and real and the SPM might fail a few times before getting it right. This can be a real challenge!

But the outcome is worth the effort and discipline. When the partnership is finally given the go-ahead, the engagement will be on the mark, will involve the right people in the target's organization and will follow the most effective course.

FIGURE 3.5   Engage stage: Steps 7–9

Step 7: Engage with the partner

Emerging from the first two stages and their six steps, we are now as ready as we can be to engage with the target. And we are feeling confident, as we know so much about them, the value case looks mutually compelling, and the 'navigation' tactics are clear. So, time to engage!

We will need to use a gradual process, as the target does not see what we can see yet and will have to uncover the truth at its own pace. It is vital not to reveal too much too soon in a rush to convince the target, but rather leave time for discovery. There may also be factors we have missed in the preparation, no matter how comprehensive. Step 7 will therefore be essential to progress the idea of the strategic co-operation in the target's organization and also to deepen our understanding of why it will be a compelling proposition.

There are two main routes for engaging with the target: top-to-top, using an initial potential joint strategic framework to be deployed within the organizations; bottom-to-top, leveraging an initial set of successfully deployed 'demonstration' activities, to prove the bigger case. Both can work; a mix of both is ideal.

A disciplined engagement results in better knowledge of the critical factors, the so-called partnership value 'hooks' for the target from the co-operation and what needs to be done to improve the attractiveness and appeal of your offering.

Step 8: Deepen understanding of the 'hooks' and refine the 'offers'

As the relationship develops, this step is about continuously refining our understanding of what appeals to the target, and then refining the value proposition and 'offers' accordingly, to make the prize of the emerging strategic co-operation mutually compelling.

We concentrate on the definitive understanding of the essential substance on which the partnership will be built and what is needed to get the partnership recognized and supported across both organizations. Many aspects are discussed day-after-day with the target and therefore become familiar to them. We are also increasingly involving our own organization's verticals and functions in the relationship and generating support for the emerging strategic co-operation.

Step 9: Jointly define and agree the SCF

This is the watershed step, the move from idea to reality. Both organizations know each other well now; they have developed a good sense of what their deeper relationship might be about and what they want from it; they value and even see each other as important and unique.

Step 9 is the turning point, the first true 'destination' of everything done so far. It is the time when both organizations formally lay out and codify their joint SCF. It is the moment when they formally recognize, with eyes wide open, the true intent and key components of a long-term strategic and important relationship. And jointly agree it! From this point on, the relationship should and will be called a 'strategic partnership'.

In fact, the best joint SCFs are expressed very simply. They include just a few strands of 'transform' value, whose combination defines both the mission and the full 'transform destination' of the strategic partnership.

Building on our earlier example of an automaker and an energy company, Figure 3.6 illustrates what an SCF might look like in their case.

FIGURE 3.6   Strategic co-operation framework: Example

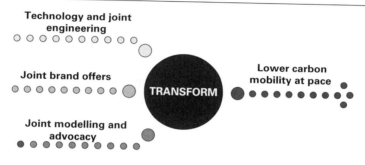

In this example, the partners' shared mission is to generate lower carbon levels from mobility. The strategic partnership's 'destination' or ultimate outcome is to be recognized as the industry leaders for this aspiration (Figure 3.6, right-hand side). By 'transforming' the way technology is developed, 'transforming' the route to market for their innovations and 'transforming' the dialogue with regulators to establish an appropriate and enabling regulatory environment (Figure 3.6, left-hand side), they are able to 'transform' the low-carbon performance of the automotive sector ... and 'transform' their own enterprise's performance strategically.

By the end of Step 9, both parties will have agreed a joint strategic framework for the partnership. The central team will internally have revised and completed the co-operation plan, to continue to be 'on top of the game'. And both parties will be determined to finalize and announce their alliance, because they will not be targets to each other anymore, but strategic partners!

FIGURE 3.7   Build stage: Steps 10–12

Step 10: Jointly syndicate the strategic co-operation

Seeing their joint future in similar ways is necessary but not a guarantee of success. Now that both organizations are convinced and have agreed to the partnership, it is time for everything really to start. This is the purpose of Step 10, which will make the agreed co-operation a well-known, defined and syndicated 'business'. There are two main activities in this step:

- Formalize the co-operation, so it can be syndicated and deployed across both organizations simply and powerfully; and define and set up the collaborative mechanisms to make it live and prosper, eg the governance process, an engagement charter and so forth.

- Announce the partnership – and, most crucially, announce it internally within each organization. Then, follow up this general announcement with targeted individual discussions with the most interested parties in both enterprises.

At the end of Step 10, the co-operation will be confirmed; both organizations will have been widely informed and actively involved; mutual tone and intents will be clear across the organizations and the majority of their silos and verticals.

Step 11: Select and install the remainder of the strategic partnership team

Now comes one of the hardest phases in the whole model. Agreeing and communicating the strategic co-operation has raised strong expectations at many levels in both organizations. Progressing the partnership further will require a determined focus to:

- develop the 'sources of value' (SoVs) and the mutual/joint 'offers' to deliver the partnership's full potential;

- motivate and support the numerous parties involved in both organizations.

It is therefore appropriate and necessary to provide the partnership with additional and appropriate levels of central human resource (in terms of both capacity and capability), to drive and support progress. Earlier would have been risky, given the uncertainty around the deal. Later would put the co-operation at risk altogether.

Two main types of roles are needed: Regional Strategic Partnership Managers (RPMs), ie similar roles and profiles to the SPM, to roll out the partnership in priority territories; and additional VOMs to supplement any colleagues brought in during Step 4, to develop and land the mechanisms and 'offers' required for the delivery of the main 'sources of value' (SoVs).

Step 12: Set up the workstreams

The practical journey towards 'transform' value will be achieved through joint structured workstreams, where leaders and experts from each of the partner's organizations will progress the activities and define the resource requirements together.

It is a prerequisite for success in establishing these workstreams, their structures and processes, that the business areas that are pivotal to the strategic partnership's mission and 'destination' are actively involved early on.

In our earlier example of the OEM–energy partnership, workstreams would be set up between technologists, marketers, strategic planners and corporate affairs leaders, with the objective to 'transform' the partners' mutual interfaces in these areas, and subsequently their whole industry.

The corporate governance structure and processes for the strategic partnership will also be launched and installed in this step. These will play an important role in 'motivating' and setting up the expectations for the workstreams, who will want to report positively to the senior management.

Experience shows that it takes determination and resilience to go through this step successfully, as leaders and team members in the workstreams are usually already very busy with other priorities. Also, many people in both organizations will often not see the potential of 'this new and difficult thing' at this early stage and some may even remain strategically or operationally doubtful – if not hostile.

FIGURE 3.8 Transform stage: Steps 13–15

Step 13: Jointly 'operationalize' the strategic partnership

Up to this point, the joint co-operation framework has been developed around a few pivotal 'sources of value'. Delivering them requires that the relevant parts of the two organizations work well together. Only if this happens will the co-operation deliver its potential. This is the motive for setting up the joint workstreams in Step 12; now in Step 13 they must be made to operate.

Teams will have to work closely together from now on. And again, our experience leads us to expect many challenges in making this happen. The involved teams had a lot to do before and might not always welcome the additional work; not all parts of the organizations will have a strong partnering experience; the journey to deliver what are very often industry firsts is not always easy to figure out.

We advise using a simple and systematic approach to alleviate most of these challenges. The breakthrough comes from getting each workstream team to jointly create their 'source of value' charter, including objectives, activity plan and governance. This is essentially a repeat of Steps 6 and 9, but focused now on each individual workstream. The central partnership team will be instrumental in this effort, notably at the start, with the SPM, RPM or VOMs convening and supporting the workstream process and making it happen in practice.

When Step 13 has been completed, all important co-operation objectives will be underpinned with a charter, leaders and team members will be identified, milestones set, and resources and governance jointly defined for each. These workstreams will be integrated within the overall co-operation governance process set up in Step 12, for approval, resource allocation decisions or other necessary management input.

Step 14: Deliver 'transform' value

If both partners have gone through Steps 1 to 13 in a disciplined and ordered way, they cannot fail to deliver both strategically and financially from the co-operation! Step 14 represents the continuous implementation and cross-fertilization of the workstreams over time, to reach 'transformational' value destinations.

Moving organizations into new territory and applying edge and intensity to their joint delivery over long periods of time takes competence, consistency and determination. The relationship must not become routine, cozy or less dynamic; on the contrary, it should be continuously re-energized, remain cutting-edge, lead in what it does, and generate increasingly material successes for the partners. If not, why bother with the sophistication of a strategic co-operation?

The good news lies in what experience has taught us: you should expect any well-run strategic co-operation to deliver considerably more value than planned – and even more than was hoped for – in the original frameworks. The two main mechanisms through which this additional benefit is delivered are:

- As organizations and people get to know each other, work well and deliver value together across multiple levels, they become confident and open to more sharing, thus pushing the collaboration further.

- As solutions and 'offers' are developed jointly, they evolve from good ('improve'), to better ('enhance'), to 'transformational' – and so does the value they generate. At some point, people can see possibilities they could not see before and realize them at considerable scale.

We have been consistently surprised at how the disciplined application of the model has resulted in much greater mutual value over time than originally anticipated. Stephen Odell describes this evolution very pertinently, so keep at it!

Stephen Odell, Executive Vice President Ford Motor Company and President EMEA

The true value of a partnership comes out when the interface between the two companies moves from a 'need' to a 'want'. Sometimes you need to interface because there is a mutual requirement and that is okay. But the moment when the relationship starts to move from a 'need' to a 'want' is when the magic potentially can happen.

I think the 'want' happens by being really persistent and by getting people at the working level to interface, because they will see the benefits. I won't because I don't know what the 'want' could possibly be between an engine developer and a fuel engineer, but I guarantee there are some opportunities there. So when it becomes a dialogue that is acceptable to both and when they move from 'need' to 'want', that is when the real opportunities come out.

Step 15: Expand to new areas, value propositions and 'offers'

So, new possibilities and ambitions are now emerging and developing from the established co-operation. Each new opportunity will require the same dedication and discipline from both partners as outlined before, transforming opportunity into success through their joint approach and work.

This is a continuous virtuous circle, when delivering the next level of impact and 'performance' involves new 'offers', leading to evolution in existing workstreams and their charters or creation of new ones. We are now in a continuous value creation and innovation loop around Steps 12, 13 and 14, making the strategic co-operation ever more important to the partners … and often to the world!

The partners have now realized their initial ambition and succeeded together, using each other's support and capabilities … and are eager for more of the same!

A case story

BP provides strong evidence of the power of this stage-gated strategic partnership development model, at both the portfolio-wide and individual co-operation levels.

As a company, BP holds partnerships deep in its DNA, with 'caring' and 'working to mutual advantage' core to its value set. Hence, the company is continuously attempting to improve and manage its partnership practice. After having rather unsuccessfully trialled a number of approaches to manage its most important commercial relationships, BP decided in 2002 to codify its model and apply it consistently and rigorously with some of its most important technology and commercial relationships.

Between 2003 and 2005, BP selected 16 strategic partner targets among the finest and largest global organizations, by working through Stage 1 consistently. Of the 16 in the original selection, 15 have developed into multi-dimensional strategic co-operations, which are still enduring and still expanding nearly 10 years later.

To date, dozens of industry firsts and progressive offers have been developed by BP and its partners, at the business–energy interface. The co-operations have metamorphosed their mutual perspective of the other, their interfaces and ways of working together, as well as having delivered 'transform' value to all involved.

The model was formally started in BP in 2003 and has now become a 'way of working' in the downstream part of the company. The success and the impact of the model are resulting in a progressive and continuous extension of its adoption and use in other areas across the company.

Partnership teams have been assembled through Steps 4 and 11, as individual strategic co-operations have been developed. They are an amazing collection of talents, both leading the co-operations and providing expertise and capability across the multiple businesses and verticals involved and the wider BP.

It is generally accepted that the value delivered to BP's partners is higher than that gained by BP. Nevertheless, the financial value to BP from the relationships has tripled over eight years and the strategic benefits are even greater.

Mike Glenn, Executive Vice President, Market Development and Corporate Communications, FedEx Corporation

"We are probably involved in more strategic partnerships than we give ourselves credit for. And based upon the relationship we have had with BP, we have taken steps to formalize those. We consistently try to standardize around a model and put it out as a way to do partnerships.

John Seifert

"I have experienced best practice when there is a systematic approach to setting context, such as: defining and setting business ambitions; describing the way things should be done; clarifying standards of behaviour between partners; and applying mechanisms for open dialogue that reveal personal biases while building mutual trust.

Winning is largely in the model!

We are now concluding this critical chapter of the book. Its simple message is: design your own version of a strategic partnership development model, use all its stages and steps diligently, and you will consistently generate extraordinary collaborations. Quite naturally, your model does not need to be the same as ours, so let's learn from our leader interviewees as they talk about strong facets of their own practice.

Viren Doshi

Being lucky is important as a strategic partner, so we have defined luck as where 'preparedness meets opportunity'. You have got to be prepared, which means: understand what the other side is; use planning sessions with colleagues; define goals and surface issues; work on how to get your ideas across in a way that is most acceptable. This helps achieve 'advances' in a relationship.

Alan MacDonald, Vice-Chairman, Citibank/Chief Client Officer

We run a partnership management process: our matrix has a strong client axis. We aspire to become the most important provider for financial services to our partners; we focus on understanding our customers' needs; we structure ourselves to match their organization; the interface is led by a dedicated managing director; we develop products to match their needs; we have three P&Ls in Citi, one being by client; we use multiple scorecards for the overall business, its efficiency, risk, etc.

Peter Foss

We continue to build our process: we have selected a number of strategic partners; we are ready to let their development run for a lot of years; we want to be clear on where growth will come from and what to do for them; we are telling the businesses to put their best folks on them; and the CEO will review these accounts on a monthly and quarterly basis.

A big part of the success will come from everyone in the partnering team adhering to, integrating and applying the model at all times. Later on in this book we will even advise that you assess team members on how they do so, as an important measure in their individual performance contract or score card.

Summary: Designing a '100 per cent success' strategic partnership development model

- Define a comprehensive strategic partnership development model for your organization. As a guideline, ours entails 5 main stages, made up of 15 individual steps.
- Even if you are not looking for strategic partnering but prefer more tactical partnerships, or simply improved external relationships, a lot of these practices could be of considerable help.
- Use the model diligently to ensure consistent success, because winning is largely in the process.
- Measure your team members on how they apply the model.

There is, of course, more to success than the strategic partnership development model alone:

- How do we succeed in defining a powerful and relevant 'destination' and co-operation framework, from almost nothing?
- How do we create and manage extraordinary relationships across both organizations?
- What do we mean exactly by 'offers', why are they so important and at the same time so challenging to develop? And how do we do it well?
- What are the mechanisms for successfully managing the strategic partnerships over long periods of time?
- Who are the people needed in the central partnering team and how do they work with the rest of the organization?

Answering these and other questions critical to success will be largely accomplished in the context of the model – and is the purpose of the next chapters of *Strategic Partnering*.

04
Selecting the best strategic partners

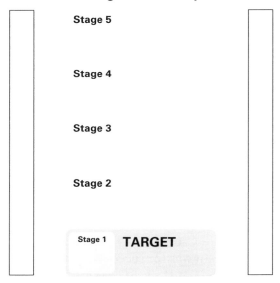

Partnership is a long, intricate, intimate dance together and nothing matters more than your own sense of balance and your choice of partner.

AMY BLOOM

This chapter establishes the imperative of selecting strategic partners with all due care and consideration. It represents Stage 1 of our strategic partnership development model and, as noted in earlier chapters, is of paramount importance. Partnering with the wrong organization has little chance of delivering enduring success for anyone involved in the alliance.

Kevin Murray, Chairman, The Good Relations Group

"We should absolutely go through a process to select a partner because there are so many things we might forget or overlook or be too optimistic about and you need to put basic checks and balances in place. A disciplined process is really quite critical, so that it is not only about chemistry but also strong logic and sound assessment.

Sir Frank Williams, Founder and Team Principal, Williams

"Any company which thinks it can manage without partners is probably dreaming. But partnering with the right people is critical, and as with many other things, 'the truth always finds you'!

Often, partners are chosen because of scale, reputation, existing links or business already done with each other, even social relationships between their leaders. These criteria need to be complemented or even replaced by a thorough examination of their high-level objectives, both strategic and financial, and of their capabilities. The attributes expected to fulfil our requirements will also guide our selection of the right partner. With a continuing emphasis on practice, this chapter will cover the following issues:

- the critical importance of selecting the best strategic partners;
- the process to be adopted for partner selection;
- the criteria and 'lenses' to be applied in partner selection;
- the lessons to be learnt from experience.

The critical importance of selecting the right strategic partner

In the preceding chapters, we established the considerable opportunities available from successful strategic partnering. However, the right conditions need to be in place to achieve 'transformational' value, and this is brought about by applying a 'leadership' management model to our portfolio of partnerships.

As presented in Chapter 3, our individual partnership development model comprises five sequential stages, the first of which, 'target', is arguably the most critical of all and the one explored further in this chapter.

It is like a marriage!

Executives often compare true strategic partnerships with a marriage. There is a lot of validity in this parallel and it is indeed helpful to think about strategic partnerships in simple social terms. For example, it would probably be hard to argue against the assertion that the selection of partners is crucial to a marriage as well as to a business alliance. In both situations, the far-reaching ambition, the long-term perspective, the deep commitment, the accountability for the human or business 'children', the dependency, the intimacy and the mutual giving are profound and extensive. Failing to find such matching fundamentals between the partner and us, ie failing to make the right partner selection, would be a major shortcoming.

Ian Robertson

Such partnerships are like marriages. Good ones are where you share objectives and both sides help to make the relationship a success. And like in a marriage, if your partner agrees with everything you say, it doesn't always ring true. Any relationship will have ups and downs and tension can be a force for creativity and energy. This is something that both parties have to be comfortable with.

Michael Johnson, four times Olympic Gold medallist, founder of Michael Johnson Performance

It is much more difficult to achieve good partnerships than you might think. You will in many cases find organizations coming together or attempting to come together and discovering after they have formed a partnership that, at the end of the day, it is not the type that builds a mutual benefit. Those strategic partnerships which actually are successful, I mean long term, are honestly rare. It might be because the partners have different cultures, or different approaches in some cases, or different goals in many cases, or they try to grow their company first, without looking at an equitable situation. So obviously, you have got to use the partnership approach when you believe all these things are close enough.

Aiming for '100 per cent success'

Still with the marriage analogy, many couples say they marry for love – but this would be a mistake in strategic partnering. Choosing partners simply because they are known to the business, they already work with us, or because 'we like them' are not strong enough reasons to partner with them.

Before any marriage or partnership, there are a few simple questions to ask:

- Do we share a common life purpose? Or in the business context, do we want the same thing, do we have the same objectives?

- Do we feel safe expressing our thoughts and feelings to the other person? In our business situation, do we trust the other party? Actually, this theme of trust comes up more than 90 per cent of the time in our senior leader interviews, as an absolute prerequisite to any partnership.

- Is she/he a Mensch? In both the private and business worlds, there is an imperative to be a 'good' person or organization, to try doing the right thing and to anchor acts and behaviours in deeply held values, which are either shared between the partners or complementary and compatible to each other.

- How does he/she treat other people? As we say on many occasions throughout this book, partnerships are about the ability to give. No self-absorbed person or organization can be a good long-term partner. More generally, the way our potential partners treat their stakeholders and staff is important and revealing.

- How will I know if she/he is the right partner? Feelings and intuitive sense have to be acknowledged of course, but they need to be considered alongside deep analysis and robust and realistic assessment.

Confronted with the importance of choosing the right partner, let's consider a likely process and some more refined 'lenses' to help us select our strategic partners. As anecdotal evidence, we remember the initial establishment of a strategic partnering programme a few years ago and the selection of our first 12 potential partners. To our CEO's question, 'how many do we believe will become strategic partners?' we answered, '12'. At the time, it appeared totally unrealistic, but a few years later, the reality was ... 12. Hence, selection needs to be approached and managed so comprehensively that the success rate is indeed 100 per cent, or as close to 100 per cent as possible.

The process for successful partner selection

Partner selection is Stage 1 of five and Steps 1, 2 and 3 of our 15-step strategic partnership development model. To ensure that the whole model works as efficiently as possible and that organizations do not waste time and effort on in-depth analysis of non-starters, we tend to split this stage into three levels, moving from broad-brush to finer analysis, gradually intensifying the effort and the enquiries.

Figure 4.1 illustrates these three steps as they apply to the broadest scenario, ie when an organization starts to establish a portfolio of strategic partnerships from scratch. The same logic and process can obviously also apply to organizations which already manage selected relationships but who are considering taking these affiliations to the next level. It also applies very well to assessing single relationships, as opposed to a portfolio.

The selection journey starts by using the existing enterprise segmentation analysis (Level 1 filter in Figure 4.1), then focusing in to narrow down the field (Level 2). It then moves into a more detailed landscaping of the pre-selected candidates (Level 3), and finally builds a first-pass '70 per cent probability' business case for the prospects (final filter). The whole approach results in strong target strategic partners, a single one in the individual selection case or a few in the portfolio case. Once past Stage 1, the target organizations will all proceed through the next stages of the partnering model towards becoming successful alliances.

FIGURE 4.1   Select and Target process

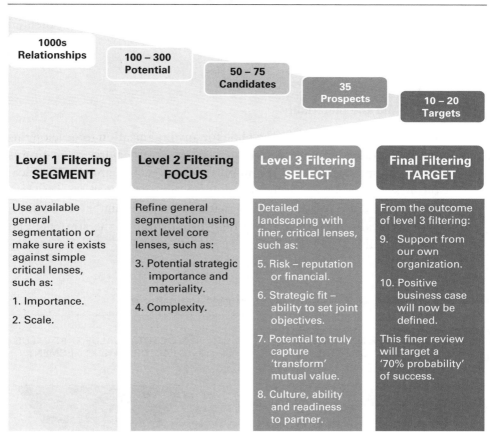

With this progression in mind, let's explore the successive levels of filtering, starting with segmentation.

Level 1 filtering: Leveraging existing enterprise segmentation

This is our first and broadest level of filtering. Prior to starting Step 1 of the partnering model, any organization or business should be strategically clear on the relevance and relative importance of each and all of their stakeholder relationships. A thorough segmentation and mapping of their political, university, NGO, customer and supplier relationships should already exist, where stakeholders are placed into high-level groupings, based on the criteria of the greatest current or potential impact on the organization's strategy.

These criteria can be as simple as:

1 Importance.
2 Scale and materiality.

It is a basic and important discipline for any organization to develop this type of enterprise segmentation analysis, so that resource allocation is strictly commensurate to the importance of each segment. A typical business-to-business customer breakdown into such categories is shown in Figure 4.2 and reflects the fact that a very small number of relationships typically represent a very high proportion of the strategic and financial value.

FIGURE 4.2   Value segmentation typical profile

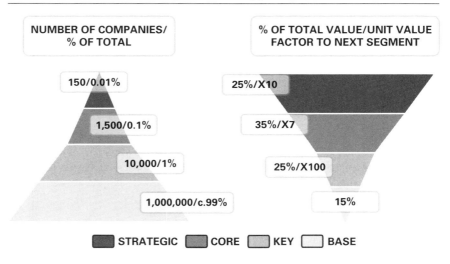

In this particular study, 150 organizations in a sample of one million account for 25 per cent of the total potential value and each of them is worth 10 times more than relationships in the next segment. It remains a puzzle why organizations often find it so hard and challenging to develop their own thorough 'third-party' segmentation and calibrate their attention and resources allocation to relationships accordingly. Indeed, investment and support should be deployed consistently, and in a disciplined way, to reflect the rational outcome of this segmentation exercise.

Interestingly, most political or business sector segmentations are extremely pyramidal, often even more than those shown in Figure 4.2. For example, in the automotive industry, seven players represent close to 80 per cent of the world's car production; in aerospace, Boeing and Airbus represent over 80 per cent of the civil aircraft global production. In these highly concentrated sectors, where a very small number of major players hold such huge importance and value, considerable thought is required to figure out how to differentiate ourselves from the pack and develop deep strategic co-operations with the few possible and the even fewer available partners. Alan MacDonald, David Marley, Martin Sorrell and Peter Foss offer complementary perspectives on the importance of the 'top of the pyramid'.

Alan MacDonald

Our ambition is to become the most important provider of financial services to our partners. A general rule is that the two or three dominant providers would have 70 to 75 per cent of a client wallet, with the leader having 40 per cent. With a high share, we can then afford to provide a deeper, better service.

David Marley, Managing Director, IBM

80 clients represent a third of IBM's business. We are dedicated to treating them as strategic partners for all of what it means and requires.

Martin Sorrell

Our top 30 clients are one third of our revenues. Most of these relationships, touch wood, have been very long term and go back 50, 60 years or more. We can't be complacent and need to provide them with the best of our 165,000 people in WPP.

Peter Foss

I would venture that 80 per cent of your business is done with 50 customers maximum, maybe not even that many. In some cases it could be that one customer is 4 or 5 per cent of your company. It is therefore much better to partner with leaders in their industries, grow their revenues and grow along with them. The great thing with building a strong partnership with them is that you can discuss openly how to help this growth.

Level 2 filtering: Focusing our segmentation further

Building on the enterprise segmentation and the first-pass filtering based on importance and scale, we should now narrow our segmentation further. Again, the 'lenses' chosen to refine the filtering will depend on the specifics of your organization, but we generally find the following two criteria useful at this stage:

3 Potential strategic importance.

4 Complexity.

Potential strategic importance

This goes beyond the fairly mechanical 'importance lens' used in the Level 1 filtering step. We now assess if there is a natural 'mission' shared by the potential partners. It includes a preliminary sense of the future rather than the present, of the opportunity versus the existing, of the possibility of 'transformational' value versus 'improve' or 'enhance'. Simply, it represents a first view on whether there is potential for this relationship to become strategically important. Deeper enquiry on the strategic opportunity will be carried out later, but this early judgement on potential is clearly key to quality filtering.

This 'lens' should also include a consideration of the potential partner's competitive and reputational positions: are they the 'best', or among the best, at what they do and what we need? Are they a recognized and respected institution and brand, because associating with reputed organizations should be a crucial component of 'strategic importance', as noted by Tom Albanese.

> **Tom Albanese**, former Chief
> Executive Officer, Rio Tinto Group
>
> "It depends on who the players are. If the potential activities and value are of scale to Rio Tinto, then the strategic partner has to be one of a scale that has the wherewithal, has the horsepower to provide the assurance. Other players may be able to make an offer I can't refuse, but that is a pretty high bar, because what I need most is a 20-year relationship. So scale matters, size matters. And then I think it is about other components – one is assurance of supply, a second is the competitive, commercial compatibility, and the third is the reputational area: 'don't embarrass me and I won't embarrass you'.

Complexity

The case for strategic partnering and central intervention comes most naturally when management complexity exists and therefore requires an actively simplifying, mobilizing and enforcing approach. Complexity can arise from and relate to:

- Geographical spread. Without a coordinating or driving strategic partnering capability, complex organizations made of multiple country presences often find it a challenge to ensure consistent application of strategies, innovations and standards as they relate to their strategic partnerships and their value-creation mechanisms.

- Multi-business. Similarly, it is never easy to persuade complex institutions made of multiple departments, verticals or functions, to put their weight behind an enterprise-wide initiative or 'offer'. Arguably, these are precisely the situations where greatest opportunities lie, to align many areas of an organization behind the simplicity of well-codified and productive strategic partnerships. Our model offers this rallying force and therefore avoids reinvention in 'every village'.

- Complex organizational structures. As they develop, most Fortune 1000 companies build complexity in their organizations, where business territories are co-owned by various areas of accountability, be it business line, functions, regions and countries, etc. Going beyond this complexity and making the best of it will be an active challenge for the development and management of strategic co-operations across the board.

We probably would not need the sophistication of a strategic partnering model if the considered partner was mono-country, mono-business and organizationally simple. In these cases, a more localized approach, be it in a geographical or organizational silo, could work equally well.

Any potential strategic partner will therefore have to fall into the upper category of this two-step segmentation effort. At the end of our Level 2 filtering, we will be left with a relatively small number of 'candidate' governments, firms or organizations who all present an obvious importance to us, an even more considerable latent value, a strategic fit and a high level of complexity. A note from experience: their true importance is often understated in this early selection phase, compared to the value that the partnering practice will unveil when the co-operation is ongoing and flourishing.

Level 3 filtering: Identifying strong prospects

Once reduced to a relatively low number of candidates, the filtering moves to significantly deeper and finer investigation. As shown in Figure 4.1, this 'landscaping' phase essentially addresses and studies the fundamentals of the candidate(s) in two main respects: who they are, and the likelihood of their openness to partner for the long term.

The key 'lenses' for selecting strong prospects

At this stage of the enquiry, we would usually employ the four following 'lenses':

5 Risk, be it on reputation, financial or other.

6 Strategic fit, likelihood of joint objectives and ability to partner.

7 Their drivers for a potential strategic partnership and the potential to mutually capture 'transform' value.

8 Their culture and likely readiness to partner.

These 'lenses' are not always easy to use of course and getting as close to a quality assessment against these criteria will be our prime objective in this particular step.

Risk

As the association will be high-profile, none of the strategic partners would want to associate with another party who potentially could carry significant risk to their reputation, financial robustness or position within their sector. A lot can happen quickly during the long lifetime of an alliance, and choosing a partner against a well-considered risk profile is strongly advisable.

This 'lens' should be tested extensively and the following considered: if something went wrong with the partner, do we believe that we would be ready to help, support and talk publicly for this organization? Because this is what true partners would do, if they believe in the genuine quality of their counterpart and as 'it is in times of challenge that one knows who true friends are'.

Jeff Immelt

A key aspect is to share risk/reward. Partners should take financial risks together and this builds a strong bond. Also look at the times when the chips are down and things are tough. Then, there is a chance to step in and do something extraordinary, say to a customer, and establish 'who is with me?' After 9/11, the airline industry was in turmoil. GE offered to invest $20–$30bn to help the airlines through the difficult period. It was a very big risk but it paid off with strong relationships.

Frank Williams

Inevitably at some point in any partnership, things become difficult for either party; however, one can't abandon one's friends when they are in trouble. Firstly, it is not an attractive characteristic, but also, ultimately, people's fortunes come and go and most will go through the tough times!

Martin Sorrell

When I talk about loyalty and commitment, it also means that, when companies have difficult times, sticking with them is terribly important. Because everything is cyclical and if you believe you are just going to get secular growth, it never happens that way.

Strategic fit and ability to partner

This 'lens' is multi-dimensional and of course pivotal. Coming out of almost all our top executive interviews, the ability to form and agree joint objectives is essential to the idea of strategic partnering. Hence the respective candidates' core spaces and strategies need to be connected and coherent. Potential partners need to share broadly similar missions and types of 'destination'. They also have to complement each other, so the core activities and efforts of one can benefit and enhance the other.

As mentioned in Chapter 2, this fit can arise from multiple factors:

- 'hand-in-glove' positions, such as cars and tyres; aircraft engines and air framers; or turbine manufacturers and utilities;

- similar strategic aspirations, such as auto, energy and government aspiring to higher fuel efficiency; or hardware, software and utilities to smart grids;

- complementary resources and capabilities, such as business process outsourcing (BPO) and IT for business services; hardware manufacturers, networks and content providers for telecoms.

Michael Johnson

One of the things that I always do at the very beginning is try to understand the goals of the potential partner; and when I can understand the other company or the potential partner's objectives, then I can much better appreciate whether or not there is a fit for me and whether or not there is synergy here. So I would say, first seek to understand the potential partner's goals!

We also believe it to be important that partners are all strong. As Ian Robertson says, strategic partnerships do not exist so that a strong organization can rescue a weak one, or two weak organizations can combine their risk. Their purpose is to bring two leading players in their sector together to build and enhance their collective offering. The players may be different sizes, but they should both be sector leaders; moreover, true strategic partnerships should always be evolving and never rest on past successes.

Ian Robertson

"Things can always be done better and if both parties in the partnership have shared goals, then there is great power in striving together to achieve these improvements. For a partnership to be a success, both sides need to be equally determined and energetic. For the most successful companies in the world, the needs and expectations between them and their partners are incredibly high – and rightly so. It is only with the highest levels of direction, focus and co-operation that these companies can stay successful.

Potential to truly capture 'transform' levels of mutual value

Some organizations will be committed to working with our competitors. Or their structures, geographies, decision-making processes, etc, will be so different to ours that a deeper co-operation would simply not be feasible or relevant. This landscaping phase should therefore provide a mapping of the candidate's assets, linkages, structures and key resources, to reduce the risk of encountering unexpected deal breakers. Using the example in the commercial world of strategic suppliers (in procurement) or strategic accounts (in selling), we will need to assess in both cases whether partnering can decommoditize our products and change them into value-added 'offers', whether we can access a disproportionate 'share of wallet' with our partner, and whether supply chains can be dependably integrated and rationalized.

Professor Dr Wolfgang Reitzle, Chief Executive Officer, Linde AG

"I am completely behind the concept of strategic partnering. It's all about identifying the right topics and defining the right scope that is not too broad and has the potential to generate positive results for both parties within a reasonable timeframe.

Andrew Mackenzie

"I think we're talking about the relationships that we would have with companies which on the whole have revenues and market capitalizations within our order of magnitude. Most of these will almost certainly have multiple relationships, involving as much being a supplier to the other and vice versa. So we're both each other's supplier and customer and we can discuss things effectively.

A frequent example of an organizational limiter can be the role of 'old type' procurement. If this extremely important function between suppliers and customers is powerful in the candidate's decision making and remains largely guided by traditional and transactional models and measures – eg price rather than value, product rather than solution – it can hinder strategic partnerships altogether. Conversely, some strategic procurement groups consider their role as integrators and champions of overall value creation, and can deliver the best of all worlds by being amazing enablers and supporters of strategic partnerships.

Culture and likely readiness to partner

Of course, the characters of two or more organizations will never be exactly the same. But the looming extensive and intimate nature of the relationships across the parties' organizations demands a strong cultural compatibility.

Andrew Mackenzie

At my level, I spend a considerable period of time on relationships with governments and my direct reports spend a considerable period of time on relationships with communities. It is all about mutual interest. I was reviewing an area recently where the geology is great, the high-level politics looks great, the market looks great. However, the community issues look tremendously challenging and the decision might be that they cannot be resolved to the satisfaction of all parties. If we have had the opportunity to put forward our case and value proposition and, for whatever reason, they have decided they don't want us there, that is okay by me. We only ever want to be operating where the community wants and supports our efforts.

Long-term 'living together' requires similar deep values and behaviours, as well as compatible ways of looking at the world and at situations. This is not to suggest that partners should be identical, as diversity and differences can of course be sources of considerable value. But they need to live well together, to engender trust, have similar intuitive responses and connected mindsets. We will reflect extensively on the cultural aspects of partnering in Chapter 12 of *Strategic Partnering*.

And finally, the killer question: are they open and fit for partnering? Not an easy question, but a critical one which needs to be assessed carefully. Indeed, some organizations will look like ideal candidates and have all of the essential characteristics, including a strong desire to partner. But they may just be unable to do so. Perhaps they won't give in order to receive; or they are overconfident and won't listen to advice; or they are not genuinely ready to be open, share some of their secrets and trust a partner.

Lord Sebastian Coe CH, KBE, Chairman British Olympic Association and CSM Sports and Entertainment

For every organization, it is how we recognize that it is not simply about the delivery of business but about being a values-driven organization and being seen as such. It is what we want people to say about the integrity of the organization. For me, the moral framework – and whether anybody likes it or not – comes from the very top and is not just a matter of writing out a mission statement or a vision, unless that is delivered in every sector of your organization.

Shelly Lazarus, Chairman Emeritus, Ogilvy & Mather

There is a real art to having strategic partnerships. There are organizations and people who are brilliant at it and there are others who are just completely hopeless.

So you'd better be careful about who you pick to partner with because you are going to have to go through a lot together. I have often thought about what makes for great strategic partnerships and there are some things that are simple to say, simple to conceive, but really, really hard to do. You have to start with trust. If two parties don't trust each other, it doesn't matter how much in sync they are. And it doesn't matter how much their capabilities complement each other if they don't trust the other person.

Frank Williams

It depends who makes the best product. In our case, for racing purposes, it depends on if you find a partner, a technical partner who is up to the job. And then, if you can, make your proposed partner a convert to the cause because, in Formula One, everybody who is involved has to give total commitment to excellence.

FIGURE 4.3 Select and Target: Scoring Examples

Stage 1 of the partnering model – Target & Select scoring examples

		Rating 1: Low / 5: High	
	Example 1	**Example 2**	**Example 3**
Segmentation			
1. Importance	3	3	3
2. Scale	4	4	3
3. Potential strategic importance and 'transformational' value	4	4	3
4. Complexity	5	5	3
Selection			
5. Risk	3	2	3
6. Strategic fit & ability to partner	4	4	3
7. Potential to capture the mutual value	3	4	3
8. Culture and readiness to partner	5	5	3
Targeting			
9. Positive feedback & inclination from the organization	3	3	5
10. Value case	4	4	3
Rating summary			
Mean	**3.8**	**3.8**	**3.2**
Minimum	None under 3	One under 3	None under 3
Conclusion	Pass	No pass – risk	No pass – mediocre

Mechanisms to finalize a strong prospect list

There is no universal scoring mechanism that combines measures, assessments and judgements on the few core 'lenses' and criteria we have just explored. Each organization should calibrate their scoring and specific weighting according to their own situation and priorities. Figure 4.3 shows what a possible scoring system could look like, reflecting the 'lenses' discussed above.

Using this scoring method, it would be wise to progress no further with a candidate, if either of the following two outcomes arise from the first three filtering steps:

- The potential partner is demonstratively bad on any of the core 'lenses'. For example, in Figure 4.3, candidate 2 scores too low on 'risk'.
- They score passably well on all 'lenses', but mediocre overall. For example, candidate 3 seems simply too average to be a likely 'transformational' partner.

The bar has to be set high – there should be no compromise, because big commitments are looming and we want 100 per cent success!

At this point, a small number of candidates will have made it through the segmentation and landscaping phases. Each of them should now be cherished like a precious gem! They have become strong prospects and deserve considerable attention, as there is clearly the potential for 'transformational' value to be realized in partnering with them.

Final filtering: Selecting our target partners

Well-underpinned prospects are now lined up with some of them highlighted as having the potential to ultimately become great strategic partners. As shown in Figure 4.3, we know a lot about them already, enough to change up a gear and finalize the selection. Hence, we will focus now on building up an early, positive business case, with focus on two key 'go/no-go' questions:

9 Our organization's support: is our own organization keen, positive and supportive of this tentative strategic co-operation and about the potential partner?

10 Business case: is the 'transform' value really there, can we be confident it can be reached and what will it take to succeed?

The support of our own organization

So far, the selection process has been conducted and run essentially through central coordination. In the case of a first strategic partnering initiative, the central team is the pioneer of the programme; in the case of an extension of the programme, they are the experienced managers of the model and bring their differentiated capabilities to the selection process.

Now that robust data exists on each prospect, it is time to engage with the interested verticals and functions in our organization. A good way of doing this, which we have used many times, is to run a one- or two-day workshop focused on one prospect, involving senior representatives of the relevant departments. It requires a lot of effort to organize of course, but it will often result in high quality insights, genuine ownership and strong support from the attending leaders. They will usually be early adopters and invaluable allies within their part of the wider organization.

A first-pass business case

The earlier filtering stages should be reviewed and tested through meaningful exchanges at the workshop, with all leaders involved. The individual 'areas of co-operation' (AoCs) and the assumptions behind the main 'sources of value' (SoVs) should be examined in depth. Examples of templates used for this AoC and SoV mapping are given in Figures 4.4 and 4.5.

The illustrative example in these two figures involves two potential partners – 'the partner' and 'us' – sharing five areas of strategic interest: technology, supply chain integration, marketing integration, risk management and new market expansion. In the example set out, Figure 4.4 represents these five areas of strategic co-operation and breaks them down into their component workstreams and SoVs. In this particular case, it might be noted that the workstreams look both connected and partly interdependent, which makes the likely potential value from partnering high, whilst accessing integrated 'transform' value might prove rather complex. The debates among the workshop participants on this case promise to be particularly interesting, animated and contributive and the partnership development fascinating!

FIGURE 4.4 AoC and SoV mapping: Illustrative example

Areas of Co-operation	Co-operation Workstreams	Sources of Value	AoC leaders Partner	Us
Technology	• Co-engineering • Environmental offer • CCC • DDDD	Partner: XXXX Estimated value range: Us: YYYY. Estimated value range	Head of Technology	JPM
Supply chain integration	• Supply chain synergies • Logistics • Product A supply • Product B supply • Product C supply	Partner: XXXX Estimated value range: Us: YYYY. Estimated value range	Manufacturing Director	FTG
Marketing integration	• Global category management • Joint B2B offer • Co-branding • PPPP	Partner: XXXX Estimated value range: Us: YYYY. Estimated value range	SVP Sales	HRN
Risk management	• Risk management • HSSE • Joint advocacy • UUUU	Partner: XXXX Estimated value range: Us: YYYY. Estimated value range	SVP Risk Head of Policy	SMC JWR
New markets	• China • India • YYYYY • ZZZZZ	Partner: XXXX Estimated value range: Us: YYYY. Estimated value range	Head of Countries	KRT SLY TAK

FIGURE 4.5 Respective importance of SoVs: Illustrative example

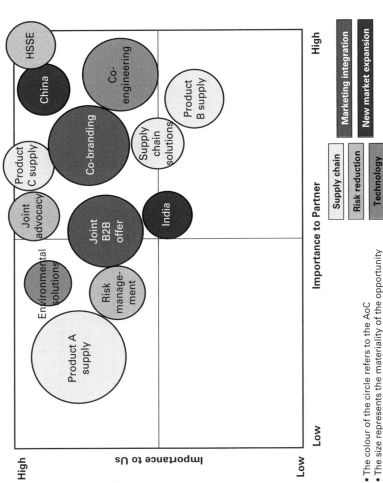

- The colour of the circle refers to the AoC
- The size represents the materiality of the opportunity

The workshops will set a number of prospects to one side into a reserve position, ie a 'no-go' or 'not ready yet' grouping. These are not totally abandoned, but they will not be a priority in the next phase compared to stronger candidates. Others will pass the workshop milestone successfully and will be declared active targets. The workshop will conclude with a first-pass business case set to provide a 70 per cent chance of success with the target, including a high-level structured codification of 'transform' value and a set of key success measures for the potential partnership. This first-pass business case will be a core and invaluable reference for the whole of the partnership development cycle.

Habemus target strategic partners!

At this point, strong targets have been identified and ratified as potential strategic partners. Dependent on the organization's decision processes, formal approval to proceed will be requested from the executive team or the corporate executive in charge of the partnering programme. Once this approval is granted, the selected targets will be designated internally as 'strategic partners'. From this point on, they will be approached and managed as such, using all components and mechanisms of our strategic partnership development model as they enter Stage 2. In practice we will now coordinate the relationship in a deliberate and centralized manner, and bring in dedicated human resources.

However, it is not yet time to rush and declare our intentions to the partner(s). This will come later, when another level of preparedness has been completed. But the target might already observe a different level of focus, attention, support and even tone across its organization in its dealings with us.

Making progress towards selecting the best strategic partners?

Let's go back to the earlier marriage analogy. We said we wanted and needed a partner with: a comparable and compatible lifestyle; a common life purpose and sufficiently similar objectives; deeply trustworthy and with strongly held values; non-self-absorbed characters; and featuring core practical considerations of importance to us. We have tested this dispassionately and analytically to (hopefully) fulfil Martin Sorrell's key priorities for successful partnering:

Martin Sorrell

The most important things in strategic partnering? It is mutual respect, sharing the same vision, leveraging each other's knowledge; it is loyalty and commitment; and it is taking a long-term view. Pro-activity and innovation are important, but there needs to be longevity, confidence and trust.

Let us summarize then our approach to 'selecting the best strategic partners':

Summary: Selecting the best strategic partners

- As in a marriage, it is critical to select your partner carefully!
- A thorough multi-step filtering process should be used, so effort is not wasted on the wrong potential partners.
- The model comprises 4 filtering steps and 10 key 'lenses'.
- At the end of this first full stage of the partnership development model, strong target(s) have been identified and will now be considered and managed as strategic partners.

Of course, time will tell but experience suggests that disciplined investigation using this process, significantly reduces the risks inherent in choosing not only the right but the best strategic partners. The model now moves from 'should we?' to 'how will we?' And the next stage will focus on doing what it takes to build mutual 'transformational' success.

05
Establishing a winning strategic partnering organization

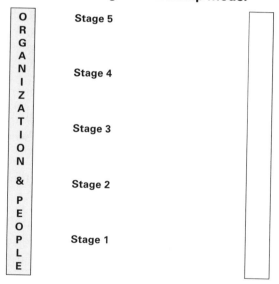

The Strategic Partnership Model

O
R
G
A
N
I
Z
A
T
I
O
N
&
P
E
O
P
L
E

Stage 5

Stage 4

Stage 3

Stage 2

Stage 1

Architecture does not create extraordinary organizations by collecting extraordinary people. It does so by enabling ordinary people to perform in extraordinary ways.

JOHN KAY

To lead people, walk behind them.

LAO TZU

Having completed Stage 1, we have now selected target partners and want to build towards creating extraordinary value together with them. Only great people operating in strongly enabling organizations will be able to achieve this and, as we enter Stage 2, we need to provide quality leadership to the nascent partnership(s). But before selecting people, let's define the type of organization we need to assemble teams, bring in talent and commence operations.

Partnering programmes often get some essential '101' organizational principles very wrong from the start and then have little chance to recover from the fundamentally flawed 'architecture'. Hence, we believe that a successful strategic partnering approach requires its own organizational philosophy and associated set of principles.

As discussed in Chapter 2, our strategic partnering approach operates under a 'leadership' management model. Here, an experienced central team is tasked with planning and progressing all the steps required to establish winning strategic partnerships, lead their execution and deliver value. The same team needs to stay in place over a long period of time to make the co-operations truly successful. Ultimately, this partnership team grows its capability to epitomize a core partnering organizational capability.

In this chapter, our objective will be to introduce the key organizational principles supporting a winning partnering strategy. We will cover the following themes:

- the philosophy of 'architecturing' a strategic partnering capability;
- our recommended organizational approach and how it fits with the rest of the entity;
- the key roles in the central partnering team, and the important distributed roles;
- the 'must have' principles for 'architecturing' the central strategic partnering team;
- selecting and bringing in people into this organizational construct to achieve success.

Philosophy of 'architecturing' a strategic partnering capability

There are two essential pillars supporting the 'architecture' of a world-class partnering capability:

- Think of and practise strategic partnering as a genuine all-encompassing discipline or business, not as a siloed competency or initiative such as selling, purchasing or lobbying when pursued alone.

- Think of the world purely through the lens of the strategic partnership, rather than from the perspective of any other group or business to which it contributes.

No compromise on making strategic partnering a fully-fledged practice and organization

This is not a 'one-off' initiative! The thrust of strategic partnering is to change norms and 'transform' the business strategically, create extra-ordinary value, run programmes which the enterprise would not be able to entertain otherwise, and convince the best leading organizations to join. This will require a strategic and long-term view, operational excellence, distinctive capability and knowledge – of the process and the partners – as well as considerable focus and resilience in applying the partnership development model. These requirements and the importance of the venture demand a fully-fledged and self-standing discipline that is established as an integral component of the enterprise.

David Marley

Our top 80 clients represent a third of IBM's total business and they all are very sophisticated organizations. They are what we call 'integrated accounts' and for many years, we have managed them through a dedicated organization. There are many aspects that make this set up including that each has a dedicated IBM managing director accountable for the relationship and with considerable authority within the company.

Alan MacDonald

496 of the Fortune 500 companies are Citi's partners or customers. Our company organizational matrix is three dimensional: client, product and geography. The point I want to stress is the existence of the client axis, which is there to try excelling at serving our partners. First principle of how our organization is set up aims at understanding their needs and then offering and delivering a full array of services globally. Our interfacing structure is built to match the partner's organization. It includes a dedicated senior leader usually based in their home town.

Think of the world through the lens of each individual strategic partnership

Everybody associated with an individual strategic partnership should be entirely driven by the practice, the business and the relationship that it represents. Achieving the thrust and potential of a strategic co-operation will require focus, passion and dedication, which only a certain type of organizational set-up will enable and truly support. In practice, the 'leadership' management model means that the enterprise strategic partnering programme will be piloted by a focused central unit. The individual relationships will be led and managed by a dedicated Strategic Partnership Team (SPT).

Let's assume that organizations A and B have entered into a strategic partnership. Everybody in organization A's SPT is fully dedicated to the relationship with B, particularly its leader, the Strategic Partnership Manager (SPM). After a while, they should all aim to be fully identified with the partnership and even go as far as being called 'Mr/Mrs/Ms B' by their colleagues right across A. Everyone in the SPT lives their role as promoting and fighting for B's brand within A. Their main objective is the delivery of the targeted strands of mutual value, milestones or financials through the collaboration, both for A and B. Only this single-minded and structured team approach will provide excellence and 'transformation'.

There are many challenges to applying these two pivotal principles with purity. For example, some organizations find it culturally and opera-tionally arduous to shift to a model where existing departments, vertical businesses or functions now have to accept 'intrusions' from the SPT into their own organizational arena. It can also take a significant amount of time for people joining the programme to adapt and reset to a new business model defined by a relationship, rather than more traditional scopes such as geography, product or asset.

These challenges can all be overcome, and even become sources of differentiated 'performance', as long as they are recognized from the start and consistently worked at. Let's consider how they translate into the actual 'architecture' of a partnering organization.

How the partnering unit fits into the wider enterprise

A defining element of our partnering organizational construct lies in the appropriate positioning of the role of the central team and the configuration of its component parts. Experience suggests that many organizations find it a true challenge to define and calibrate such teams adequately and set them up for success.

A dedicated strategic partnering team to action the 'leadership' model

The role of the central Strategic Partnering Unit (SPU)

In Chapter 2 of *Strategic Partnering*, we defined the 'leadership' management model. In this set-up, extensive and ultimate accountability of the partnership is held by a separate central Strategic Partnering Unit (SPU) or division.

Its function is to achieve what individual entities in the enterprise could not accomplish by themselves, in bringing the full potential of the organization to the relationship and delivering extraordinary value to the involved partners. This mission encompasses the design of the co-operation strategy, the core value propositions, the governance and relationship management, the main deals, the standards of execution and the active monitoring of 'performance'. The division also has the authority to mobilize resources and chair joint workstreams, ensuring that strategic goals are being pursued and momentum maintained.

It is this set-up which results in excellence and far-reaching 'transformational' value objectives. Using this model, 'improve' and 'enhance' value will be delivered in the early years, on the way to the aspired 'transformational performance'.

Building the separate, specific and focused strategic partnering unit

As shown in Figure 5.1, the unit is fully autonomous, reporting straight into the board and/or the enterprise executive committee through their accountable executive champion.

FIGURE 5.1   A separate and focused unit with access and 'clout'

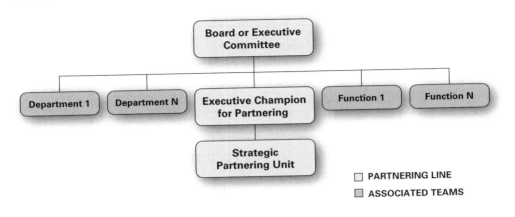

Peter Foss talks about the importance of giving 'clout' and an independent positioning to the partnering unit:

Peter Foss

When I started doing the partnership effort, which was almost 10 years ago, I realized that the accounts viewed me differently because I was coming in as a corporate person. They viewed me more as a customer than as someone trying to sell them something. In this unique position I was indeed able to say: 'look I'm here to help you understand my company better and in doing so, I'd like to understand yours better, and in our discussions we are going to find some areas in which we feel our companies will benefit together'.

It worked increasingly well because many realized that they needed to get more people into the game, support the relationship to work harder, really unleash the power of the company and apply it to another opportunity in order to be increasingly successful. So it is like unleashing the whole power of the organization, as opposed to a vertical part of it, I guess.

Our observation of various other models applied by governments, NGOs, universities or companies shows the occasional use of alternative practices where the SPU is either:

- Hosted by one of the enterprise's groups, vertical businesses or functions, arguably the one with the most obvious immediate strategic or financial material benefit from the partnership. We strongly discourage this approach as: at some point, a bias will inevitably develop towards this entity's interests and the overall enterprise perspective may be weakened or lost; deep knowledge and expertise on the rest of the organization is not necessarily held there; confusion can arise because the visible senior leaders of strategic partnering are also those of this hosting entity.

- Split among multiple units. Again, experience does not advocate this option, as it carries most of the challenges mentioned above. Additionally, some of the operating processes that make strategic partnering successful cannot be easily developed and enforced with a divided approach. The learning and development of deep capability occurs most effectively through a single, joined-up unit.

Each individual strategic partnership is led and supported by a dedicated Strategic Partnership Team (SPT). Each SPT includes a Strategic Partnership Manager, with the number and roles of other team members decided according to the importance, complexity and materiality of the co-operation. The central SPU is therefore mainly the sum of these SPTs, as it integrates the portfolio of strategic partnerships plus, as discussed later, a very small shared functional team.

Focusing and excelling in a few selected activities

Five core missions ... plus one

Part of the power of the model is to be extremely clear on what the team members in the central SPU, and by inference members of each individual SPT, do ... and equally importantly, don't do. This precision will ensure they become experts – hopefully world-class – in their core activities, and deliver a distinctive and extraordinary contribution to the rest of the organization. As represented in Figure 5.1, here is what we believe these five priorities and core accountabilities – plus one – should be.

FIGURE 5.2   5 + 1 key missions of the partnering team

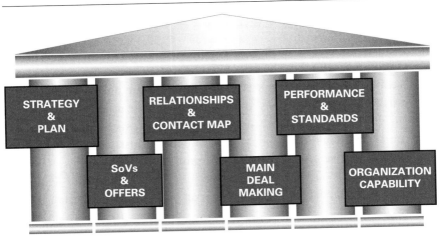

Establish and set the strategic partnership strategy and plan

As with any enterprise or business, each individual strategic partnership requires a clear strategy, the purpose of Chapter 8. Strategic partnering being mainly about the unknown, the innovative rather than the incremental and big rather than small, the effort behind and attention to strategy are arguably even more critical than for established activities or businesses. Once the strategy is set, the SPT will deploy it across the organization, such that maximum sustainable value is created and the partnership objectives and required resources are aligned.

Develop the core value proposition and value-added 'offers'

Value is where everything starts and finishes with strategic partnering and experience shows that developing the 'sources of value' (SoVs) is the most complex challenge to these programmes. We will reflect on how to achieve this in Chapter 9 of *Strategic Partnering*. The SPT will have ultimate accountability for the overall value proposition and offer to the partner. Even more importantly, they will coordinate, support and monitor the development of sophisticated, differentiated and compelling 'offers', so that the strategic partnership is justified and underpinned by deeply rooted substantive value.

Define and manage the partner-to-partner contact map: hold selected critical relationships

As detailed later in Chapter 7, there can be tens or hundreds of individual relationships between partners. Moreover, the success of the partnership will rely to a large extent on a set of well-ordered governance and joint operating processes. The SPT will have accountability for defining and managing the overall contact map and making the rules and standards of engagement clear to all involved. Clearly, the Strategic Partnership Manager and his/her SPT colleagues will also hold a number of critical relationships themselves.

Lead the negotiation and completion of the main deals

As individual strategic collaborations develop, it is likely that formal deals and contracts will be required for some 'areas of co-operation'. We are ambivalent about the impact of such formal agreements, as we have seen extraordinary alliances develop without a single deal or contract, while others needed more formality. In the case of strategically important deals, the SPT leads and will have accountability. Indeed, negotiations will optimally be managed through leveraging the SPT's unique aptitudes, including its focus, capacity, expert knowledge and day-to-day familiarity with the partner.

Be accountable for 'performance' and set standards for the execution of the partnership

In this model, the SPT and more specifically the Strategic Partnership Manager, have ultimate accountability for the overall 'performance' of the relationship. Observation shows this is not the case in many alternative partnering models, primarily because organizations often struggle to define an effective 'performance management process'. In Chapter 11, we will examine how 'performance' is assessed and allocated, and how the SPT's accountability for strategic and financial value delivery is crucial to reaching 'transformational' value. This accountability will also encompass monitoring 'performance' and intervening as required, as well as setting standards for the delivery of the partnership across the organization's verticals, geographies and functions.

Grow the organizational capability

A sixth core mission should also be mentioned, and arises when the partnership operates at portfolio rather than individual strategic partnership level. In this case the SPT is empowered to own and grow the enterprise partnering capability. This activity is arguably life critical to the central Strategic Partnering Unit and very important to the rest of the organization, where best practice will be shared on 'offer' development, relationship management, etc.

Hold a clear and distinctive position in the organization

In complex organizations, clarity of role, respective accountabilities and rules of the game make a considerable difference to successful working as 'one team' and delivering outstanding results. The section above hopefully provided some clarity on what the SPT should and should not do. This should eliminate areas of confusion over accountabilities with other departments, business units, geographical divisions, etc., whose main role will be their contribution to the development of 'offers' and the physical 'local' delivery of the partnership's SoVs.

Equally, the SPT should not confuse accountabilities with the enterprise's central functions, such as R&D, public affairs and manufacturing, which are controlled elsewhere in the organization. It will often be tempting for the SPT and their colleagues to move across boundaries; this should be strongly discouraged as it will hinder the full enterprise's mobilization and effectiveness.

Interfaces with the verticals, business units and geographical divisions need to be codified and processed, with vertical and functional organizations operating within the parameters agreed with, and finally set by, the SPTs, as described later in this chapter.

Key roles in the strategic partnering organization

Strategic partnering will only succeed if the whole organization gets mobilized behind the programme and actively manages each of the important entity and individual relationships within the partner's organization. Tom Albanese talks about this multi-level engagement:

Tom Albanese

"There needs to be a strong involvement and alignment at different levels:

Firstly, the people who do the stuff on the ground, so that these persons of both parties who are on walkie-talkies, whatever they are doing and whatever they are saying, can actually trust each other. So, literally, the truck showing up into the yard.

The second would be at the commercial level, where there is an off-site relationship which really sets the rules of engagement in commercial terms.

And the third is almost more a diplomatic relationship that can see through the day-to-day issues on the ground, and also the day-to-day issues in the commercial negotiations, and can have a strategic discussion.

So each have their role and those who don't have enough time to get involved with what is going on with the guys with the walkie-talkies, still play their role strongly.

As shown on Figure 5.3, the partnership will involve leaders and team members in the central partnering unit and others in the wider organization. Any partnering model should include a clear scope and accountabilities for each role, and methods to reach the magic of unifying all disparate units in a horizontal effort in service of the partnership success.

Let us review these critical and pivotal roles to success, starting with those in the central strategic partnering team.

The central strategic partnering team

With an objective to build a strong impact team, while staying simple and efficient, the central team (light blue in Figure 5.3) is made up of just four main roles:

- **The Strategic Partnership Manager (SPM):** There is one dedicated SPM for each individual strategic partnership. The centre of the partnership, he/she is accountable for the co-operation strategy, the 'offer', the relationship – including convening for governance reviews – its 'performance', and heading up the partnership team. Some organizations, such as IBM, also refer to them as the senior 'point of all escalations'. He/she is recognized by both partners as holding the pivotal role between the two organizations.

FIGURE 5.3 Key roles in strategic partnering

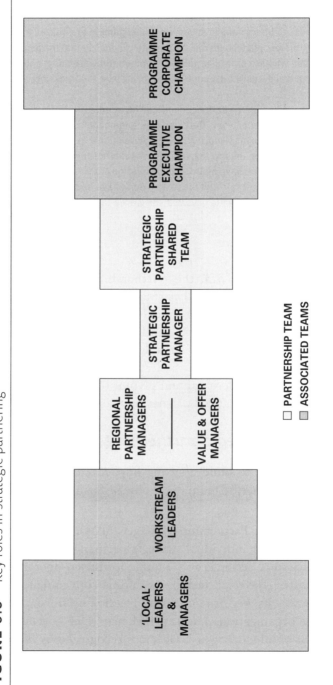

PROGRAMME CORPORATE CHAMPION

PROGRAMME EXECUTIVE CHAMPION

STRATEGIC PARTNERSHIP SHARED TEAM

STRATEGIC PARTNERSHIP MANAGER

REGIONAL PARTNERSHIP MANAGERS

VALUE & OFFER MANAGERS

WORKSTREAM LEADERS

'LOCAL' LEADERS & MANAGERS

☐ PARTNERSHIP TEAM

▨ ASSOCIATED TEAMS

As Viren Doshi says, their passion and entire professional existence are defined by the partner and the partnership. SPMs need to be amazing professionals and people, as will be discussed in the next chapter.

> **Viren Doshi**
>
> My title is 'Senior Vice President, Client Service Officer'. My client is my market; my client is my business.

- **The Regional Partnership Manager (RPM):** The role and accountability of the RPMs are very similar to those of the SPMs, although applied on a regional basis and by delegation of the SPM for that region. The RPMs, who fulfil core roles in the SPT, are needed when leadership is required on strategic work, comprehensive 'offer' development, extensive relationship management and material 'performance' delivery for the partnership in the region. They are not to be confused with managers in vertical or regional operations, who will also contribute to the partnership but will have different priorities.

- **The Value & Offer Manager (VOM):** These roles are often the key missing piece in many strategic partnering organizations. Value creation and related 'offers' will be central to the origination, continuation and success of any strategic partnership. But it is always a big challenge to innovate; more so between two organizations; even more so on a sustainable, continuous, rapid and large-scale basis. The critical tasks of the VOM will be to ensure that the joint workstreams have structure, objectives and momentum; to support the internal experts, so they keep focused on critical 'offer' development; to interface with the partner's experts to test assumptions and progress the selected SoVs, applying the day-after-day practice; and to enable and monitor high quality relationships. We wouldn't establish a strategic partnering organization without VOMs!

- **The Strategic Partnering Shared Team (PST):** The whole focus and most of the resources of the central partnering team should be biased towards the individual partnership teams. Nonetheless,

FIGURE 5.4   A small partnering functional shared team

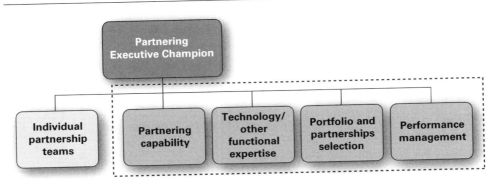

as shown on Figure 5.4, a small and very focused shared team is required at SPU/portfolio level, to provide leadership and support to the few critical areas where sharing makes sense:

- partnering capability build, a critical need for the whole central SPU and each SPT;

- technology or other shared functional expertise required across the partnerships;

- portfolio and potential partnership assessment, to lead the Stage 1 selection process and support the development of individual partnerships in their journey throughout the 15-step model;

- 'performance management', whose importance will be established in Chapter 11 both for internal and partner purposes.

The 'informal team': roles critical to strategic partnering outside the central team

Many other roles in the rest of the organization need to be mobilized and are equally important to success. This is the 'informal team', and consists primarily of four roles (dark blue in Figure 5.3):

- The **Area of Co-operation/Workstream Leaders** (ACL): As for the VOMs, with whom they share connected activities, their importance is usually understated in most strategic partnering organizations. They are leaders and representatives of the organization's verticals, functional areas, etc, where the co-operation will develop and create mutual value. In practice, they will take leadership of the joint workstream for their area and associate with their equivalent in the partner's corresponding area. They can be functional leaders, eg reputation, lobbying, technology, supply chain; or business/operational leaders, eg sector, business unit, procurement. Without the championing of their area of co-operation and their team's engagement, value would not be generated and the partnership idea would have no real substance.

- **Local Partnership or Delivery Managers:** As AoCs and SoVs develop and the importance and materiality of the partnership grow, a significant number of roles will be involved across the organization, to contribute to 'offers', lead on delivery, create relationships, etc. This network can ultimately grow to include hundreds of people and will liaise and coordinate with the individual central partnership team, to act in line with strategy, enrich the co-operation and deliver within the required standards. As no formal link usually exists between the central team and these roles in the matrix, rallying their support will require good quality engagement processes and the delivery of tangible business benefits to them, beyond the sense of 'being good citizens'.

- The **Executive Champion (EC)** for the partnering programme: The individual SPTs report to the senior enterprise executive accountable for the programme. He/she will be the executive voice for strategic partnering across the organization and will have accountability for the partnerships portfolio, resources and overall 'performance'. Where tensions arise between the central SPU and other departments or verticals (eg on respective strategic priorities, resources and funding, short- vs longer-term) the EC would intervene to agree the way forward. Most importantly, the EC will 'protect' the Strategic Partnering Team from the pull and demands of the wider organization. Too often, enterprises are inward-looking and extremely absorbing of their people's time. Conversely, the SPT members need to be out there with the partners and available to them in a day-to-day approach. Hence, the EC should shield them from the internal pull, so they can accomplish their mission. The EC also plays a central role in the relationship map, developing an enduring relationship with the relevant senior executive in the partner's organization and co-leading the executive champion governance with him or her.

- The **Corporate Champion (CC)** for the partnering programme: Ideally a member of the main board and at least of the executive committee, the CC ensures the alignment and support of the enterprise to the overall programme and the individual strategic partnerships. He/she sets the tone for strategic partnering in the organization. Throughout the development of enduring relationships, the CC also acts as the co-chair of the Chairman or CEO level 'corporate champion' governance (see Chapter 7) of some individual strategic partnerships, selected for their relevance, importance, high visibility or material value.

John Browne

I think that all leadership acts are about setting the tone and providing a role model, whether it is the leader or someone else in the senior team, for everyone to follow. So, the number one rule is to set the tone, the number two rule is set the plan, number three is make sure people are incentivized and rewarded to deliver, and number four is deliver. You need to be seen to be doing that, be seen to get it right and part of the way of being seen to get it right is always to repeat stories – 'we did this well, we did this badly' – all that you do during a performance review. It is those sorts of things that apply in almost any leadership act and, I think, very strongly when managing partnerships.

As the corporate champion simply cannot – and should not – lead all the individual 'corporate champion' governance, good practice is that other members of the board or the executive committee play this role, bringing their weight to the individual partnership(s) they commit to while getting direct exposure to and experience of the partnering programme.

'Must have' principles for setting up strategic partnering teams

So, strategic partnering will have greatest chances of success if a central team is established with a clear ethos and distinctive accountabilities; if it is composed of a few key roles; and if it operates using well-codified and tested processes. Experience has taught us a few 'must have' principles for designing and organizing the central partnering team:

One strategic partnering organization, one senior leader, one single team

As noted above, centricity and expertise are the name of the game! A single central strategic partnering organization will enable world-class capability development and deployment. Single individual partnership teams will provide the right focus on each relationship. One senior leader, the SPM, will ensure that each individual alliance benefits from powerful and enduring leadership. One single team for each strategic co-operation will provide the expert resource and dedication to develop the partnership to mutual 'transformational' value. In trivial terms, let's organize so that great people 'live and die for their strategic partnership'. Lord Coe talks about his 'One Team' approach in the London 2012 Olympics Organising Committee.

Sebastian Coe

Everyone involved was taking pride in being a part of the London 2012 journey and knowing what that journey was about and knowing what their part and their role in that journey was. You know, it is a story that is probably not true, but, famously, it is often told that when John Kennedy went to Cape Canaveral, sadly before it was called the John F Kennedy Space Center, the first person he meets is the caretaker. And he shakes his hand like a good politician and says, 'what do you do?' And the guy turns to him and says, 'I'm part of a team trying to put a man on the moon'.

I wanted to feel this same level of involvement and pride in my organization at LOCOG. It didn't really matter whether you sat on the reception or you were the chief executive, you had one objective and that was to create the right environment for the athlete!

A few roles entirely defined and dedicated to the strategic partner; almost no shared team

We believe that almost all partnering resources should be deployed in direct support of individual strategic partnerships, as they are the thrust of the whole case and consideration. There should be no bureaucracy and very few inner interfaces. Hence, everything will be focused on what it takes to succeed with the partnerships.

Clearly differentiated activities from the rest of the organization

We have mentioned '5 + 1 core activities' which the partnership team should focus on. Remaining single-minded, team members will reach functional excellence in the six primary practices of strategic partnering.

This focus will equally provide a remarkable and healthy clarity on respective accountabilities between the central team and other parts of the enterprise. Organizations can develop considerable anxiety and get fixated on trying to clarify the respective roles and accountabilities of their various entities. Once some basics have been established, it is vital to stop agonizing on this matter, operate the model and rely on intelligent and willing team work. Figure 5.5 shows a comprehensive example of how respective accountabilities can be defined between a central strategic partnering unit and the rest of the organization. This may prove a simple and balanced guideline when you establish your own partnering model.

A very flat organization, ideally only two levels

This principle is both critical and not easy to achieve and stick to over time. The determined guideline is to keep the strategic partnering team extremely flat, ideally with no more than two organizational levels in the team itself, as shown in Figure 5.6:

- Level 0 is the executive champion for the strategic partnering programme.
- Level 1 consists of the partnership SPMs and a few shared team leaders.
- And Level 2 makes up their entire teams.

The main rationale behind this principle resides in the fact that success requires senior leaders and managers, empowered to represent the full organization, developing senior relationships, and capable of decisions with and in front of the partner. This will not happen if the partnership team members are buried in the depths of the organization. And no capable senior leader would even consider joining the central partnering team if he/she had limited responsibility and visibility. It is therefore vital to keep the structure very flat and SPM's access to the top of the house straight and simple.

FIGURE 5.5 Central strategic partnering team vs other departments: Respective roles

Core Mission	Central Partnering Team	Associated and Involved
Strategy and plan	• Develop the individual partnership strategy and plan, in line with main involved departments' participation and competitive strategies and financial frameworks.	• Develop and implement the department plan for the partnership, consistent with overall strategy. • Communicate, implement and deliver the partnership strategy.
Value proposition and offers	• Understand partner's needs and define the focused offer development process that 'packages' the full organization's offer, to win. • Finalize the value proposition and offer, ensuring they meet partner's and departments' objectives.	• Develop specific offers to meet partner's needs, consistent with the partnership strategy and department's brand and channel strategies. • Place and deliver the department's offer components to the partner and provide feedback.
Relationship	• Define rules of engagement, design and manage the cross organization contact map in coordination and with input of the departments.	• Within the contact map, manage the department's specific relationships and on-going partner contact.
Performance	• Set and meet mid-term and in-year strategic milestones and financial targets, consistent with the partnership strategy. • Jointly monitor and communicate performance.	• Set the same milestones and financial targets as the central team, consistent with partnership strategy. • Provide resources to deliver plan and activities.
Deal making	• Define the deal strategy and deal parameters in consultation with departments. • Ensure deal is executed.	• Execute deal within an agreed framework and targets.
Capability	• Develop strategic partnering capabilities with a consistent transfer approach and geographical spread of the model across the departments.	• Identify and develop target groups for strategic partnering management capability development.

FIGURE 5.6   Each strategic partnership led by two-layer team

A challenge to this principle arises when the portfolio size grows, in which case the EC may not have the ability any more to lead or oversee all the SPMs. In this situation, incidentally a nice problem to have, we would advise setting up coherent sector spaces – otherwise called practices – where strategic partnerships are collected together coherently by industry. In each of these spaces, and without changing the two-layer principle, a 'premium inter pares' SPM assumes some of the leadership account-abilities for the other partnerships. But no SPM loses their critical direct links with the EC in regard to the partnership strategy and their personal development.

Excellence, excellence and ... excellence

The whole partnering model is predicated on doing and achieving the 'extraordinary'. Only excellence will trigger and deliver the required highest standards of inputs and outcomes. The partnering system demands outstanding application. The design of the partnership strategies, the 'offer' development and relationship management require mastery. Hence, the partnering team members have to combine strong leadership and deep functional expertise. Strategic partnering is about excellence ... and acts as a school for excellence.

A winning strategic partnering organization

Our general observation is that organizational structures and related operating processes for strategic partnering are seldom designed optimally. When asked, executives often comment that 'going all the way' necessitates significant organizational changes and the introduction of substantial new ways of working across the enterprise. This is surely a part of the story, another being the frequent lack of clarity on what works and what doesn't, on the primary and winning principles rather than the secondary ones.

We should not understate the cultural and operating shift required to reach excellence in strategic partnering. A key one at the convergence between the 'leadership' operating model and the 'organization' model presented in this chapter is the genuine application of the inverted hierarchical pyramid, as represented on Figure 5.7.

FIGURE 5.7   The strategic partnering inverted pyramid

The strategic partnership is led and assumed by the SPM and his/her team. They support the AoC and SoV leaders to develop 'offers' and value for and from the partnership. The informal team and the enterprise executives play a major enabling and guiding role to the partnership.

Let us summarize how this chapter attempts to guide the constitution of an enterprise partnering organization and its evolution over time:

Summary: Establishing a winning strategic partnering organization

- Set up strategic partnering as a fully-fledged and core organizational component of the enterprise, not a compromise.
- Think of the world through the lens of each individual partnership.
- Apply the 'leadership' management model.
- Create a unified, separate, specific and focused strategic partnering unit (SPU).
- Ensure that the SPU focuses and excels in six areas of expertise: strategy, value proposition, relationships, main deals, 'performance' and capability development. Don't let any other activity divert you from these.
- Bring only a few high capability people into the partnering team; ensure that the vast majority of them are focused on single partnerships.
- Keep your partnering organization very flat, with no more than two layers.
- Be clear on what the roles are in the central partnering team and in 'the informal team'.
- Strive for excellence throughout the journey.

We are now organizationally ready to bring in the talents who will practise alchemy and turn the partnering idea into something extraordinary. Let us take on the objective of matching the roles we have just defined with the fantastic people we absolutely need.

06
Developing world-class strategic partnering human capital

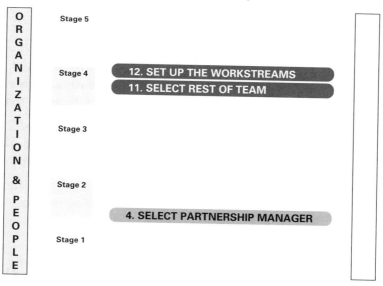

The Strategic Partnership Model

ORGANIZATION & PEOPLE

Stage 5

Stage 4
12. SET UP THE WORKSTREAMS
11. SELECT REST OF TEAM

Stage 3

Stage 2

4. SELECT PARTNERSHIP MANAGER

Stage 1

Far better is it to dare mighty things, to win glorious triumphs, even though checked by failure ... than to rank with those poor spirits who neither enjoy much nor suffer much, because they live in a gray twilight that knows not victory nor defeat.

THEODORE ROOSEVELT

Judge a man by his questions rather than by his answers.

VOLTAIRE

Applying and bringing the strategic partnership system to fruition requires very special talents and skills. Arguably, more than in many other endeavours, succeeding with strategic partnering and turning a little into a lot depend upon considerable ingenuity, knowledge and emotional intelligence from those involved.

Indeed, human capital is at the very heart of successful strategic partnering. This is not just any human capital though, as the mix and volume of the personal qualities necessary to effect a complex and enduring relationship are somewhat different to those for more traditional businesses. For example, a high measure of resilience and humility both come top of the desired attributes.

In this chapter, we consider the necessary leadership, expertise and personal attributes required in the key strategic partnering roles. We then describe mechanisms to select and develop such skills, either from deep within the organization or reaching out to the outside world in search of the winning team. Finally, we discuss the team's culture and values, as a major source of collective and individual impact. Subheadings include:

- Who are the right talents? We will discuss how a strong set of personal attributes is required. We will describe the essential competencies and qualifying experiences for Strategic Partnership Managers, Value & Offer Managers and other important roles.

- How will we identify and select our team members? We will share a suggested process to identify such skills within or outside the organization, ensuring an 'absolute' fit between people and roles.

- How will we further develop talents for excellence? Finally, we will consider a framework for professional and personal development.

Who are the right talents and what are their essential qualities?

High-performing leaders and managers in strategic partnering will epitomize a special blend of leadership, functional expertise and personal attributes. Actually, everything about our partnering team members starts with the last point, ie who they are as people, as individuals. Remember Chapter 4, when we were considering and selecting strategic partners. As in a personal relationship, we needed the partner to be 'a Mensch', ie a 'good' person trying to do the right thing and guided by deeply held values. It is very much the same for people in strategic partnering, as reflected by our interviewee leaders.

John Seifert

When strategic partnership is at work, the people in the mix (not always the most senior ones) set the context for what is in the best interest of the brand and organization as a whole. These people are fearless about working horizontally, challenging conventions and breaking down barriers for the greater good of the organization. They put the good of the enterprise ahead of their own goals, accomplishments, and success over time.

Sebastian Coe

I had been there as a working broadcaster and journalist, as a vice president of the largest Olympic sport, as a chairman of a bid and I had seen it through more optics than probably most people. So, I knew how complicated London 2012 would be and it saved me a lot of time, because I knew two things: I had to have robust secure relationships that you could absolutely rely upon and I had to have the smartest people from their sector who understood the complexities of the stakeholder landscape.

Shelly Lazarus

In terms of dealing with professional service firms, my observation is that the most talented individuals in these firms want to work on those projects where there is a strategic relationship and not someone simply 'ordering up a print ad'. So a client who is smart will think about what kind of talent they are getting within any professional services firm and if they continue to be smart, they will know that the best people work on the strategic relationships and the less good people work on the one-off projects.

A very strong communality of personal attributes

Having led and observed hundreds of professionals leading or managing partnerships, it has become clearer how similar the personalities are of those people who do best; and how those who are missing some critical personality traits find it less natural and even hard to excel, let alone succeed. Not that it is impossible, but certainly much harder.

So, what are the personal traits required for success, whatever the precise role in the team? Figure 6.1 is an attempt to capture these attributes:

FIGURE 6.1 Consistent human attributes across the partnering team

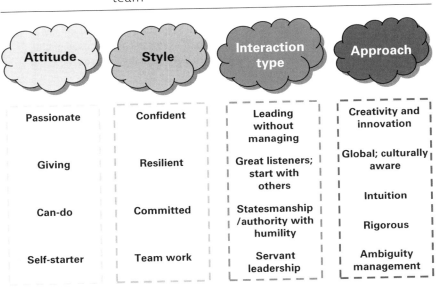

Without going into great detail, let's unpick a few core categories. For example, we have observed that strategic partnering team members need a considerable amount of generosity, humility and lack of bias, to ensure they always consider the perspective of others rather than mainly their own. There should indeed be very little ego in these people! As an interesting combination, they will also possess an amazing inner strength, and a mixture of confidence, relentless resilience and deep commitment. And they will demand a great deal of themselves, striving passionately for excellence and the right outcome for the 'cause', combined with a remarkably positive attitude.

> **Peter Foss**
>
> I look for people that have a lot of self-confidence, are very comfortable with themselves and have excellent listening skills. They need to be curious about things and always ask questions and look for new and better ways to do things. They should know how to probe without being irritating, to understand what is important to the partner. And they really listen, so they get the insight into what the other person is really saying. And then, they are able to pull that information together into a meaningful plan to work together.
>
> The great partnership team player has strong interpersonal skills, as you really need to work with and at the same time lead people; and others should want to work with that person. Because if you are going to lead a large opportunity across a large company and if you call someone, you want that they answer the phone or call you back.
>
> You have to have a true desire to win, an innate desire to be a winner. Not to the point of being abrasive, but with a certain amount of aggressive behaviour to win, although well managed. And these winners will want to move quickly, as there is a lot of value in speed, in rapid resolution of issues and fast penetration of opportunities.
>
> Finally, they have to be big people. If you really want to do strategic partnering, you need someone who has been around a number of years and has built some relationships. I think it would be very hard just to pop in and start from scratch. It is important that they are pretty senior people and that is a big change from the way we used to think about such things. But if 80 per cent of your business is done with 50 partners max, how could you not afford to have your really best people on strategic partnerships, those who excel in the skills that we talked about!

It is quintessential to highlight the need of being able to deal with and manage ambiguity extremely well. After all, strategic partnering roles are all about the unknown and the new, about a large number of relationships all pursuing diverging agendas. Very often, there won't be rational answers to plenty of questions and our team members need to weave through this uncertainty without being distracted from their mission and 'destination'.

> **Shelly Lazarus**
>
> Somebody said to me one day, 'Do not even try to enter this business if you are not comfortable with ambiguity.' Business development is filled with complexity and ambiguity. And the more complex and ambiguous something is, the more you are going to need strategic partnerships. As an aside, I don't know how many people would raise their hand when you ask, 'Do you like complexity and ambiguity?'

Discussing people's attributes is not about making judgements. And we are not suggesting that these traits are better or worse than others, or that they make some people better or less good than others. What experience tells us is that people with these particular personal attributes are a more natural fit for success in a strategic partnering role. And it is indeed this optimal fit between a person and a role that we are looking for, which in practice means that these attributes are a defining part of our selection 'lenses' and central to the assessment process described later in this chapter.

Strategic partnership manager (SPM)

The Strategic Partnership Managers make or break strategic co-operations. In our model, they are given the central role and accountability for the partnership. They are expected to combine the right leadership skills, strong expertise and to fully focus on practising the 'leadership' management approach to reach 'transformational' value. They are the modern leaders, as defined insightfully by Jill Ader.

Jill Ader, Member of the Board, Egon Zehnder International

The sources of individual authority in organizations vary with their culture and with times. Traditional legitimacy comes from the individual's position in the entity's hierarchy. Another essential source of authority may arise from one's functional expertise. And a third from the ability to rally others behind a vision, a mission and strongly held values. In today's world, there seems to be a major shift towards the last of these and a defining advantage to the leaders with high engagement skills, leading by example, making value-driven choices and building great relationships with their multiple stakeholders.

Let's look first at the core profile and capabilities and then add some experience-based wisdom to the selection, development and management of SPMs.

The SPM core profile and capabilities

The SPM profile stands as a combination of the personal attributes shown in Figure 6.1 and the leadership and functional abilities represented in Figure 6.2.

Without aiming to comment on all parts of Figure 6.2, which is hopefully largely self-explanatory and of some help for your own profiling, let's summarize the SPM key competencies:

1 A strong strategist, capable of vision and disciplined planning.

2 An entrepreneur, able to lead the development of new material value propositions and link activity to value.

3 An experienced business leader, with strong 'customer-driven' business acumen and 'having seen it before'.

4 A diplomat, with distinctive relationship capabilities.

5 An ambassador, able to 'navigate' through all types of situations across partners' organizations – including the resolution of issues – and epitomizing cultural empathy.

6 A politician, able to feel and leverage the moving context internally and externally, using strong communication skills.

7 A deliverer, used to 'passing the finish line' and finding strategic insights in 'performance'.

8 A negotiator, with strong 'selling' experience.

9 A coaching-type team leader.

Unlike in more traditional approaches, deep knowledge of the partner's industry, market, products or services is not an absolute must. Nor is there an absolute need to have resided in some of the partner's key regions, with the absolute exception of their home country. Individuals who combine most or all of the above and use the strategic partnering model diligently will catch up fast on these gaps. The selection grid will therefore only refer to a reasonably connected experience base and include sector- and geography-specific knowledge only as a plus.

FIGURE 6.2 Strategic Partnership Manager: Essential capabilities

Core mission	Core activities	Core profile and capabilities
Strategy and plan	• Develop the individual partnership strategy. • Ensure partner and internal alignment behind the strategy.	**THE ENTREPRENEURIAL STRATEGIST** The SPM will need to project well afar, be strategically ambitious and clear and see opportunities that others don't.
Value proposition and offers	• Have ultimate accountability on the overall value proposition and the individual material offer components. • The SPM is the main 'support and challenge' leader across the partnership's workstreams.	**THE BUSINESS LEADER AND DIPLOMAT** The SPM will guide the transformation of value substance between the partners. He/she will need to align many parties to see and support the invisible and new.
Relationship	• Define and manage the contact map. • Ensure extraordinary relationships are built. • Convene the corporate governance processes. • Develop and maintain selected key individual relationships.	**THE AMBASSADOR AND POLITICIAN** Representing one party to another, the SPM will need all qualities of an ambassador. He/she might even be based at the partner's premises. The SPM role will require considerable influencing and to create familiarity day-after-day.
Performance	• Set mid-term and in-year strategic milestones and financial targets. • Hold ultimate accountability for strategic and financial delivery: intervene as required.	**THE DELIVERER** Nothing will take the eye of the SPM away from a fierce determination to deliver for both partners.
Deal making	• Ensure the deal strategy and parameters are clear. Ensure conclusion of the target deals. • Ensure the deals are executed.	**THE NEGOTIATOR** The SPM guides and leads teams as appropriate on terms and process of umbrella or material deals.
Capability	• Ensure the required strategic partnering capabilities are in place and being developed day by day to succeed with the strategic partnership.	**THE COACH** The SPM supports and challenges the team members, continuously developing people.

Some wisdom on the selection, development and management of SPMs

Over the years, we have drawn conclusions on some winning practices about SPMs, listed below.

SPMs are from here

As they aim to develop extraordinary relationships and lead the involved parties through 'transformation', SPMs need to be Germans when the partner is German, Japanese with Japanese partners, American with American partners, Chinese with Chinese partners, etc. Senior local leaders can understand their counterparts far better than anybody else. As their partnership will probably be global or at least regional, it does not mean the SPMs shouldn't be globally aware and culturally sensitive as well. But nothing will replace local knowledge, intuition and the ability to hear the weak and more subtle signals!

SPMs need to be fully empowered

As suggested repeatedly in this book, SPMs need to be genuinely and deeply empowered. It will not always be easy for CEOs and senior executives to truly delegate and, when meeting with their equivalent numbers in partner organizations, to operate within the SPM's guidance and position him/her highly. Using an analogy, the SPM should be like a priest in the army, talking to a general with the rank of a general and to a soldier with the rank of a soldier. It is critical that the SPMs operate with a mindset of needing to fully deserve such empowerment and are also experienced enough to use their authority wisely. For instance, they will need to be natural at 'saying what we do; doing what we say'.

Two core profiles

Consistently, SPMs whom we have seen succeed have been personally 'big' and businesswise 'senior' people. These roles are not for average performers or inexperienced individuals. Two main profiles often perform well:

- Experienced mature leaders, with 20–25+ years of leading businesses successfully, of types that required extensive interfaces with other parties, and combining this deep experience with an intact appetite to remain a fierce deliverer, as noted in Figure 6.2. These profiles usually bring considerable strengths to the 'experienced business leader', 'diplomat' and 'coaching leader' capability areas.

- Leaders with shorter experience of 12–15 years, who are on a fast-track career path and combine strong emerging abilities in all essential capability areas. They are eager to 'transform' themselves through the strategic partnering experience and model, to accelerate their personal and professional development. These profiles usually excel as 'entrepreneurial strategists' and in the development of new material value propositions and offers.

Better to go with nobody rather than with an unsuitable SPM

Only professionals who present a very strong combination of the capabilities and attributes defined above offer a significant chance of success as SPMs. As discussed later in the selection process section of this chapter, it is important to resist all temptations to select a SPM who would not offer enough of these characteristics. It will always be better to alter the pace of development of a partnership than to go with the risk of the wrong SPM, as this could lead to mutual disaster!

They will all need to learn!

As close as selected SPMs are to the ideal profile, none will have the capabilities required in full when joining the strategic partnering team. It will take 12 to 18 months for the best to 'get it'. The essential guideline to newcomers will be: understand, learn and apply the strategic partnership model; be humble and reconsider what you believe you know and combine it with the strategic partnering model to raise your practice to a new stronger 'transformational' level. Let's hear from Ian Robertson on the determination they will need to demonstrate.

Ian Robertson

People need a hunger, a hunger for success. Complacency must be avoided at all costs. We expect our teams to get up in the morning energized and ready to shift the needle, not to say 'aren't we doing well'. This is essential to be a good partner in any co-operation between organizations. If one partner is more passive and only reacts to the actions of the other, then the relationship starts to fail. Neither can lose the fight to press forward and challenge constantly.

No SPM should change role before four to five years

A typical business cycle takes four to five years: understand in Year 1; seed in Year 2; grow in Year 3; harvest in Years 4 and 5. It will also take 18 months for the best SPMs to master their role and a minimum of three years to reach expert level. The partner will also expect strong continuity in the relationship and joint partnership leadership, to build on the established trust. For mutual advantage, both business and personal, a standard practice in the strategic partnering team will therefore be a strong stability in roles.

Let's admit it: great SPMs are rare people, bringing and growing into a strong combination of many critical attributes. They present a considerable opportunity, a significant risk and a true investment. Hence, looking for and developing them should be a top and everlasting priority!

Value & Offer Manager (VOM)

As real substance and 'sources of value' (SoVs) will be defining to any co-operation, the people who create and develop these, the Value & Offer Managers (VOMs), are central to the strategic partnering model and team. VOM profiles stand as a combination of the personal attributes shown in Figure 6.1 and leadership and functional abilities represented in Figure 6.3.

The VOM key competencies

1   A strong strategist, capable of vision for their 'offer' area and of connecting their effort with the wider plans.

2   An 'engineer', not literally speaking, but able to bring a rigorous scientific approach to creating the unknown.

3   A subject matter expert: unlike SPMs, VOMs need a deep understanding of their own and their partner's sectors, as well as how they interface.

4   A politician, as they need to overcome at least three major obstacles: work by influence rather than direct authority, guide people to look for the unknown, and operate across organizations.

5   A deliverer, as value and progressive 'offers' are the name of the game for the partnership.

FIGURE 6.3 Value & Offer Manager: Essential capabilities

Core mission	Core activities	Core profile and capabilities
Strategy and plan	• Develop individual workstream strategies. • Position the workstreams, value proposition and offers in the overall partnership strategic context.	**THE STRATEGIC ENGINEER** The VOM will need to be strategically clear on the destination and possibilities of the joint offer development. Objectives will need to be consistent and material to both organizations' strategy.
Value proposition and offer development	• Single point of accountability for the development of advanced offers. • Lead innovation in the interfaces between party A and party B.	**THE SUBJECT MATTER EXPERT** The VOM will lead the transformation of value substance between the partners in selected areas. He/she will need to be or become expert in these areas and be naturally deeply innovative.
Relationships	• Develop and place the value proposition and offers with the partner. • Develop the value proposition and offers with the internal teams. • Develop and maintain outstanding external and internal individual relationships.	**THE POLITICIAN** The VOM will guide and influence other leaders and experts to achieve things they never did before. This will need all the qualities of a great politician, to help people 'see what they don't see' and create familiarity day-after-day.
Performance	• Set mid-term and in-year strategic milestones and financial targets for the offers. • Hold accountability for setting the delivery parameters, and strategic and financial delivery.	**THE DELIVERER** The VOM will be guided by and have deep practice of how to deliver sources of value through advanced offers.
Deal making	• In case contracts are required, ensure the deal parameters are clear and conclude them.	**THE NEGOTIATOR** The VOM will negotiate and close contracts.
Capability	• Ensure the required capabilities are in place in the partner's and his/her own organization so the value proposition and offers are developed.	**THE DIPLOMAT** The VOM will work persuasively with the parties so the appropriate human resources are in place.

6 A negotiator, to agree the necessary contracts. A somewhat different negotiation type though, based on creating familiarity 'day-after-day', rather than a 'smoky room' approach.

7 A diplomat in and out, as he/she critically represents the organization with many important counterparts at all levels across the partner's structure, and needs to get them to do what they would not naturally consider doing.

Principles to make VOMs successful

Much of the experienced-based wisdom applicable to SPMs also applies to the VOMs, notably:

- VOMs need to be strongly empowered;
- they need to be senior and sufficiently experienced;
- it is better to go with nobody rather with an unfit VOM;
- they will all need to learn;
- no VOM should change role before four to five years.

However, and less importantly than for SPMs, VOMs will not necessarily need to be locals. The language of expertise being universal, the VOM authority and impact will come mainly from their functional capabilities and their ability to get teams to join forces to achieve a common goal.

The roles of successful VOMs are simply extraordinary, because they are to a very large extent the human centre of the strategic partnership. They stand at the heart of future technological, political and market progress in the sectors they serve, hence the need for their strategic ability. They are experts in multiple areas, although not the most experienced in any one, hence becoming indispensable 'translators' and connectors between multiple groups. They are central to value creation, and to the sustainability and success of the strategic partnerships. Nobody is born a natural VOM and, through learning from their role, they will develop absolutely unique capabilities, making them vital in any organization and business.

Interestingly, our observation suggests that most partnering organizations in play don't even include such roles as VOMs. Or certainly don't position or recognize them at the level they deserve. Great VOMs are rare and indispensable to the partnerships and they will require undivided attention, from selection to supporting their personal development.

Other strategic partnering roles

As described in Chapter 5, a few roles other than SPMs and VOMs will be critical to success, operating either in the central or in the extended 'informal' strategic partnering team. We are referring mainly to the regional strategic managers, the central shared team, the 'areas of co-operation' and workstream leaders, the local and delivery managers and the programme executive champion (see Figure 5.3).

As defined in Chapters 5 and 11, the central shared team includes a small group of 'performance' managers who are able to provide an integrated picture of the partnership by aggregating and supporting all SoVs from the distributed parts of the organization.

We recommend a similar attention to the selection and engagement of these critical contributors, as for the SPMs and VOMs. As represented in Figure 6.4, they will need to operate at expert level in some of the partnering capability areas and above a minimum threshold in all others. Anything less than full commitment to the partnership from any of these roles will have a detrimental effect on future success, hence the deep care and attention required.

Not all individuals involved will be experts or strong in some of the critical areas of capability.

- Those individuals operating in the central Strategic Partnering Unit (light blue in Figure 6.4) will first have to emerge successfully from our discretionary selection process, which will ensure they are fit for the role. Their focused 'in job' day-after-day exposure and experience will then take them gradually through their development path.

- The development itinerary will of course be different for those individuals who report to other parts of the organization (darker blue in Figure 6.4). For them, an appropriate multi-step plan is required. It begins with some element of selection, as we simply can't involve a person who lacks some of the critical capabilities in a partnership. The SPM, RPMs and VOMs will then stay close to those selected, notably in the early days, to set expectations and lead by example. Finally, the inclusion of partnership-related objectives in the informal team members' 'performance' scorecard, including their personal adherence to the model, will play an important role.

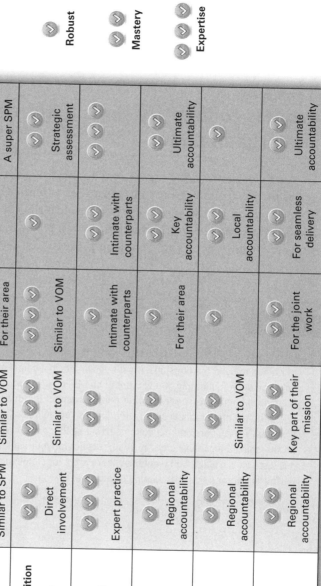

FIGURE 6.4 Essential capabilities for other partnering roles

Core mission	Regional partnership managers	Strategic partnership shared team	Workstream leaders	Local leaders and managers	Programme Executive Champion
Strategy and plan	Similar to SPM	Similar to VOM	For their area		A super SPM
Value proposition and offer development	Direct involvement	Similar to VOM	Similar to VOM		Strategic assessment
Relationships	Expert practice		Intimate with counterparts	Intimate with counterparts	
Performance	Regional accountability		For their area	Key accountability	Ultimate accountability
Deal making	Regional accountability	Similar to VOM		Local accountability	
Capability	Regional accountability	Key part of their mission	For the joint work	For seamless delivery	Ultimate accountability

Robust

Mastery

Expertise

Having now analysed the capabilities required of those whom we want to join the strategic partnering journey, we are better placed to finalize the competency maps to be used in the selection process itself. As we are looking for distinctive and exceptional talent, let's consider the guidelines which can help make the recruitment approach successful.

Process to identify skills within or outside the organization

As for all aspects of the model, we advise using a thorough process to select the talents needed for the central or extended strategic partnering team. Making the wrong assessment could bring considerable risk and expose both partners to mutual failure. Ian Davis passes on his observations regarding partnering people in professional services:

Ian Davis

"Organizations often recruit for people who they think have the capability, the attributes to build relationships. Most consultants in my field of experience tend not to be very dominating, not to want to be CEOs – some do, but not on the whole. So natural humility, respect for other people, respect for ideas is easy in this area. The principle of mutual advantage, working in very fluid, collaborative ways is also easy for lawyers and consultants because that's what we do and most are partnerships themselves anyway. Also, respect for your seniority is nothing, it is just you are older. So I would say there are a lot of advantages in terms of partnering across skill sets within professional services.

Drawing on our experience, here are a few principles on which to base the design of a recruitment process.

Use the competency maps as the basis for assessment

Considerable attention has been given to developing a clear set of attributes and competencies that are considered essential to success. They should be used diligently as the basis for assessment and the ultimate selection of people leading or participating in strategic partnering. In practice, these criteria can be gathered into assessment grids to support selection panel interviews and deliberations. Each organization will develop its own version of these grids and we have no particular preference as to their format, provided that the content is extremely rigorous.

A senior expert capability leader

The importance of building, developing and managing adequate human capability for strategic partnering is so critical that it is advisable to appoint a dedicated 'capability director' to lead its construction. He/she would be an experienced senior leader, a seasoned business person with strong people credentials rather than a pure HR specialist, and would be selected as having similar attributes and competencies to others in the central partnering team. He/she will be a cornerstone of the small strategic partnering functional shared team introduced in Chapter 5. Their role will be entirely focused on the development of the human capital indispensable to lead the enterprise's partnering strategy, providing the right level of attention and quality to this vital activity.

A dedicated and stable expert panel

From talking to different organizations, it is clear that selection itself can happen in many ways. However, our preferred process is one of a dedicated panel, who would over time develop a deep understanding of the strategic partnering model and the human attributes and competencies required to implement it. The ideal scenario is one in which the panel remains stable, with panellists holding their roles over a long period of time. In doing so, they develop a uniquely insightful view of a large number of candidates, internal or external, resulting in a powerful benchmark for selection.

As best practice, the panellists should come from a variety of sources in order to bring a robust blend of perspectives. They might include, for example: the programme Executive Champion, senior leaders in the strategic partnering team, senior retirees from the partnering team, external head hunters, etc. Subject to need, they would typically meet and interview candidates once or twice a month.

A thorough five-step selection process

Clearly, it is vital not to risk bringing an 'unfit' candidate into any role. Given the strategic importance, reputational commitment and intimate relationship with partners, the business risk attached to doing so would be very significant. Equally, the personal consequences of not succeeding would be detrimental to the individual concerned. In order to optimize the quality of selection, a series of selection filters should be considered, as represented on Figure 6.5.

FIGURE 6.5 Rigorous people selection process

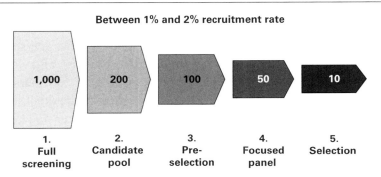

Between 1% and 2% recruitment rate

1,000	200	100	50	10
1. Full screening	2. Candidate pool	3. Pre-selection	4. Focused panel	5. Selection

The implementation method and outcomes from each of these five selection filters are as follows:

- **Mapping and screening:** roles are clearly mapped and the capability director screens all potential candidates within the organization on a regular basis. He/she establishes a 'search' network to consult and work with routinely and closely. His/her approach would involve: the Strategic Partnering Team feeding in insights and evaluations about people they work with; contacts resulting from the enterprise or the Strategic Partnering Unit communications; word of mouth; job postings; leadership and HR, as they work on individual career pathways and development; head hunters for external candidates, etc. This extensive screening results in a first-pass potential pool of candidates.

- **Desk-based filtering and pooling:** following the assembling of comprehensive data on the individuals derived from the first-pass screening – internal databases, annual assessments, CVs, direct feedback, etc, – a desk- and conversation-based exercise is performed, resulting in some candidates being removed from the pool. Others come through this filtering process successfully, making up a robust candidate pool for the next phase.

- **Pre-selection:** The capability director or delegate conducts pre-selection interviews. These can be face-to-face or held via video or phone. This exchange aims at pre-testing the candidate's attributes and capabilities against the grid, thus pre-qualifying individuals who score highly in most categories, and eliminating those who do not.

- **Focused panel interview:** the pre-selected individuals meet with a panel for a full day of interviews. Ideally these sessions will be held face-to-face, though where candidates are geographically very distant, they might be run via video-conference or telepresence. The panel will split into subgroups and conduct extensive evidence-based interviews, each focused on different sets of attributes and capabilities. The average interview time for a candidate on that day could range between three and five hours.

- Selection: ultimately the panel will get together and hold extensive assessment and challenge sessions on each of the candidates. These deliberations will result in a well-founded decision and will include detailed feedback to the candidate, whatever the outcome.

Let us hear Gerhard Resch-Fingerlos on his experience of such approaches to selection.

Gerhard Resch-Fingerlos, Partner, Spencer Stuart

There are so many roadblocks and impediments to good partnership management. So, you need to do it very well and I have been thinking about what it means in practice.

My particular story is 10 years of building a full partnering human capability from scratch. In this case, a selection panel made of six interviewers meets every month to interview pre-selected candidates. We split into three groups of two and each group assesses the candidates against clear criteria for over an hour. When all candidates have had their three interviews, the panel members meet for a 'convergence' workshop, to form a view on the fit between interviewees and roles. The panel is composed of two current executives, two retirees chosen for their expertise and two Spencer Stuart partners. So why is it working so well?

First and foremost, it is about consistency. Every month for the last 10 years, the core selection team has always been the same, and that is extremely unusual. I don't know of any other situation that has the same consistent quality.

Then, after the first two years when it may have been a bit less clear, we agreed on a common capability and personal attributes framework. And we also said:

'okay, this is the common framework and we will use it to work and build our benchmarks'. What we benefit from is the long-term consistency of the panel people themselves, as well as in the way they apply the tool. It is the combination of both that makes a complete difference.

We stick to an old-fashioned type of interview, one which has now been used in the market for 30 years. We use competency- and evidence-based interviewing. We have defined the business drivers very precisely and are focusing on just those. So we can clearly separate the wheat from the chaff when we interview, and because we are so focused, our tools work and are very powerful.

Our track record of recommendation and 'on-the-job' success is quite consistent, meaning the people that we recommend have a high probability of being successful. There is never 100 per cent success, as we know in real life, but we are getting very, very close to an incredibly high level of reliability in our judgement, which means that what we predict will usually happen.

So why is the whole concept so valid? The secret is in the 'convergence' workshop. It is not so much the hour that each of us spends with the candidate – yes, it is important and is good for data gathering. But the quality develops in the workshop session between the panel members. There is a dynamic in the room that provides different angles and perspectives on individuals and, because of this 360-degree view, we get quite a realistic profile. And it is about the uniqueness of the people making up the panel: not that they are unique as individuals, but it is the uniqueness of their interaction that makes the quality of judgement so pertinent and consistent.

Also, over time, we have developed such a high level of proficiency in the interview process that we focus on the real drivers and do not get distracted by the noise. The outcome is consistency and the quality comes from having worked together through this process and with this selection grid for so many years. Now, people who look at it from the outside might challenge us and say 'well guys, it is a bit old-fashioned what you are doing, not state-of-the-art', but I think it is state-of-the-art because of the dynamics that we have created amongst the panellists.

So there are a couple of things that truly are unique in this market. One is the timescale. When we do this with other companies – and I have relationships with many – the process lasts for months, at best a few years, but never 10 as it has done here. All the other relationships that we have worked on at Spencer Stuart, particularly when it comes to benchmarking exercises, observations, assessing candidates and helping our clients to make deployment decisions, are of a shorter nature and less consistent.

So, in a nutshell, what made this case different is the consistency, which is unbeatable. And you can't replicate that. It is nothing you can copy and paste anywhere else. It is the unique chemistry among the panellists. It is their own benchmarks developed over years, which are very tightly knitted into the business drivers. And all of this is a unique combination and makes the outcome itself a benchmark.

It should be noted that such a process can and should be applied equally for both internal and external candidates.

Ensuring an 'absolute' fit between people and roles

Let's examine a few practices that enhance the chance of getting the enterprise strategic partnering human capital not only right but best-in-class.

A very selective process

In cases where an organization decides to deal systematically with the selection of its strategic partnering team members and adopts a thorough multi-step process similar to the one just presented, the risks of failure should be very low. That said, the task and the challenge to implement it well remain significant and are not to be underestimated. As shown in Figure 6.5, experience suggests that only 1 or 2 out of a 100 in the original pool will make it to the team.

As mentioned before, the consequences of failing to select the right team members are so serious that a higher rate of conversion would be likely to mean compromise ... and therefore be somewhat worrying.

The future boss not to be involved

It is common practice in organizations that bosses and heads of teams usually lead and define the selection of the key individuals making up their team. We discourage this habit here, so that the decision is made on absolutely objective criteria, with no personal or business bias whatsoever. Hence, the selection process will be outsourced by leaders, usually SPMs, to the Capability Director and the panel who will form their judgement completely independently.

It does not mean that the future boss will not be involved at all though. He/she will have the final say, ie once the panel has reached its final position, the SPM or other recruiting leaders will approve or veto the appointment. Experience suggests that objection at this stage is exceptional.

Full independence of choice, with no influence from the rest of the organization

The selection process needs to be run fully independently and exempt of any influence. Often, important roles in an organization would be filled with the guidance, 'help' and influence of leadership, HR committees or other ad hoc processes, using common selection criteria across the enterprise. These criteria are helpful to the strategic partnering process in setting preconditions, but are not in themselves sufficient. Remember that we are looking for a strong fit against defining parameters and this is what the panel should uniquely base its judgement upon. Shelly Lazarus explains why common selection criteria are simply not good enough for strategic partnering.

> ### Shelly Lazarus
>
> "Who is not good at partnering? First of all, there are people who need to be the smartest person in the room. They are not good at partnerships because they don't have inherent respect for others. If you believe that you're smarter than anyone else, how can you be respectful to somebody else's opinion?

Protecting independence of decision is not always easy. How many times does the following question arise: 'why didn't you bring Mr/Mrs/Ms X in, as he/she is great and one of our stars?' The response is: 'because there is not enough fit between their profile and the specifics we are looking for'. Or: 'why did you bring Mr/Mrs/Ms Y in, as he/she is not a candidate with the highest rating or potential under our common criteria?' The answer to that is: 'because he/she presented a strong fit with the required capabilities and attributes'.

Unanimity in the panel decision making

The way the panel makes its decision is also important to the final outcome. Extensive collective consideration of each candidate is recommended during what Gerhard Resch-Fingerlos calls the 'convergence' workshops, where we also advise that unanimity be sought. So, there should be no compromise, and 100 per cent agreement among the panel members.

Hard test the candidate's passion and determination

The final step involves the candidate him/herself. As discussed before, strategic partnership roles are rather untypical: on the one hand fascinating, on the other challenging and demanding. They demand a lot from the team members, including many changes in the way they are accustomed to operate, think and act. This is not easy for them and, as noted earlier in Figure 6.1 on 'attributes', it will take resilience, determination, a can-do attitude and even passion, to name just a few required personal traits.

The final critical test before making an appointment will therefore focus on the candidate's passion and determination for the role. Candidates should be driven by their deep interest in and affinity with the partnering practice, its opportunity and learning. They should not be led by other aspirations which, respectable though they may be, are not what will pull and push the successful SPMs, VOMs and others in the SPT every day, to become the human focus of strategic partnering within the organization. Let's read from Paul Deighton on the strong pull that people should feel for the partnering 'magic dust'.

Lord Paul Deighton, Commercial Secretary to HM Treasury

On building the teams to deliver and manage London 2012, the key thing for us was to develop people's confidence and trust that we had the basic competence to deserve to be the holders of the Games' 'magic dust'. Once people realized how precious this was, they would relieve us of it if we were not doing an excellent job, or they certainly wouldn't join in. Once they realized we were doing a good job, they were happy to partner up with us because we could take them to a very special and positive place.

Let's step back: individuals have been selected on the basis of their strongly tested knowledge and capability base, as well as personal traits. This makes us very excited about them joining the partnering team. We are equally aware that they will need to learn a lot and significantly 'transform' their professional practice, to be ultimately successful. Let's consider how this might happen.

Guidelines for developing professional and personal talents

As part of the strategic partnering system (represented in Figure 6.6), we suggest that there are five principles and actions involved in enabling individuals to be increasingly successful in their new roles. Let's hear from John Seifert about the importance of investing in the partnering capability.

John Seifert

We have probably 10 times the number of people and 3 times as much money invested in areas designed to foster strategic partnerships. This imperative influences our recruitment, evaluation and retention of top talent. It also guides our choices for thought leadership and new organizational capabilities as the world shifts.

FIGURE 6.6   Key sources of learning and development

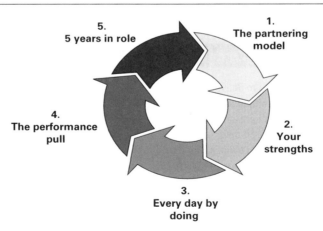

Let us reflect on each of the five main sources of learning and personal development.

1. The model, the model, the model!

This has been mentioned before and we cannot repeat it enough times: each team member should delve deep into the model from the very start, understand it thoroughly and make systematic use of it. Experience shows that when applied diligently, the learning and success curve is simply so much steeper and faster. Of course, this is easy to say: newcomers have their own ways of doing things; the question of why the model is different and more robust than their own process is a legitimate one; and the model may look like something they seem to know already. It will take coaching and support from leaders and colleagues to hone a dedicated approach to the model.

2. Build on strengths

The team member has been appointed following a demanding selection process, whose thrust was to assess his or her fit with target attributes and capabilities. Of course the first weeks and months will be disorientating, but it is important to proceed with confidence and build on the obvious strengths demonstrated through the selection process.

3. Everyday learning by doing

This is the key developmental method and it works! Firstly, many opportunities exist in the model to learn from others through applying the model's processes, such as 'support and challenge' (S&C). As described later in detail, these S&C sessions are unique platforms to test a partnership strategy, an 'offer' or a 'navigation' approach with expert peers. It creates an accelerated learning opportunity on all of the six strategic partnering team's core mission areas (see Figures 6.2, 6.3 and 6.4), through extensive challenge ... and support from trusted sources. It also enables considerable transfer of knowledge and best practice from leaders and colleagues to the individual.

> ### Ian Robertson
>
> Partnering leadership training should be on-the-job. Developing the right leadership skills and credentials every day is essential in our work and even more so where a partnership is concerned. The clarity of shared objectives and the ability to paint a picture of what success will look like are vital.

Also, the central partnering unit is high powered, composed of senior people, rather small in size and with a very flat organization. With the same criteria true for each dedicated partnership team at an even smaller scale, their members operate very closely together and have the opportunity and luxury of continuous mutual feedback. Finally, the role of leaders is often viewed as that of a coach, notably acting as qualified and competent 'supporters and challengers'. Let's hear from Viren Doshi on coaching and sharing.

> ### Viren Doshi
>
> It is important to give the right mentoring, so I do it for our partners and for principals on client handling and client relationship building. I give a module and then we have questions and answers – we call it the 'fireside chat' before dinner. We sit there and people ask questions: 'Oh, but they're not buying, what should I do?', 'How do I deal with it? How do I get access?', 'Nobody knows me, they do not answer my calls, how do I meet them in the first instance?' So all kinds of very different problems come out.
>
> Clearly, ours is an apprenticeship model where you, as a seasoned person, have to take somebody less senior with you, so that they can see what you do. I had the benefit of a mentor for many years and now I need to do the same with our younger partners.

4. Leverage the 'performance' pull

Part of the beauty, excitement and pain of strategic partnering roles is the imperative to strategically sustain the mutual commitment between partners as an absolute requirement for 'performance'. As we will see in Chapter 11 on 'performance' management, there is no place to hide on progressing mutual value creation in these positions. This emphasis on delivery acts as a powerful personal development tool, as individuals have to figure out how to fulfil the expectation of continuous and then 'transformational' value delivery.

5. Stay in the role long enough

As noted earlier, it is vital to stay in a role for a minimum of four or five years (and potentially longer) if and as the role fundamentally changes with the partnership 'transformation'. Indeed, each year of the business cycle is different and critical to further learning. As the five years unfold, maximum personal development occurs in tandem with accessing 'transformational' value. Hence, our practice is to require an absolute commitment to spend four/five years in the role, as an imperative precondition to any appointment.

Conclusion: Developing world-class strategic partnering human capital

We now have the benefit of comprehensive principles and processes, to create, maintain and improve the whole organizational capability and human capital to make our co-operative approach a success. In practice, these enable us to select and bring in the needed SPMs and VOMs from Step 4 of the partnership development model onwards. We can and should also apply this practice to recruit the direct or deployed human resources required throughout the other stages of the partnership model.

Let us summarize our approach to building the winning strategic partnering human capital.

Summary: Developing world-class strategic partnering human capital

- The individuals joining the strategic partnering team are rare and precious talents.
- SPMs, VOMs and other roles share a strong commonality of personal attributes, such as generosity, humility and resilience.
- They also offer and come in with already established leadership and subject matter expertise.
- The required attributes and areas of expertise are codified in 'competency' maps and made central to our recruitment.
- A thorough 5-step selection process is used to identify and test candidates. Only 1 or 2 out of 100 will come through, but we will be confident they are fit for the role.
- In addition to being very selective, the selection process is highly codified, thorough and fully independent.
- Team members will develop and grow by embracing and applying the strategic partnership model diligently, learning by doing, having the strong daily support of colleagues and staying in role long enough to lead and live through a whole business and learning cycle.

Having worked through Chapters 5 and 6, we are now able to equip and sustain our partnering strategy with a clear organization staffed with strong leaders and experts. This is significant progress, one that many organizations never make satisfactorily, let alone successfully. Use this part of the model, and your chances and rate of success with strategic partnerships will be deeply 'enhanced' – dare we say even 'transformed'!

07
Building extraordinary partnerial relationships

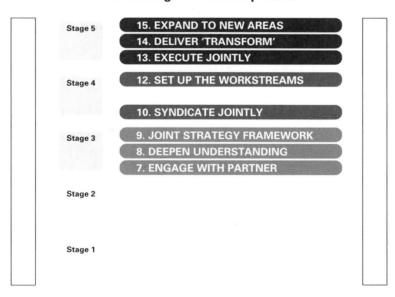

The Strategic Partnership Model

Stage 5
- 15. EXPAND TO NEW AREAS
- 14. DELIVER 'TRANSFORM'
- 13. EXECUTE JOINTLY

Stage 4
- 12. SET UP THE WORKSTREAMS

- 10. SYNDICATE JOINTLY

Stage 3
- 9. JOINT STRATEGY FRAMEWORK
- 8. DEEPEN UNDERSTANDING
- 7. ENGAGE WITH PARTNER

Stage 2

Stage 1

The right relationship is everything.

JP MORGAN CHASE

Extraordinary relationships do not guarantee the success of strategic partnerships but they do act as essential and powerful enablers. As humans, we gain assurance from creating successful relationships, as they form the foundation of our social and domestic lives. As professionals, we tend to share the same desire to create successful relationships, but let's test this: have you ever met an executive who admitted he or she was bad or average at relationships? And would you say that all your business relationships are excellent? It is one of those areas where everyone is an apparent expert!

Why should we be any better at developing relationships in business, where we often may not have direct influence on those we meet? And even if positive relationships exist, are they truly underpinning 'transformational' value creation?

Extraordinary relationships, at both organizational and individual levels, are core to any successful partnering. In fact, they are at the heart of our partnership development model throughout Stages 3, 4 and 5 ... and for the full duration of the co-operation. They require careful planning based on clear and mutually beneficent outcomes, close nurturing, and will need to evolve over time if they are to be sustained. In this chapter, we explore:

- Why extraordinary relationships are required to build successful business partnerships.

- Why success requires the building of two parallel and complementary levels of relationships: organizational and individual.

- What is at the heart of extraordinary relationships, both corporate and individual.

- How to go about creating these strong and enduring bonds.

To make this process reliable and repeatable, we offer proven rules to help develop such relationships, providing firm and sustainable foundations to successful partnerships. We will show that a systematic approach to relationship building can define the success of strategic partnering, and will offer a set of processes and rules which, when used consistently, ensure an active, enduring and fruitful partnership.

Extraordinary relationships often involve extraordinary people, and it is a true challenge to define this intensely human undertaking as a set of workable and practical processes. However, failing in the discipline of relationship building puts at risk our ability to secure 'transformational' value. This is why this dimension of strategic partnering sits at the convergence of art and science, of heart and mind. Shelly Lazarus reflects on some key aspects of the relationship magic:

Shelly Lazarus

"There is inherent generosity in people who are good at forming strategic relationships. If you are self-absorbed, self-congratulatory or you have got to be the smartest person in the room, it is really hard to have a relationship. Deep relationships are about sharing.

Great relationships and partnerships also need deep mutual respect. You can disagree with someone for whom you have great respect, because it is not personal. You know, it is a little like unconditional love you feel for children. We have established that we have total respect for each other and because I am so respectful of you, you are now allowed to completely disagree with me because it is not going to affect our relationship. It is just that you are going to express a point of view that I will listen to and respect because it comes from you. And in general, I am going to respect the view, the brain, and the heart of another person with whom I am in a deep relationship.

Relationships are changing ... and remain the same

Relationships are changing ...

Hyper-connectivity encourages a myriad of relationships to blossom and flourish merely through a series of powerful digital communications, social platforms and simple electronic interactions. Facebook is building, replacing and destroying social interactions all at the same time. Easy come, easy go. At least 20 per cent of marital relationships owe their origins to the internet. In 20 years' time, this could exceed 50 per cent. One can learn almost everything immediately about another person through the wire.

The same is true in business. On the one hand, relationships tend to become less enduring. Virtual communities ebb and flow through the web, making interactions ever more transitory. Business becomes more volatile with the average half-life of a Fortune 1000 company decreasing from 90 years (in the early twentieth century) to a mere 25 years today.

So too employment contracts, which have dropped from decades to years (and even months). Don't plan to retire with your current firm, as chances are that they won't exist by the time you come to the end of your career.

Yet the new abundance and availability of data through digital, social or mobile channels place insights and knowledge at the heart of relationships. For public or private organizations, these technologies provide continuous, considerable and high-quality insights into what others want or are doing. For individuals, it makes people more important, more central, and easier to understand and communicate with.

... and relationships remain the same

Despite this revolution, the fundamental rules of relationships have hardly changed over the last few millennia. In our domestic lives, real value remains in achieving long-term relationships. We frequently start marital relationships with, for example, two jobs and separate incomes, two sets of interests soon followed by the demands of child rearing and home making, all of which last for two or more decades and require a true partnership. And when careers have progressed and kids leave home, another cycle starts. Clearly, the foundations on which successful relationships survive and offer happiness allow a couple to 'navigate' through many years of changing circumstances. How many of us are actually fully prepared for such a challenging journey?

Similarly, business relationships must evolve through a complex set of challenges to achieve longevity or 'strategic partnering'. Real business value arises only when such relationships progress through the following stages: 'improvement', 'enhancement' and finally 'transformation'. As discussed earlier, there are an ever increasing number of reasons why businesses need to interact to form partnerships and build up associated value networks. As in the case of individual people, creating long-lasting business relationships is complex and becomes ever more challenging, given the modern age 'easy come, easy go'. And perhaps, even close to impossible ... except if one works systematically at it. And when one does so, the reward is simply massive!

Why develop extraordinary relationships? Issues and solutions

Relationships are at the heart of the world leaders' agenda

The IBM 2012 Global CEO Study, resulting from interviews with over 1,700 CEOs and senior public sector leaders from around the globe, places relationships at the heart of each and every one of their 'three imperatives essential for outperformance'.

As identified by the CEOs during the study and represented in Figure 7.1, these three key imperatives are: 'empowering employees through values'; 'engaging customers as individuals'; and 'amplifying innovation with partnerships'. Obviously, these three vital sources of progress and value for the CEOs are about improving, enhancing and hopefully 'transforming' relationships with their most important stakeholder groups.

FIGURE 7.1 Global CEOs' three imperatives: All about relationships

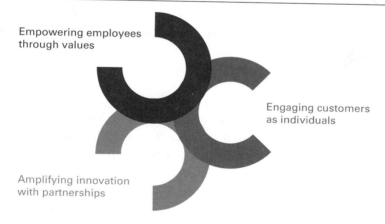

Empowering employees through values

Engaging customers as individuals

Amplifying innovation with partnerships

SOURCE: IBM Institute of Business Value, *Global CEO Study*, 2012

- With regard to the first imperative on 'human capital', the relationship between organizations and employees, as well as between one person and another, is changing constantly. The practice of these relationships needs to be redefined and renewed. A considerable opportunity exists to increase empowerment, provide space for initiative and reward loyalty.

- With the second imperative – 'customer relationships' – the new transparency and knowledge present the opportunity to create much improved 360-degree offers to customers to fulfil their needs. Technology also provides the platform to improve communication with people as individuals and make it both timely and value adding.

- Last but not least, 'partnerships' feature with increasing prominence on the world leaders' agenda. As revealed by the study, only 4 per cent plan to do everything in-house, while 53 per cent are already partnering to innovate (over 60 per cent in government, education and healthcare) and close to 70 per cent aim to partner more extensively now and in the near future. Interestingly, the main change comes from 'how' they think and want to manage their relationships, as 'the next frontier for openness', 'accepting the cultural shift', 'building trust' and 'sharing control'.

As discussed in Chapters 1 and 2 of *Strategic Partnering*, the importance of partnerships, and especially strategic partnerships, is growing continuously. And we seem to agree that the key question is 'how' to succeed. The world's decision makers place great emphasis on relationships, and they are actively considering how to remodel their organization's partnering practices.

Issues and solutions

Most of us seem quite clear on the critical importance of relationships, on the positive contribution of great ones or the show-stopping nature of poor ones. So what are the issues and how to remedy them?

No ego, no 'self' in the mix

As confident professionals, we tend to think that we understand a lot about building successful relationships – both corporate and individual. And as 'egocentric' creatures, we are keen to bring all our personal experience to the table when we embark on strategic partnerships. But the high rate of failure in personal and business relationships weighs heavily against us in this respect. Extraordinary relationships that are built to achieve breakthrough delivery and stand the test of time require a very different approach and behaviours than simple personal belief and good intent.

Prioritizing substance over 'feel good' factor

What we need to overcome is the very human belief that relationships are valuable in their own right. How many times have we heard something like: 'I know him/her, so we will get to where we want'; or 'We can't do this because it might get in the way of our excellent relationship'. Extraordinary relationships that form the basis of successful strategic partnerships must be based on facts, practical actions and tangible business benefits and outcomes – not just human warmth and respect. A golden rule to follow is that successful relationships should be developed consistently in the service and pursuit of real substance and proven needs and value of the partnership.

We cannot stress enough that relationships are 'not in service of relationships', ie not built purely for their own sake, but purposefully to support the development and delivery of clear, well-articulated business strategies and associated 'sources of value' (SoVs).

Assume that your local grocer is extremely friendly but has a limited range of products. You would rather go to the next shop that stocks all your requirements, even if they don't smile as much. Actually, we are looking for both here: on one hand the value or the offer, and on the other hand the smile!

Stephen Odell

I think one of the themes of a successful partnership is consistency of both parties over time. So, not just through difficult economic times but also through change of leadership or through a business going through its own strengths, opportunities or difficulties. Because often friendships come out of partnerships but friendships can sometimes equally be rather unreliable, because people can be friends or not be friends or, they can be friends and then stop being friends. For me, a successful partnership has to operate through consistency of purpose.

A purpose to all engagements

This brings us to a key point of action: make sure that no single contact is made without a clear business purpose and/or to achieve a desired outcome, as suggested by Andrew Mackenzie.

Andrew Mackenzie

> It has to be seen as a fundamental relationship, and it shouldn't just be about having nice lunches, but it's actually about talking and getting down to the essence of business and why we work together.

Being human, we tend to develop relationships for their own sake. It is often easier and more comfortable to reach out to people intuitively rather than go through the painful effort of expressing detailed intentions. There is a misconception that 'relationships will make it all'. In the cold light of day, people inevitably revert to their own interests, to the substance behind any relationship. Hence we believe in the value of bringing a clear discipline into the way relationships are managed. As the old saying goes: 'there are very seldom free lunches in life!'

The authority of saying no

If you have a great partnership, or a major supply position with another company, how comfortable will you feel about saying no to one of their 'important' requests? Introducing mutuality as a rule for any extraordinary relationship should not let one party become beholden to their partner.

Relationships should be shaped to create both 'an authority' and a joint 'right' to say no, a powerful ability to choose with no major consequences to the relationship, as noted earlier by Shelly Lazarus.

In short, extraordinary relationships are hard to fashion and to sustain, but lie at the heart of any successful partnership. And they are very different to what one usually experiences in day-to-day life, or in the way people usually practise relationship building. Just look at the low yield generally associated with executive network contacts. These interactions tend to generate more noise in the system than productive partnerships, solutions or value. As humans, we need to reframe our experience and intuitions, and bring in some discipline if we want to 'transform' the statistics in our favour.

Extraordinary relationships for strategic partnering

Governments, companies, agencies, NGOs, universities and other institutions are made up of people, processes and structures – bound together by culture and purpose. When organizations enter into a strategic partnership, they need to build relationships at two different levels: corporate and personal. Over time, both the people and structures will change dramatically. Even purpose and culture may evolve in response to external conditions. An enduring strategic partnership needs to survive these changes and to do so, cultivate extraordinary relationships and build them structurally and consistently at two parallel levels:

- between organizations;
- between individuals.

Building extraordinary relationships between organizations

Corporate relationships are defined by the processes and mechanisms set up and used by the partners to work together and, equally, to govern their strategic co-operation. They create mutual 'obligations', a rhythm and efficiency to the partnership. As we will recall from our strategic partnership development model in Chapter 3, a strategic co-operation cannot be declared such without it being firmly underpinned by institutionalized operating and governance processes. And as Ian Davis says, it won't truly exist until it has become institutional:

Ian Davis

There are some process points about how you make partnerships strong and then process steps to make sure that the partnership adjusts its mission as necessary and remains fact-based.

The question is sometimes: who is partnering with whom? Because in the end, for a partnership to work strategically, it must transcend individuals and so if you are designing such a partnership, you can't be dependent on a CEO or a CFO or head of IT, and be at risk every time you change the relevant executive. You see that a lot in IT, big IT systems and then the CTO goes and the organization recruits somebody else who changes the paradigm. That's not a strategic partnership. It was just a relationship between an individual and a company. So, strategic partnerships in the end have to be institutional.

Well-structured and managed corporate relationship processes will prove vital to value creation. They will help teams to work together; they will create momentum; they will ensure decisions are made; they will enable personal relationships to develop and mature. They will also help mitigate many of the critical impediments to success raised by our interviewees earlier in Figure 1.2, including the dependence of the partnership on just a few individuals.

Let's hear from Jeff Immelt on the power of a system that builds multiple-level relationships.

Jeff Immelt

The relationship should be mission-based, work across the business and create many focal points. One question is: how do you make it a system? You need to assign people from each side to build a working relationship and develop something together. Also, they will not let the relationship be put at risk by ensuring that no conflicts or issues get overlooked.

You need to develop relationships at many touch points in the companies. People change positions, so you need multiple relationships for continuity, including at the top of the company where there is less movement. Continuity helps you make good strategic decisions.

Building extraordinary relationships between individuals

Individual relationships include each and every personal interaction that is developed between different members of the partnering organizations. There can be tens or even hundreds of them in the case of partnerships between complex institutions.

People make partnerships. And people will do it with people. Success comes from developing personal connections at all levels of the partners' organizations. And being only human, most of us will do better with people we know, trust, respect … and like.

Apologies for a brief aside at this point. Over the last 35 years, it has been the authors' immense privilege to meet, develop ground-breaking strategic partnerships, go through the fire and experience amazing personal relationships with extraordinary leaders and people. Lying within the strict ethical boundaries set by governments and corporations, these relationships have offered repeated mutual 'transformational' value. Moreover, many years of building trust, respect and considerable affection have led to cherished friendships, as well as magic personal fulfilment. Wherever you are in the United States, Asia, Africa, Australasia, Germany, the United Kingdom or Europe, thank you all infinitely for being such great 'Mensch' and such good friends!

Paul Deighton

It was extraordinary that the experience people went through together for London 2012 created such bonds that will last a lifetime. Whether it was building a venue, providing a service to a venue, being a volunteer, running hospitality programmes or simply being at an event and watching a piece of history, this all left an indelible imprint. I found the people who helped to deliver the Games are the type that would do absolutely anything for each other and to help others succeed in whatever they are doing next because of what they have been through together. A huge trust developed because you shared such a powerful experience and relied on those other people to get something done in the most extreme circumstances. And it happened!

In summary, deep relationships need to be built and become outstanding at both a corporate and individual level, to achieve a successful strategic partnership and access 'transformational' value. This requires a structural as well as a people-based approach to relationship building. So, what are the advised methods and disciplines in both areas?

Building extraordinary relationships between organizations

How does an organization approach building unparalleled relationships in practice, particularly at the enterprise level? CEOs and leaders very often struggle with setting up a model for this, so here are a few principle and process ideas, which will hopefully be of some help.

An enterprise-wide approach

On occasions, large corporations will launch strategic initiatives with parts of other firms, while they are in competition, conflict or even litigation with other departments or business units of these same companies. Given the scale of some organizations, a paradox like this is eminently feasible. But does this sound like a sustainable situation? Clearly this cannot constitute a firm basis for long-term success. We believe that strategic co-operations must be built and constructed across the entire breadth of the involved parties.

Clearly, institutions need to act in a holistic manner when strategic partnerships are being planned. The left hand needs to know what the right hand is doing. Strategic relationships are likely to occupy board-level time and attention. Nothing should distract from the core strategic intent.

A structured approach

Governments and Fortune 1000 corporations are very complex organisms, made of multiple business units, multi-layer stakeholders and multi-geographies, and are functionally diverse. Such complexity demands a structured approach to building corporate relationships.

The main enablers of this systematic and structured approach are the dedicated strategic partnership teams, principally the Strategic Partnership Managers (SPMs) and Value & Offer Managers (VOMs). As we remember from Chapter 3, they are brought in as early as possible in Stage 2 of the strategic partnership development model and the team is extended in Stage 4. One of the SPM's first priorities will be to work through the areas of opposition between the respective organizations, and how these can be managed in the context of the emerging joint strategic intent.

Peter Foss also advocates a structured approach and an influential role for the partnership team:

Peter Foss

To unleash the whole power of the organization, we need to develop a process between large partners that isn't just about two people. For example, the chairmen get together and they have a nice dinner and a nice discussion and then go away and everybody goes back to work. It can't be a singular event like that, it has to be broken down into multiple pieces that reach far further into each participating organization.

> And that is why the people who build and do partnerships have to have enough insight into their organization and frankly enough ability to get people to listen to them and to act, to break down a lot of barriers and persuade the people running the individual businesses to go beyond their own immediate agenda.

Using the simplified example of a two-organization partnership, the initial status of interactions will usually resemble the left-hand side of Figure 7.2. Such complexity does not help a high-quality relationship. The partnership team will therefore structure and organize the multiple interfaces to resemble the right-hand side of the figure. Specifically, the SPM will own and manage a dynamic contact map that defines all these links. As in chess, he or she will deploy each 'piece', optimizing their influence and capability and making the whole approach coherent, efficient and productive.

One of the main benefits to the partners of such a structured approach is to 'internalize' complexity. In offering a one-stop-shop access through the partnership team, it 'transforms' the partners' ability to develop the most productive distributed relationships at all necessary levels of their respective structures. The partnership team will also set the tone, resolve issues and 'clear the air' internally as necessary, so the interactions between partners are high quality and promote co-operation and value wherever possible.

Ideally, both partners should develop a similar strategic partnership organization. In practice, the strategic co-operation team of the initiating partner should seek to invoke a mirror-image team structure within the target organization. These dedicated teams coordinate efforts between the involved corporate, vertical, business and function levels, to ensure a productive and harmonious working relationship across both organizations.

This similarity in partnering structures is a 'nice to have' but not a 'must have'. When it exists, such is the potential power of communication between organizations that teams in partner A come to see their namesakes in partner B as direct colleagues with similar missions. When it applies to a lesser extent, notably in the early days of a partnership, the highest priority is to ensure that AoCs are established across the co-operating organizations, coordinated and supported by partner A's SPM and assigned VOM. Because it will be the AoC leaders and their teams who will truly and materially progress value creation.

FIGURE 7.2 Strategic partnering and the new age of relationships

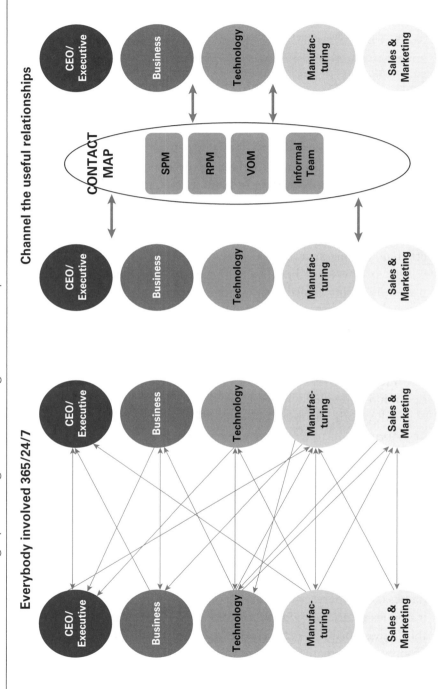

A governance routine

Matching structures and organized interactions are vital but insufficient on their own to achieve the desired outcomes. Partnerships also require governance and oversight. The greatest success comes when a joint executive governance process is established and functions well. This ensures board linkage, strategic oversight and a mutual 'obligation' to progress the co-operation and deliver against agreed objectives.

The executive governance process is put in place with the partner(s) from Step 12 of the strategic partnership development model ('Set up the Workstreams'). This joint mechanism governs the development, implementation and delivery of the mutually agreed strategic co-operation framework (SCF), as defined in Chapter 8 of *Strategic Partnering*. The Corporate and Executive Champions have decision-making authority on the SoVs in the SCF. Governance meetings are routine, structured and carefully planned to support the 'navigation' of the SCF.

> ## Mike Glenn
>
> "You have to have executive sponsorship. There is a saying that I am fond of quoting and that is: 'what interests my boss, fascinates me'. And so, having the level of executive sponsorship in any type of relationship keeps the partnership people and others in the organization engaged in the discussion and the dialogue. And then, you set goals that are well-defined and achievable, develop a scorecard to measure those goals and hold the team accountable for delivering on results. Finally, you review quarterly, twice a year, annually, whatever the needs of the relationship are and this oversight and the accountability that goes along with it will make a considerable difference.
>
> At a very senior level, I would say there are probably 10 strategic partnerships at FedEx. There, it's absolutely critical that we have a relationship at the very highest level of the organizations where both parties are committed to serving the other. A member of our strategic management committee is the executive sponsor for that relationship.

Governance is often seen as the 'sacred cow' in any corporate partnership. In practice effective governance is necessary, but it is far from sufficient on its own to build enduring relationships.

An enterprise-wide relationship participation framework

In summary, the enterprise relationship is built on a clear structure made up of different levels, roles and routine processes. A schematic framework of these different levels of governance relationships and interactions is proposed in Figure 7.3. Unless an organization has filled every box, it is probably still some way away from an extraordinary enterprise-wide relationship.

FIGURE 7.3   Multi-layer enterprise-wide participation

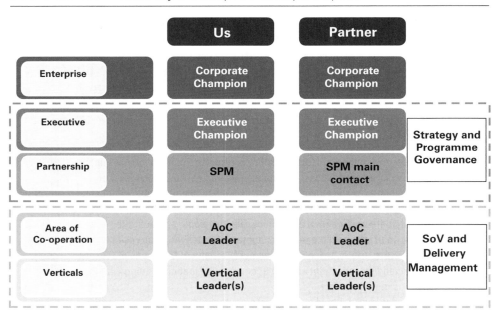

This is very much like the game of chess, with the main participating organizational groups and individuals facing their counterparts and playing their specific role in the governance and management of the relationship. The various structured relationship levels are shown from bottom to top of Figure 7.3:

- **The verticals, business and function leaders and operators:** relationships at this level drive effective operations across all areas of the partnership. They range from the 'people with the walkie-talkies', to leaders co-operating on operational planning or performance reviews. They are the vital **pawns** of the chess game; when one is missing or wrongly deployed, the chances of failure scarily increase.

- **The multiple AoC champions and experts:** this is the level at which the joint activities are defined, developed and where innovation occurs. They are the business people, technologists, marketers, manufacturers, advocacy leaders who jointly create the innovation, the 'transformation' and the co-operation value. Their central role and relationship make the AoC champions the heroes of the partnership and the **rooks, knights and bishops** of the chess game, as they bring the combination of expert robustness, agility and innovation to the partnership.

- **The partnership champions:** together, the SPMs and their teams lead and run the partnership, structure and support the cross-organization relationships and ensure that all critical interactions and activities run smoothly. They need a particularly high-quality relationship with their peers and at chess, the SPM is **the player** not a piece.

- **The Executive Champions:** they provide the vast majority of executive intervention and support, including the defining executive relationships and governance activity. In chess, the Executive Champion is the **queen**.

- **The Corporate Champions:** they provide enterprise oversight, ensure that corporate importance is given to the alliance, enforce alignment to corporate strategy and establish board linkage. In chess, they represent the **king** and Peter Foss acknowledges their critical role in the partnerships:

Peter Foss

It is game changing when your CEO says: 'look, these relationships are what is important to us and I am going to measure and reward you for putting your best people on this effort, because I know that these 50 companies represent 80 per cent of our business and the future of the company's growth. Therefore, we are going to put major effort behind them'. If it becomes important at the top, if the top speaks that way and measures it, like in a quarterly review or something equivalent looking at these top relationships, then it becomes important to the company.

Once the structures and accountable people are in place, these multiple-level relationships need to be consummated through an ordered series of interactions. And then, the enterprise partnership builds and evolves through the routine of these regular connections.

Establishing joint processes

Establishing shared governance and AoC structures, joint activity plans, mutually committed resources and aligned key performance indicators (KPIs) secure the partners' active involvement and commitment. A routine of joint reviews with agreed objectives, agendas and formal follow-up will ensure alignment and create 'obligations' across all five main layers of the partnership's relationship, governance and management: verticals, AoCs, partnership teams, Executive and Corporate Champions. Figure 7.4 provides an example of the principles and practice for the configuration of the engagement processes.

FIGURE 7.4   Hierarchy of enterprise relationship processes

	Implement	Design	Lead	Strategize	Transform
Level	Verticals	AoC	Partnership	Executive	Enterprise
Title of meeting	Operations meeting	AoC steering committee	Partnership review meeting	Executive Champions review	Corporate Champions review
Attendees	Operating and delivery teams	Leaders of the AoC and involved teams	SPMs and/or RPMs	Executive Champions and SPMs	Corporate and Executive Champions; SPMs
Purpose / Role	Ensure operations delivery to standards	Ensure planning and progress of the AoC	Ensure planning & progress of partnership	Provide leadership to partnership	Ensure corporate importance and linkage
Frequency	Daily; ad hoc	Ad hoc; every 1 to 2 months	Week hook up; month formal	Quarterly	1 or 2 times per annum

For good practice, the vast majority of the partnership-related interactions should happen at the operational level, in the 'areas of co-operation' (AoCs) and activity implementation. Corporate Champion reviews are occasional and 'an event'. Hence the following indicative pattern of activities:

- hourly, daily, weekly, monthly and quarterly series of interactions in the implementation groups, ie the involved verticals and departments;

- frequent AoC champions interactions, as guided by the requirements and progress of their joint workstream;

- daily partnership champions (SPM, VOM) interactions, with weekly formal reviews across the streams of co-operation;

- quarterly or twice a year Executive Champions reviews, providing strategic oversight to the co-operation. They include the Executive Champions, co-operation champions (SPMs) and their teams and AoC leaders, as appropriate;

- annual Corporate Champion governance review, gathering the two Corporate Champions, Executive Champions, plus guests invited on a very focused basis, all convened and supported by the SPMs in charge.

This enterprise-wide relationship structure and routine will foster and organize dynamic connections at each level across the partnering organizations. It will ensure that systematic and enduring progress is made and that the partnership is not put at risk from changes in personnel. It is vital to guard against partnerships becoming largely or solely dependent on an individual.

Kevin Murray

So often, we see partnerships founded and based on the key individuals who formed those relationships, who developed the trust, who shared the common purpose, who delivered outstanding results, who thrived together and succeeded. And then they move on to different roles in the organization. And the people coming up behind them don't have that sustaining level of trust that drove it … and then it starts to fall apart.

John Seifert

"When we experience a change of management in a client organization, and the new player(s) believe that, for whatever reason, our support is in service of a particular individual's interests at the expense of the client's, we risk losing their confidence and trust in our motives. We always need to be on side with the best interests of the client overall, and avoid (at all costs) taking the political side of one party over another.

Frank Williams

"A major problem we might have is that you form a strong relationship with a company and the people in it and then a key person changes. Now, we no longer have the personal relationship but also the new person thinks that it is their duty not to do whatever the predecessor believed in. At the end of the day, we are talking about people and, in my experience, what is very fundamental is 'a shared goal and the continuity of personal relationships'.

Building extraordinary personal relationships

Evidently this is all about people and it is people who make a partnership!

They are the leaders and actors at all levels of the co-operation, including being behind the corporate relationship processes and mechanisms. They are the convergence between art and method. A successful enterprise relationship is built on the sum of many extraordinary personal relationships – deep relationships that have the power to transcend the individual.

These quality individual relationships enable business opportunities by providing advantaged access, unlocking barriers and championing the co-operation and AoCs. But it is vital to remember these are not relationships for the sake of relationships; they are mapped with incredible precision to match SoVs, with full cognizance of all decision-making authorities and their influence.

This comes about by applying the discipline of systematizing internal and external relationships, being deliberate about 'who to who' relationship building. Developing and using rigorous contact maps makes a considerable difference here.

An extensive and comprehensive contact map

Engaging with the partners and 'navigating' across their organization towards the objectives should be pursued consistently and be tightly engineered. A systematic approach comes through developing and using comprehensive contact maps, which include:

- External contacts mapped to internal stakeholders, to manage structured external relationships across the partner's organization. To succeed over the long term, it should define what the required relationship is, ie who it involves, the purpose and frequency of engagement, as well as the space and boundaries, for each participant. The external contact map should also indicate the planned activity and status of the relationship building and targeting. This is a living document and should be a key tool developed, owned and managed by the SPM.

- Internal contacts required to deliver the joint activities and SoVs. These relationships need to be formalized with the appropriate business leadership. The scope of the relationship and delivery expectations should also be made clear.

A simple illustrative example of an external contact map is provided in Figure 7.5. Some may include hundreds of names. Its construct is principle-based:

- Each individual identified as key in the partner's organization has a tagged contact in ours (dark blue box). They usually have a similar position or rank in the partnering organization.

- A deputy, or 'next contact', is named for each of these key contacts and a relationship will also be developed actively between the key partner contact and this deputy (mid-blue box).

- The SPMs and RPMs will develop multiple relationships across the partner's organization, although often as 'junior' relationship holders (light blue box). They will be in the background, ready to provide strategic context, organizational support and continuity in case of people changes.

A multiple-layer relationship will therefore be established, without losing the clarity and purity of the overall approach described in Figure 7.2. This is the best of all worlds, as it combines focus and assurance.

FIGURE 7.5 Comprehensive external contact map

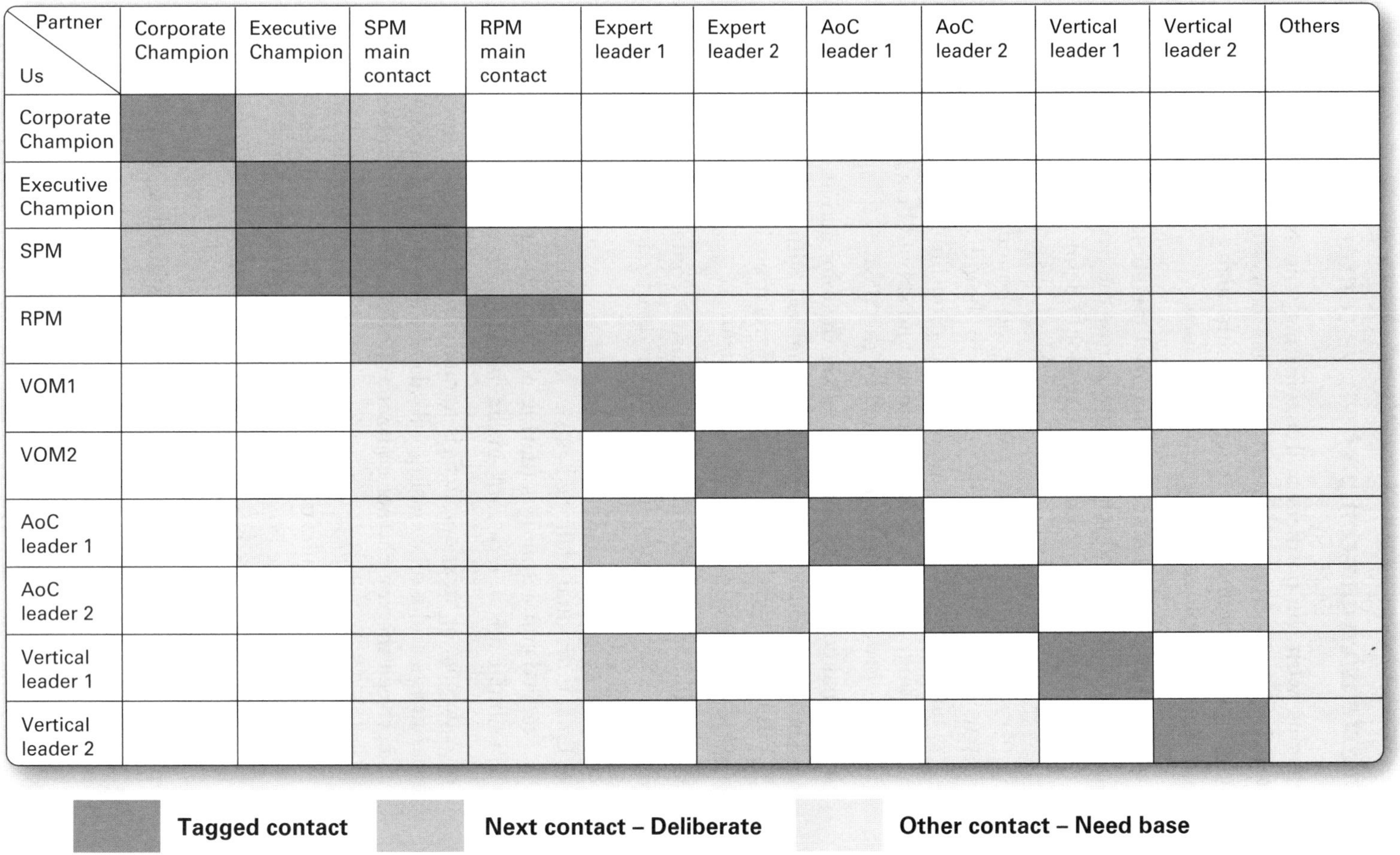

Partner / Us	Corporate Champion	Executive Champion	SPM main contact	RPM main contact	Expert leader 1	Expert leader 2	AoC leader 1	AoC leader 2	Vertical leader 1	Vertical leader 2	Others
Corporate Champion											
Executive Champion											
SPM											
RPM											
VOM1											
VOM2											
AoC leader 1											
AoC leader 2											
Vertical leader 1											
Vertical leader 2											

Tagged contact   Next contact – Deliberate   Other contact – Need base

The human factor

People relate to people. The dream scenario is when personal connections develop among peers at every level, including top executives. When this happens, teamwork builds outside both organizations' firewalls and results in proactive and collaborative entrepreneurship and innovation. This is what Stephen Odell calls 'the move from a need to a want'.

People feel pride and a real sense of fulfilment in a combined business and human achievement. How many times do we hear from the most successful partnership leaders: 'these guys on the other side are wonderful; we have fun exploring our joint business; they are often easier to work with than our own people, because the cross-organization chains of command are more flexible and we have more space to build and operate'.

Frank Williams

If our relationship goes back many years, has always been stable and trusting, it means that the communication is easier and much more natural between the parties. I have always believed in the importance of communication and ability to work with key people in a very open manner in order to achieve success.

Kevin Murray

It is about integrity, authenticity, honesty and that means sometimes saying the things that are unpalatable but which you truly believe, so that people know where you are coming from. I have seen a lot of relationships that are trusting relationships where people don't actually agree with each other but they trust each other. So there is no hiding of points of view, there is no sophistry when it comes to what they really think and believe and how they feel. So, 'you may not agree with me, but I know how you think and that means I can trust you'. So sometimes being trustworthy is about saying the necessary difficult things.

Undivided 365/24 personal attention to your partner

Truly enabling personal relationships that endure need time to develop, responding effectively and anticipating the needs, requirements and drivers of the partnering individuals. They demand personal attention and considerable foresight. If you don't think of your partner during your sleepless nights or on Christmas Day, just wonder if you are truly in a partnership!

Building extraordinary personal relationships also requires a consistent attitude of being always professional, principle-led, available, friendly, firm on facts, inviting and involving; of conveying passion and sophistication and being able to take others with you; of exhibiting positivity and excitement; of being genuine, natural and creating a trustful environment.

Martin Sorrell

If you asked me what defines a strategic relationship, I would say it is that your competence, let's say your common sense, is such that your partner is willing to use it outside the normal boundaries of your business relationship. So, if they have a problem, they would think to call me or somebody in our organization to discuss it and get some help. The best client relationships we have are when people say: 'This happened yesterday – what do you think?' It may have nothing to do with what you are doing for them. Let me use a bizarre example. A client rang me up and said: 'It is my anniversary. You know New York – recommend me some great place'. It means you have a relationship where the confidence, the trust, the openness are so strong that you just ask somebody for advice.

Friendship is probably the wrong word. But if you trust somebody, if you have been through fire together and you value somebody's advice, you would tend to think about that person as being somebody who could help you in other areas. Because you so admire or appreciate what they have done for you in that area, you think they might be able to help in this other area.

Extraordinary relationships require systematic regular communication with key individuals at all levels of the partner's organization. Let people in and openly share your world, for example relevant market insights, your strategic considerations, and important developments for you and your organizations. They will give back a hundred times more!

Zero compromise on relationship-building key principles

A few principles are vital to trigger and achieve extraordinary relationships. Failure is almost inevitable if even one is missing.

Carefully select who gets involved in relationships

This is an essential and often challenging requirement. Great relationships build with time, because they rely heavily on deep trust and familiarity. The owners of a relationship should therefore dedicate themselves to it, make it a priority and commit to a regular pattern of activities and contacts, ideally over the long term.

In many cases, impatience prevails and relationships are initiated or developed internally or externally with the wrong people who may become filters and limiting forces to the partnership. 'Go slowly to go quickly' and take the time to target who to associate with. We will discuss this fine targeting in Chapter 10 on 'navigation'.

There is often a tension about the role of senior executives, who legitimately want to interact with their counterparts, but can seldom afford to commit the necessary investment and disciplined attention to the relationship. Or who simply don't have the temperament. Reluctantly, this reality has to be recognized when it is there, otherwise there is a risk it will destroy rather than create value.

Ian Davis

Quite a lot of organizations and quite a few CEOs are not really emotionally capable of partnering. It is a tough but true assertion. They just can't do it and we have seen that in real terms. You need to have an attitude of interdependence. Most companies don't like that because it is somehow a weakness or feels uncomfortable. Secondly, this notion of mutual respect doesn't always sit easily with people. In the end, a lot of senior people are very competitive and you need the collaborative mindset here, to be able to look beyond that individualism and corporate competitiveness.

Nevertheless, you can have very forthright organizations that become strategic partners when there is complete mutual respect. They don't do what the other does and there is admiration for the other organization. But generally speaking, there are quite a few individuals and corporations who are not temperamentally well suited to the fundamentals of strategic partnering.

Empower your SPMs

The more powerful the Strategic Partnership Manager, the stronger and higher value the partnership. They are the leading agents of the co-operation, day after day after day. CEOs and senior executives have neither the time nor the closeness to really manage this thoroughly. So the role of leadership is not to run or be the authority to the partnership but to guide, help, be supportive, and put their weight behind the relationship, notably by empowering their co-operation leaders.

How many big leaders truly do this in our corporate world of hierarchy, power, ego and self-assurance? How many unconditionally trust and diligently follow the SPM guidance on when and how to interact with their partner? How often do we see the spotlight put on the co-operation manager rather than the CEO? Big and busy leaders: stay away and follow the model to empower your champion!

Takeshi Uchiyamada, Chairman of the Board, Toyota Motor Corporation

You know, with just a few exceptions, usually people are not fired because of their failures in business. So if the leader says: 'I will delegate the power to you in order to progress the operation, but when you make mistakes, I'm responsible, as the chief, I'm responsible and then I will take responsibility for the failure', this kind of attitude will really deepen the relationship with your partners and your colleagues.

Viren Doshi

I think a strategic partner is somebody who's actually quite independent or feels independent to do the right thing. They should have enough command and respect to be able to honour what they promise, because a strategic partner who comes and talks to you but carries no weight back in their organization cannot deliver anything. So you have to do bigger things and when you speak on behalf of the firm, you have to deliver them. That to me is a hallmark of a good, serious senior strategic partner.

He or she has enough independence of mind to be representing or getting in the shoes of the other side and not always worrying about his or her own personal agenda or targets. It is a bit of a cyclical thing and you have got to reinforce that cycle of trust and keep building on it. Clearly, it doesn't happen overnight and it doesn't happen with strangers. You might have the best product but if you don't have credibility, you can't make somebody take it. Of course, our business is a little bit different, as we don't supply products – our product is the people, the ideas and the knowledge. For this to work, credibility and relationships really matter!

Day after day after day

This is the 'hidden gem' amongst all the other points in this chapter. Relationships should be built and managed with purpose day after day after day. The SPM, the partnership team, the AoC leaders (and others as appropriate) work at the relationships 'day-after-day'. In doing so, they create familiarity and authority, as if people were working in and for the same organization. Only those who develop this everyday reality will be able to shape and 'transform' the partnership into extraordinary value.

Best-in-class relationship practice almost negates the need for negotiation. Great partnerships replace negotiations by ensuring objectives are set and delivered through the familiarity of the 'day-after-day' connectivity. A little communication and progress each day and the desired outcome soon appears logical, then possible and finally obvious to everybody!

'Day-after-day' trust building also largely removes the word contract from the partnership vocabulary, as noted by Frank Williams and Viren Doshi.

Frank Williams

It is not simply about a contract that says, 'We will do this and you will do that'. It is about the emotional investment, it is because you have people working for you who say 'we understand we are fundamental to what you do and we will be performing at the highest level of our technology'. On many occasions, we have just gone ahead on the basis that people said, 'it will be done', and it has been. And others who will say, 'My word is my bond' but there are actually not that many people whose word really is their bond!

In order to get the best out of people, they need to be emotionally involved and committed. Formula One is a superb environment which energizes people to be winners and to most definitely avoid being losers.

Viren Doshi

Many aspects of strategic partnerships don't rely on legally binding contracts. It's more a mutual understanding of: 'Look, I'll look after you, you look after me.' It's fascinating but this is how it is.

If issues arise, the everyday communication resolves these promptly, before they become obstacles. This provides to use 'soft' ways, avoiding public confrontation and containing them to the relevant people and areas concerned.

This 'day-after-day' commitment is the main reason SPMs will succeed where their remarkable CEO and leading executives may not be able to, for reasons as simple as availability, reactivity, focus and familiarity.

Prepare, prepare, prepare

We will come back to the need for a detailed 'navigation plan' of the partnership in Chapter 10.

But for now, take your time, target well, do not engage before you are clear who your true counterparts, the real decision makers and the most likely silent objectors are. Often people rush to engage with the most obvious person(s) in the opposite organization: providers to purchasers, technologists to technologists, CEOs to CEOs, etc. Suddenly, access gets channelled through traditional silos and practices and game changing may become difficult, if not impossible. So observe, learn from others, only engage when you are clear on how you will 'navigate' through your relationship, as guided in Stage 1 of the partnership development model and discussed in Chapter 10 of *Strategic Partnering*.

Successful relationship management always requires well-prepared storylines. Formulate the content with clarity and from the partner's perspective. Test the content and your narrative internally, using 'support and challenge' sessions, for quality and consistency before you start 'navigating' through it with the partner. As a result, the engagement will now turn into a clear 'story' that is thoroughly related to targeted individual(s) in the partner's organization. It should not be a 'show-and-tell' of your capabilities – strategic partnership is not about 'bragging' – but a description of mutual advantage and solutions that will make a significant difference to your partner.

With the partner engagement planned so carefully and deeply informed, the outcome is almost predetermined. In essence you should be able to go to meetings and write the minutes before they happen!

Truth from the mouths of children

A children's author had already developed a full appreciation of what extraordinary relationships are, what they mean and how to build them. He had fully understood that they:

- require a strong intent and true effort; time and patience; processes, rites and routines;

- result in mutual benefits, uniqueness and extraordinary value for each organization and the individuals involved;

- hardly ever stop, because they are built around depth of mutual knowledge and appreciation, with each party being a key part of the other's life.

The author was Antoine de St Exupéry, writing the story of a little prince and his fox for children. Or, perhaps the story of extraordinary relationships for leaders…

Antoine de St Exupéry: *The little prince*

It was then that the fox appeared. … 'I am a fox,' the fox said.

'Come and play with me,' proposed the little prince. 'I am so unhappy.'

'I cannot play with you,' the fox said. 'I am not tamed … Taming is an act too often neglected. It means to establish ties … To you, I am nothing more than a fox like a hundred thousand other foxes. But if you tame me, then we shall need each other. To me, you will be unique in all the world. To you, I shall be unique in all the world. One only understands the things that one tames … And you will need to be very patient'.

The next day the little prince came back.

'It would have been better to come back at the same hour,' said the fox. '… One must observe proper rites … Those are actions too often neglected …'.

So the little prince tamed the fox. And when the hour of his departure drew near, the fox said 'Go and look again at the roses. You will understand now that yours is unique in all the world …'.

The little prince went away, to look again at the roses. 'You are nothing' he said. '… No one has tamed you, and you have tamed no one. You are like my fox when I first knew him. He was only a fox like a hundred thousand other foxes. But I have made him my friend, and now he is unique in all the world.'

'… My Rose is more important than all the hundreds of you other roses: because it is she that I have watered; because it is she that I have put under the glass globe; because it is she that I have sheltered behind the screen; because it is for her that I have killed the caterpillars; because it is she that I have listened to, when she grumbled, or boasted, or even sometimes when she said nothing.'

And he went back to meet the fox. 'Goodbye,' he said. 'Goodbye,' said the fox. 'And now here is my secret, a very simple secret … It is the time you have wasted on your rose that makes your rose so important … Men have forgotten this truth,' said the fox. 'But you must not forget it. You become responsible, forever, for what you have tamed. You are responsible for your rose …'.

'I am responsible for my rose,' the little prince repeated, so that he would be sure to remember.

Conclusion: Building extraordinary partnerial relationships

Partnerships are fundamentally about people and their relationships. But if they are only built on 'chemistry', they won't last and won't deliver 'transformational' value. As Enzo Ferrari, the founder of the iconic Ferrari automobile maker, noted with his trademark humility, 'I need to go now because today, genius has been replaced by team work'.

So let's break collaboration boundaries; let's broaden the scope of partnerships; let's think like disruptors; let's innovate together as a system. To achieve this, we need to develop the capabilities that 'transform' relationships, foster relationships at each level across the partnering organizations, use technology to make connections more personal, tackle the governance issue by sharing control and provide more flexible chains of command in the partnering space.

In our cooking analogy, we have just made a major step towards preparing the best sauce. We have carefully selected the ingredients and, above all, made sure their combined chemistries work together wonderfully. With patience, precision and flair, there is little doubt about the best outcome.

Let us summarize how to develop the bases of extraordinary relationships.

Summary: Building extraordinary partnerial relationships

- Relationships are at the heart of the world leaders' agendas and priorities.

- They are a vital dimension and enabler of 'transformational' strategic partnerships. Success requires relationships at both enterprise and individual level to be outstanding.

- Despite their confidence in this space and for multiple reasons, organizations and people find it hard to develop extraordinary relationships. It takes both method and art.

- Relationships are developed in the service of substance and real business. Make sure that no contact is made without a clear business purpose and/or to achieve an outcome.

- Relationships in the service of strategic co-operations need to be built and constructed across the breadth and at multiple levels of the involved organizations.

- A structured approach should be taken to building enterprise relationships. It includes a multi-layer approach; a governance routine; a participation framework; joint processes; and a thorough schedule of interactions.

- An extraordinary enterprise relationship is underpinned with many extraordinary personal relationships. Systematize internal and external relationships using rigorous contact maps.

- Make your individual relationships very personal to your partners and peers. 'Transform' the quality of relationships by combining a traditional approach with modern tools offered by technology.

- Don't compromise on key principles and practices to succeed: carefully target and select your relationships; empower your partnering team; build relationships day after day after day; prepare, prepare, prepare.

- Building extraordinary personal relationships requires the right and consistent attitude and behaviour. They are deep, personal, enduring and developed over time.

- A child and his fox understood about extraordinary relationships: most of us can too!

The last three chapters have dealt with organization, people and relationships, vital areas in strategic partnering, and areas where organizations and leaders often struggle. But once you have designed and established a clear partnering organization, a strong team and quality relationships, you can truly rely on these solid foundations to confidently engage in detailed activity planning, en route to mutual 'transformational' value creation.

This is the purpose of the next three chapters, tackling the toughest challenge of all: how to create value in the strategic partnership.

08
Forming a clear strategic partnership mission, 'destination' and plan

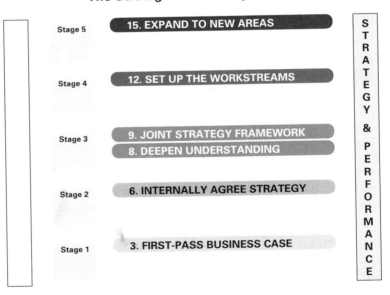

The Strategic Partnership Model

Stage 5 — 15. EXPAND TO NEW AREAS

Stage 4 — 12. SET UP THE WORKSTREAMS

Stage 3 — 9. JOINT STRATEGY FRAMEWORK
8. DEEPEN UNDERSTANDING

Stage 2 — 6. INTERNALLY AGREE STRATEGY

Stage 1 — 3. FIRST-PASS BUSINESS CASE

STRATEGY & PERFORMANCE

If you don't know where you are going, you'll end up someplace else.

YOGI BERRA

The issue is not about seeing big or small, but to see far away.

CLAUDE LELOUCH

The three next chapters of *Strategic Partnering* examine the creation and delivery of substance and value from a partnership. This is about the 'how' to develop and access 'what' the partners need to do to create 'transformational' value. Ultimately, it is about the journey and methods to develop and deliver the partnership 'sources of value' (SoVs), through the ordered and staged progression of the strategic partnership model.

Hence, we will discuss 'how' to develop the SoVs of the partnership in practice (Chapter 9), and the 'navigation' from the origination of a strategic partnership to successfully 'placing' the SoVs across the partner organizations (Chapter 10).

Before this, there obviously needs to be a meaningful 'destination' for the strategic partnership. In the absence of a robustly tested ambition, the strategic partnership would lack focus and lose its way, as is so often the case. In Chapter 2, we set the objective for the partners to reach portfolio-wide 'transformational' value and introduced six main sources for unparalleled value creation. This chapter defines the approach needed to design a powerful and concrete 'destination' relative to these six areas, as well as a workable activity framework for succeeding with the partnership.

Sebastian Coe

"In hindsight, creating the vision was the most important thing. You tend to think that the most important reason you create a vision or a mission statement is that it is what you need to do to win the next piece of business. Actually, yes we did create a very good vision to capture the imagination of most of the IOC members. But the real value of the mission was that it is your roadmap; it is your North Star.

We work in organizations that are overtly commercial and the London 2012 Organising Committee of the Olympic Games (LOCOG) was no different. But we had a mission and how often a siren voice around that table would just cut through and say, 'Guys, shouldn't we do it?' Because, if you play fast and lose the vision, then what hope have you got in a stakeholder landscape of other people holding to that? So, the vision actually is not just the pitch, the vision is what you deliver against, on an hour-by-hour basis. It is your roadmap and it will keep you healthy. It will keep you healthy and safe.

Designing a partnership 'destination' has many parallels with architecture, capturing the conceptual design before detailed planning and construction can commence. Early quality design is at the heart of all successful strategic partnerships, but is extremely difficult to do well. It demands a unique methodology and requires a select breed of professionals – the SPMs and VOMs operating as 'value architects' – to do a great job of defining 'the destination' of the partnership and the related critical components of its strategic framework.

Chapter 8 continues the cook book theme of *Strategic Partnering*, focusing on the practical design of the partnership goal and plan – the end-game of your menu and meal. It covers:

- the need to develop a well-thought-out strategic framework from the start of considering a partnership;
- the unusual but arguably necessary process for developing this strategic framework;
- what the framework actually looks like and its critical components;
- how to document, codify and implement the various threads of the partnership strategy;
- the disciplines required to craft a successful partnership strategy.

Because our partnering system approaches and manages each individual strategic partnership as a full 'business', with the partner as its scope, it is no surprise that the strategy and planning process appears to have similarities with that of a traditional business. But this is only the visible 'tip of the iceberg', as considerable differences exist in the specific challenges of partnering in practice, such as: the strategy and plan applying to the unknown; the exclusive focus on business development; and the mutuality, ie the fact that partnerships are not about 'us' but about 'them and us'.

What is a 'partnership strategy'?

A vital strategic design, but also a challenging exercise

There are plenty of studies exhorting partnering and how it is possible to achieve more for your business with partnerships. Many insights are provided on the 'why' of partnerships, but seldom is there extensive sharing on the 'what' – the deep substance of an alliance – and even less frequently on the 'how' – the methods to develop rich substance.

This imbalance between the 'why' and 'what' may come as a surprise, as partnering value will only result from the co-operative substance, from its 'what'. Perhaps less surprisingly, many leaders find it challenging to penetrate and talk about the 'how' and the novelty of untypical value mechanisms. Indeed, it is rare in public or private administration that success is so deeply determined by the ability to 'see' critical 'details', those which will prove defining to the partnership development process. In itself, this is not an issue, as reviewing the 'details' is not necessarily the role of leaders, but it should not be surprising if a CEO prefers to talk about established businesses and their incremental progress rather than the development of strategic partnerships, at least in the early stages.

A similar challenge lies at the next level down in the organization, where people are responsible for providing the leadership and support to the co-operation development. Despite appreciating that a partnership has value and brings growth potential, the 'what' and 'how' can be very hard to grasp. Many people feel disorientated and threatened on having to create an extraordinary 'unknown' with partners and do it through capabilities they are not very familiar with either. Hence, it is very difficult to create an actionable pathway to a successful strategic partnership, unless it is approached with great method.

In short, we need to tackle the considerable challenge to design 'what' a partnership stands for, 'what' it will deliver and 'how' to reach a goal of substance – because it is all about the new, about step-outs, about the horizontal (rather than the 'simpler' verticals), about others and not simply about 'us'. This chapter recommends a high level of discipline in forming the partnership's strategic approach and includes a number of counter-intuitive and unconventional practices to do so. Ian Davis reflects on how purposeful partners need to be about their joint intent and strategy.

Ian Davis

We are onto a complex topic here and we need to know: when is a partnership a partnership and when is it truly strategic as opposed to opportunistic? When you are partnering, there needs to be dependence or co-dependence because you get something that you cannot get through some other forms of relationship management. Usually, people would partner because they can't get that skill or that access or that relationship through a simpler buy, hire or source approach.

One needs to be very analytical about this, very purposeful and structured about what you mean and what you are partnering for.

The components of a successful partnership strategy

We see seven main components to a successful encompassing partnership strategy. As represented in Figure 8.1, these strands are split into two levels: the enterprise partnership strategy (light blue) and the workstream strategy (dark blue):

- **The enterprise partnership strategy:** its four threads include the development and codification of a mission and a 'destination', a strategic framework and a plan for the partnership.
- **The workstream strategy:** the successful development of substance and related SoVs requires us to originate individual workstream charters, individual SoV charters and the description of and roll-out plans for the resulting 'offers' or innovations.

The main focus of this chapter is the enterprise level of the partnership strategy represented on the left hand side of Figure 8.1. SoVs, 'offers' and innovation are explored in the next chapter of *Strategic Partnering*.

The process of developing a fully encompassing partnership strategy

Yogi Berra, the famous Yankees baseball catcher, and Claude Lelouch, the celebrated French film director, say respectively: 'If you don't know where you are going, you'll end up someplace else'; and 'The issue is not about seeing big or small, but to see far away'.

Being clear and right early on, as you 'navigate' towards the partnership 'destination' and strategic framework, is extremely challenging. Yet unparalleled high rates of success and exactness can be achieved through systematically developing the seven strategy components in Figure 8.1 fully intertwined with the strategic partnership development model.

As represented in Figure 8.2, each stage of the model improves the clarity of the partnership's strategy relative to the earlier steps. The whole idea and beauty of the process is to 'cut the elephant into slices', with each slice dealt with in turn, building on the insights of the preceding ones. Hence, this methodical step-by-step progression turns a major and apparently impossible strategy task into manageable parts.

FIGURE 8.1 Seven components of successful partnership strategy and plan

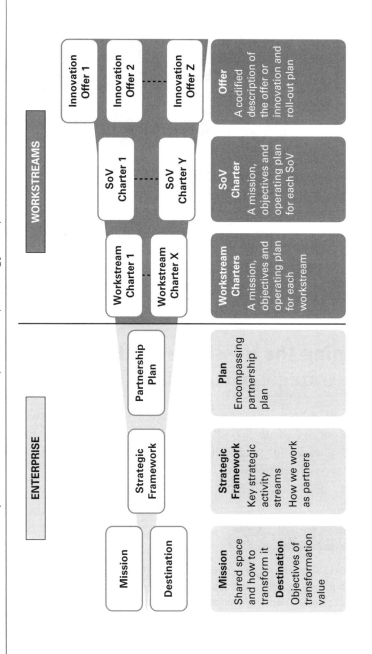

FIGURE 8.2   Thorough strategy developed along the partnership model

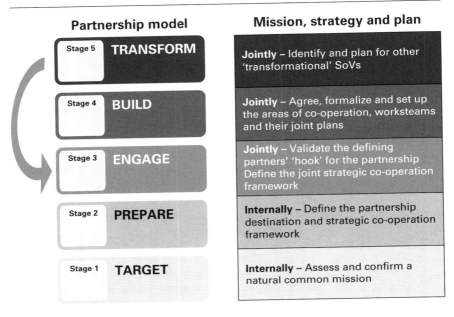

Defining the mission and 'destination' of the strategic partnership

Clarity on why to enter into a strategic co-operation, as well as a good understanding of its broad 'destination', is consistently mentioned by leaders as essential preconditions for considering and then committing to this type of relationship.

Francisco Garcia Sanz

"At Volkswagen, the major part of material costs come from suppliers. As a consequence, suppliers and the OEM share a great part of the responsibility to fulfil customers' requirements, such as quality, flexibility, innovation, costs, etc. These requirements can only be fulfilled if first tier suppliers and the OEM work together in a long-term partnership, which enables both parties to achieve their respective strategic goals. This requires a close and co-operative relationship between first-tier suppliers and the OEM.

A clear mission

As shown in the first column on the left-hand side of Figure 8.1, a potential partnership starts with assessing if a natural common mission exists between the tentative allies, primarily a reflection of the joint or connected space they contribute to, and how their co-operation could 'improve' and even 'transform' this space.

Lord Coe relates how a natural joint mission existed between him, his father and technical experts, who all brought a critical angle to every aspect of his training, to make the partnership advance and result in world-beating results.

Sebastian Coe

To me, partnership is the only way you make progress. Everything I have ever done has been done in partnership. If you look back at my earliest days in my athletics career, track and field is quintessentially an individual sport. My father was my coach and he knew this wasn't a solo journey.

He brought the most extraordinary skill sets to the table and that was a partnership! Those guys were still there 15, 17 years later when I retired, because we all bought into absolutely the same vision and the vision was really clear. There was no ambiguity about it, it wasn't soft-edged, it was to turn me into one of the best middle-distance runners of my generation, and do it legitimately and with integrity.

My father had an engineer's obsession about taking things apart and putting the elements back together so they work better. We worked with people who bought into the vision and could bring those very clear and discrete skill sets to the objective.

A natural joint mission exists in all cases when there is a key material interface between organizations and their sectors. Examples mentioned in Chapter 1 include: governments and healthcare, infrastructure or energy providers; aircraft engine manufacturers and air framers; mass retailers and leading global FMCG companies; automotive and energy companies; utilities and rotating equipment providers; chips and PC/tablet developers, just to name a few. A natural mission exists and considerable potential can arise from strategic partnering between those and many others, but it is seldom sufficiently explored and even more rarely developed to full potential.

Continuing with the use of our earlier example of an automaker and an energy company, the mission for this particular partnership could be stated as:

> PROVIDE LOW CARBON MOBILITY THROUGH ADVANCED AND AFFORDABLE ENGINES AND ENERGY

As discussed in Chapter 4 and schematized in Figure 8.1, a key objective of Stage 1 of our strategic partnership model will be to identify and test this joint mission and confirm the true potential for 'transformational' impact and value from the potential co-operation. These will need to be thoroughly assessed and explored, with potential partners not selected for further development until there is evidence of a clear and stated complementary mission.

The question is often not 'whether' to develop strategic partnerships in service of that mission, but 'who with'. Anecdotally, we remember a CEO of a leading global industrial company saying, 'given how deeply we depend on each other, it would be criminal not to partner strategically between our sectors; our real question is who to do it with?'

A clear 'destination'

Assuming that material interfaces and joint spaces exist between organizations, this alone does not suffice to justify a partnership. As shown in column 1 of Figure 8.1, there also needs to be a material and realistic potential for the co-operation to impact deeply on that space and create 'transformational' value for both partners in the joint or adjacent spaces.

Michel Taride

Key success factors of a strategic partnership are: the complementarity of products and services (in our case, the 'travel chain' category); clear strategic alignment and commonality of goals; a strong brand alignment; shared values; and, importantly, great personal relationships at all levels from the CEO down to the front line.

Then the 'magic' comes from mutual trust and the permanent attention from senior management. For example, the Deputy CEO of Ryanair is a demanding but great supporter of Hertz. Success is built on exclusivity, a long-term perspective and of course 'performance' delivery. Partnerships are not successful when organizations are short-termist and biased mainly to one partner's objectives.

The nature and scale of this value will define the 'destination' of the co-operation and it is critical to clarify this purpose internally at an early stage, with a strong first pass in Stage 1 and a fully-underpinned pass in Step 6 of our strategic partnership model.

In the example of the car manufacturer and the energy company, the 'destination' for the partnership could be formulated as:

> A STEP CHANGE IN CO2 EMISSION (X PER CENT), THROUGH THREE NEW GENERATIONS OF TECHNOLOGY OVER 10 YEARS, SUPPORTED BY REGULATORS, JOINTLY MARKETED UNIVERSALLY.

A thorough process to provide clarity on both mission and 'destination'

As Ian Davis was saying, there is a need to be analytical and structured about what both parties are partnering for. And it might look simple and intuitive, but do not be misled by gut feel and a simple 'feel-good' factor. Both play a role but the strategy needs robustness for the partnership to be 'bomb-proof'.

John Browne

Strategic partnering is providing something which is of mutual advantage to both parties, that they couldn't do otherwise and couldn't do separately. And normally, it is for the long term.

I think in all cases you should be writing down exactly what you mean by mutual advantage and in effect measuring the advantage. It is not something warm and fuzzy, it is something important and rather analytical.

Defining the strategic framework of the partnership

This is the pinnacle of the partnership strategy design. As represented in column 2 of Figure 8.1, once such a strategic framework has been developed and agreed internally in Step 6 of the model, there will be clarity on the intended AoCs, the potential value and the respective roles and contributions of each partner. Once a joint strategic framework is agreed with the partner(s) in Step 9, it will be formalized and the parties will declare themselves to be 'strategic partners'.

The most powerful and aspirational strategic frameworks always consist of two components: the partnership substance framework and the partnership ethos framework.

A joint substance

This will be about strategically and simply defining the AoCs, which are core parts of the mission and vital to building and reaching the 'transformational destination'.

Continuing to use the automaker and energy company example, Figure 8.3 offers an illustrative example of what the strategic framework between the partners might look like.

FIGURE 8.3   Strategic co-operation framework: Example

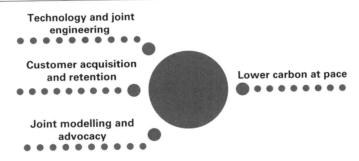

At this critical stage of the strategy development, the existence of the true potential, materiality of the value and the 'transformational' nature for each of the partners should have been verified. In practice, the next priority will be to test the accessibility and deliverability of the tentative value of the strategic partnership.

A joint ethos

Equally important as the clarity of partnership substance, the allies must set the tone, behavioural expectations and rules of engagement for the relationship. This will provide definition and invaluable guidance to everyone involved and accelerate the development of the partnership across the organizations.

This isn't strictly about defining the 'partnership culture', but is in essence what the partners will have in the back of their minds when they develop a joint ethos. Alternatively, it could be considered as the 'soft formula' for the partnership practice.

Figure 8.4 offers a simple illustrative example of a joint ethos framework.

FIGURE 8.4   Joint ethos framework: Example

POSITIONING

We aim at demonstrating leadership and creating a joint competitive advantage.

We will be fully compliant with legislation and enhance our relationships with society and communities.

WAYS OF WORKING

Our ways of working will be unique and 'hard to copy'.

We will take a bold and proactive view on all the joint possibilities.

The focus will be on 'how I can make things happen' rather than about 'should I get things to happen'.

Relationships will be friendly and dialogue straight and real; we will share our doubts openly.

We will approach value creation as if we are one, rather than from each partner's individual perspective.

We will operate locally but ensure global strategy and coordination.

We will measure and benchmark what we do jointly and transparently.

Testing the strategic and enduring role of each partner

It is now crucial to summarize and assess the partners' respective capabilities, strengths and areas of input into the strategic framework, so their role and mutual contribution to the other partner(s) is well understood and each play and fulfil their part fully. Michael Johnson notes the critical importance of connected missions between the partners and their respective ability to bring the best to the relationship.

Michael Johnson

"At Michael Johnson Performance, our mission and what we do every day is looking for ways to help athletes to be better. We are on the front end, on the innovative side and the cutting edge of all different types of technology, including developing new training methodologies that help athletes perform at their best and reach their full potential.

There is a very, very similar ethos at Nike when it comes to athletes, how to help them perform better, how to develop and provide a product that helps them to be more comfortable, to be more confident. I think the similarities between Nike and Michael Johnson Performance are very evident. It is what is needed in the best partnerships like ours with Nike, which are formed when you are able to identify fundamental similarities.

Matching our key motives to partner, with the target organizations' capabilities

In Chapter 1, the key motives for partnering were described in four categories: access to critical capabilities or resources; access to relationships or markets; access to greater security or lower risks; and access to invention potential. To help further with understanding the SoVs and to underpin our partners' assessment, Figures 8.5 and 8.6 provide a breakdown of these four categories into a detailed and practical inventory of the 'most frequent' motives for partnering.

Specifically, Figure 8.5 refers to 'access to critical resources, capabilities and innovation'. It is only if the envisaged partner is capable of providing such access important to the strategic framework and to our needs, and if such access is on offer, that we should consider partnering. Taking the reciprocal perspective, we also should not partner if we are not able to bring our fair contribution to the target organization. As noted in the IBM CEO study mentioned in Chapter 7, 53 per cent of the 1,700 CEO interviewees are partnering to innovate.

FIGURE 8.5   Key motives for strategic partnering (1)

ACCESS TO CRITICAL CAPABILITIES OR RESOURCES

- **Technology**
  Integrated technology

  - Transport OEMs (air, road, rail) and component manufacturers
  - Transport OEMs and energy companies
  - Chips and tablets/smartphones/PC manufacturers
  - Telecoms, network and software companies

  Product and application technologies intertwined

  - Utilities and power equipment providers

- **Finances**
  Investing for the other

  - Governments and private sector for infrastructure or services
  - International oil and gas companies and resource owners
  - Small technology companies and big corporations

- **Entire functionalities**
  Providing a full part of others' value chains at optimal costs

  - Client users and IT, accounting, transactions full outsourcing
  - Online marketers and logistics

- **Resources**
  Providing missing resources

  - Industrial companies and engineering expert companies

ACCESS TO INVENTION POTENTIAL

- **New business models**
  Transforming business

  - Utilities, software providers, hardware providers for smart grid
  - Telecoms hardware and content providers

Equally valuable are the categories in Figure 8.6, with key partnering motives including 'access to critical relationships or markets; and potential to markedly reduce risks and exposure'. Our enquiry at this stage will again aim to verify that the prospective partners' capabilities in these areas can contribute deeply, differently and in an enduring manner to the strategic framework and our requirements. Incidentally, close to 50 per cent of existing large-scale partnerships are developed among competitors, largely driven by these motives.

FIGURE 8.6   Key motives for strategic partnering (2)

ACCESS TO RELATIONSHIPS OR MARKETS	
• **Governments; agencies** Obtain government or agencies' decisions	• Defence and military manufacturers and governments • Energy companies and governments • Pharmaceutical, communications, etc firms and agencies
• **Communities** Obtain community support	• Construction companies and local governments • Mining companies and mine site communities
• **New geographies** Enter new markets	• Global firms and local leaders in regulated markets
• **New channels** Access customers at scale	• FMCG companies and distributors • Franchiser and franchisee • Airline alliances
• **New customer segments** Accessing customers at scale	• FMCG or retailers and loyalty programme management firms

ACCESS TO GREATER SECURITY OR LOWER RISKS	
Shared risk Often competitors Grow business	Banks for a major customer or investment Resource companies (eg mining, energy) for a major investment Pharmaceutical companies for developing and distributing a new drug
Assured supply Secure business	Industrial manufacturers and essential cyclical raw materials suppliers Food companies and raw materials Suppliers of essential equipment or components

Confirming the strategic and enduring role of each partner

Having now identified and tested each of the relevant individual strategic drivers for partnering, we use a summary matrix to finalize our decision (see Figure 8.7). The Y axis defines the key motives for partnering (listed above), as they relate to the strategic framework. The X axis indicates the partners' respective strength and position for each motive to partner.

When applying the matrix to the continuing example of the automaker and the energy company, it shows firstly that most of the motives for partnering are relevant to the strategic framework and therefore make a further assessment worth progressing. The result shown on Figure 8.7 (in the 'Joint' column) also represents a strong and truly balanced position between both partners in most areas. There is an 'Input' position

FIGURE 8.7 Respective partner's strengths to deliver the strategic framework

KEY MOTIVES TO PARTNER			
ACCESS TO:	ASSESSMENT: INPUT	JOINT	LEAD
CRITICAL CAPABILITIES OR RESOURCES			
Technology		✓	
Finances		✓	
Entire functionalities		✓	
Rare skills		✓	
INNOVATION POTENTIAL			
New business models	✓		
RELATIONSHIPS OR MARKETS			
Governments; agencies		✓	
Communities		✓	
New geographies	✓		
New channels			
New customer segments		✓	
SECURITY OR LOWER RISKS			
Shared risks		✓	
Assured supply		✓	

from the energy company to the OEM on new geographies and new business models. This reflects the stronger starting point and leading role for the OEM in these particular areas.

But apart from these two acceptable imbalances, the potential partners are good to go in this example!

Creating a winning plan for a strategic partnership

We turn now to column 3 of Figure 8.1. Having identified a mission, 'destination' and strategic framework for the partnership, developed unilaterally in Steps 3 and 6 and jointly with the partner in Step 9, we should now move to activation, enrolment and concrete value creation.

The strategic partnership plan is the internal repository of everything that defines the co-operation, approached and managed as a fully-fledged business. It tells the full 'story' of what the strategic framework really means and how it translates into knowledge, objectives, activities and individuals' roles. It guides people and actions.

> **Viren Doshi**
>
> Each main account has a plan developed in a planning session which is led by a client service officer and which includes different account team members. This is also the forum where performance at, and approach to, key accounts are reviewed in detail.

Continuously improving the partnership plan is a priority activity for the SPM and his or her team. As mentioned later in this section, the plan will also be at the centre of the relationship between the partnership team and its Executive Champion, who will review it routinely and be its ultimate formal approver.

Components of the strategic partnership plan

As represented in Figure 8.8, the partnership plan comprehends all business dimensions of the partnership.

FIGURE 8.8 Six-area strategic partnership plan

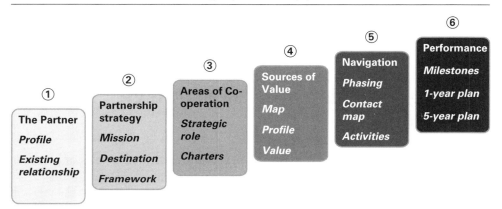

① **The Partner**
Profile
Existing relationship

② **Partnership strategy**
Mission
Destination
Framework

③ **Areas of Co-operation**
Strategic role
Charters

④ **Sources of Value**
Map
Profile
Value

⑤ **Navigation**
Phasing
Contact map
Activities

⑥ **Performance**
Milestones
1-year plan
5-year plan

Jeff Immelt

"There needs to be a purpose. The relationship should be mission-based and there must be a goal, a big goal. Then you need to work across the business with many focal points and make it a system, with processes and metrics.

The plan can be structured around six main complementary areas: they make up the full co-operation narrative and can act as an activation guide.

1. The partner

The importance of understanding the partner(s) is crucial. In fact, SPMs and their teams spend considerable time and effort upfront and before engaging, to understand the partners' main drivers, portfolio and decision-making processes.

The partner profile will therefore collect not just facts and data, but also provide guidance on the 'hooks' for the other party. It will reflect existing relationships, either as platforms to be leveraged and built upon, or issues to work on and resolve.

Peter Foss

"My efforts are always aiming at getting a better understanding of how companies work inside, what is important to them, what their strategies are and then how we can best help them to reach the so-called 'win–win'.

And if you don't get to know companies well enough and when you don't really understand their decision-making process and what is important to them, then you may miss the target because it is either not important to them or it is not relevant to the direction that they are taking their business in.

So we try to understand this and then pull that information together into a meaningful plan to work together. And those elements make things work in that, first of all, you have to be able to get access to the right people, otherwise you are not getting anywhere.

2. The partnership enterprise strategy

The strategic partnership and its plan are founded on the three pillars of the co-operation strategy, ie its mission, 'destination' and framework. All internal participants to the alliance, ranging from the Corporate Champion to large groups of people in the informal team, will be able to immediately access the 'story' of the relationship and set their own actions in the right context.

3. The areas of co-operation (AoCs)

This is where the real work takes place to develop the substance and the value of the strategic co-operation. The plan includes a map of these AoCs, linked to the partnership strategic framework.

It is advisable to work on individual AoC charters systematically, using a standard format. A one-page summary should be extracted from the comprehensive charter, to become an integral part of the partnership plan. With this, it becomes easier to discern how each workstream is contributing individually and see the integrated 'transformation' of the partners' joint space or interface emerge.

4. The 'sources of value'

Similarly, the plan will include a map of the SoVs, as they refer to their AoC and as illustrated earlier in Figure 4.4. The portfolio of SoVs will be assessed through a number of 'lenses', including their respective importance to each partner (Figure 4.5). Finally, individual charters of the key SoVs will be described on a standardized, one-page SoV summary, keeping track of progress and a dynamic perspective on the related dependencies of and to other SoVs.

This planned approach guides strategic clarity, as well as focuses action and interventions. In the illustrative example in Figure 4.4, the technologists will be able to steer the efforts in their SoVs, in light of progress made with related SoVs in the marketing and risk management AoCs. They will also be able to input and respond to issues raised by their colleagues, to improve cohesiveness and leverage across different areas and SoVs.

5. The 'navigation'

'Navigation' will be the whole purpose of Chapter 10 of *Strategic Partnering*. It is another crucial dimension of succeeding with strategic co-operations. The partnership plan will force a disciplined approach to the multiple dimensions of successful 'navigation', be it for the whole of the partnership, an AoC or a main SoV.

Key elements of successful 'navigation' include: the steps and pre-conditions for engagement; the 'story'; the people involved; the phasing of individual interactions; the timing of actions, etc.

6. The 'performance'

A key element of the 'destination' and 'navigation' for the partnership, 'performance' measurements are integral components of the co-operation plan. They provide the planning and budgetary requirements to the wider organization, notably in the form of a one-year and five-year plan. Equally, they offer uniquely insightful strategic guidance to the co-operation activities and their progress. This will be reflected in key input milestones, which will help guide, anticipate and access progress towards 'transformational' value.

Anecdotally, we remember the example of a specific partnership, which we developed over a period of ten years. It started from the worst possible position, with the envisioned partner opposed to almost any relationship. A decade later, both organizations are deep partners and have set a benchmark for strategic partnering in their joint spaces and industries. Without a clear upfront milestone map, where each stage of progress could be tracked and assessed, it is doubtful that the organization would have kept at it, particularly through the unavoidable leadership and people changes over such a long period of time.

Knowing the mission and 'destination' and keeping resolutely to our 'navigation' plan turned the challenging start into a deeply valued strategic partnership.

How the plan is developed and its essential role throughout the life of the partnership

As mentioned earlier, considering and managing strategic partnerships as fully-fledged businesses is a critical success factor.

Strategic partnerships are unusual but fully-fledged businesses

It is not a typical business, as its scope is defined by one or a few partners rather than by a more classic service, product, geography or asset; it is shaped by us and them rather than us only; it is entirely focused on development and invention, with little or no installed physical base.

However, it is absolutely appropriate to approach and lead partnerships using the best of modern business management practices.

Viren Doshi

> "The partnership, that's my market!
> And you cannot do business without mobilizing individuals towards that agenda, even if they don't all have the same single-minded motivation that you have. This itself is a key skill.

Living strategic partnerships as full businesses starts with the design of a comprehensive and high-quality strategy. As we are stressing in the chapter, there should be no relaxation at any stage with respect to a thorough, high-quality strategy development.

A complex and challenging exercise

The challenge of getting a partnership strategy right can be tough and fraught with difficulties. Imagine you are given the name of a governmental institution, a company, a university or an NGO, with a simply stated task: build an extraordinary, value-added partnership between them and us. It can appear almost impossible to even know where to start.

As challenging as it is, the potential rewards of good strategic planning can be stunning and our experience is that it is always worth giving it the necessary determination, depth and time. Key to success is understanding the partner, developing clarity on the joint mission and strategic deliverable, conceiving the joint activities and milestones required to trigger 'transformational' value, and finding the best routes to collective agreement.

An iterative approach

It is impossible to 'see what we can't see' from the start. A winning approach relies on accepting that the plan will not be perfect first time, that it requires patience and potentially multiple iterations. Many people are actually apprehensive about even beginning the process, often because it is so undefined. However, a great deal of progress can often be made with the first pass and the quality rises quickly with successive iterations.

The strategic plan will then be continuously refined and adjusted, with a formal review every year.

An involving practice

A strategic partnership plan is owned by the SPM and the partnership team. They research, develop and leverage all necessary and relevant knowledge and capability, wherever it comes from. Ownership, however, does not signal working in isolation, quite the contrary.

The enterprise partnership team will need to involve others at each appropriate step, from within the organization, from the partners and the external world.

As mentioned earlier, the role of the Executive Champion is important in the strategic planning process. He or she will ultimately approve the partnership plan and ensure alignment with the organization's strategy and choices. They will also be important in securing commitment and ownership to the partnership from the organization.

Applying the partnership development model to win strategically

In Figure 8.9, you will recognize the seven components of the partnership strategy, with the enterprise level steps which we just discussed shown on the left-hand side (light blue).

Strategic clarity will improve along the steps of the model. As noted in Chapter 4, the central partnering team will develop a first-pass plan in Step 1, through extensive research. This plan will be tested particularly rigorously in Step 3, when the '70 per cent chance of success' business case is developed with extensive input from multiple organization leaders.

By Step 6 of the partnership development model, the SPM and partnership team will have developed a refined framework and plan for the co-operation. This is a critical milestone in the model, when the organization will formally approve the strategy through its own decision processes. This 'go-ahead' will trigger engagement with the other party(ies) from Step 7 and lead to insightful and significant enhancements of various components of the partnership framework and plan.

By Step 9 and after conscientious application of the partnership development model, the business planning will be high quality, thanks to and despite the apparent complexity of the process. The key is to place these various aspects of strategy design at the heart of the partnership development model and leverage each and all steps to progressively achieve greater clarity on the strategic framework and the plan.

FIGURE 8.9 The partnership strategy: Key 'enterprise' milestones

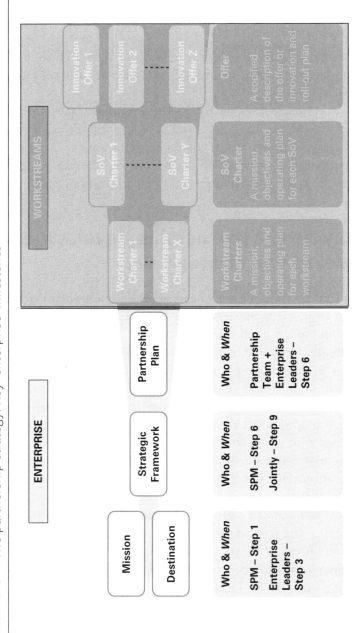

Conclusion: Forming a clear partnership strategy and plan

Leaders may champion publicly and quite freely a few selected aspects of partnerships – their principle, their outcomes and the relationships they generate. Very rarely is there any coverage of the partnership strategy, its true substance and essential processes, or the 'destination', the inputs and other critical dimensions of the 'how' of partnering. These are mainly 'delegated to the ranks'.

In truth, these are quite difficult to champion publicly, because they are hard to conceive, hard to progress, hard to get right, hard to talk about. Yet they are what generates truly 'transformational' partnerships and creates unparalleled value. Tackling these challenges would help the 70 per cent of government or business CEOs who want to 'transform' their partnership capability to achieve their aspiration.

Here is a summary of the guidelines from Chapter 8, on how to systematically develop and progress a comprehensive partnership strategy and plan, so that substantial mutual added value is generated.

Summary: Forming a clear strategic partnership mission, 'destination' and plan

- Value-added substance is the single motivation, justification and *raison d'être* of a strategic partnership.

- Accessing 'transformational' value requires a clear and exact partnership strategy. It is very hard to get it right and success requires approaching each strategic partnership as a fully-fledged business, with the need for a top quality strategy.

- Front-end loading effort to bring clarity to the mission, 'destination' and plan will prove invaluable in successfully developing partnerships. This early clarity will be crucial in raising the relationship to the level of strategic partnerships.

- In our partnering system, a co-operation strategy comprises seven components: four of them are enterprise-level, namely the partnership mission, its 'destination', the strategic framework and the plan.

- The mission and 'destination' define the essence, space and ambition of the partnership. The strategic framework establishes the areas of activity where substance will be developed, together with a joint ethos and way of working.

- Testing the true, enduring and differentiated contribution of each partner to make a big difference to a 'transformational' strategic partnership is an integral part of the plan.

- The strategic partnership plan will guide all involved towards 'transformational' value throughout the years.

- Because the plan will be pivotal to enduring value creation, it is vital to get it right. Leveraging the benefits of the iterative strategic partnership development model is best practice.

- By applying the model with strategy at its heart, the SPM and partnership team will progress seamlessly towards extraordinary value and achieve what competitors cannot.

This was a true cook book chapter. The partnership strategy process may appear a bit heavy or even bureaucratic to some on paper. But its reality is a lot simpler and experience tells us that you can achieve un-paralleled outcomes by applying this recipe.

09
Developing compelling partnership 'value propositions' and 'offers'

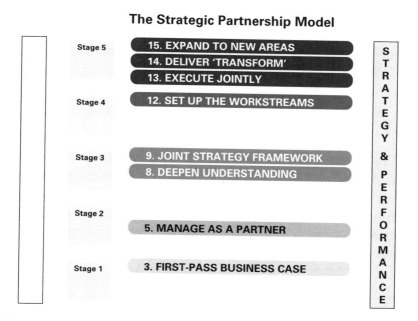

The Strategic Partnership Model

Stage 5	15. EXPAND TO NEW AREAS
	14. DELIVER 'TRANSFORM'
	13. EXECUTE JOINTLY
Stage 4	12. SET UP THE WORKSTREAMS
Stage 3	9. JOINT STRATEGY FRAMEWORK
	8. DEEPEN UNDERSTANDING
Stage 2	5. MANAGE AS A PARTNER
Stage 1	3. FIRST-PASS BUSINESS CASE

STRATEGY & PERFORMANCE

> Excellence is the unlimited ability to improve the quality of what you have to offer.
>
> **RICK PITINO**

> He who fights may lose. He who doesn't fight has already lost.
>
> **BERTOLT BRECHT**

If you read only one chapter of *Strategic Partnering*, then this is the one! The mission, 'destination' and strategic framework developed using the previous chapters' approach provide high value objectives and key activity threads for the intended partnership. They are the indispensable North Star and roadmap to any partnership, and utilizing the prescribed methodologies will ensure much greater chances of success. However, there are other aspects that need to be added to the approach to reach the aspired 'destination'.

It is time to translate the latent potential of the partnership into real and material value, through a series of tangible joint activities developed in the context of the partnership strategic framework. These joint activities convert concept into hard reality, with clear business value as the outcome.

As represented on the right-hand side of Figure 9.1, progressing towards value encompasses:

- the installation and activation of the agreed workstreams – internally first and then jointly – as they arise from the partnership strategic framework agreed in Steps 6 and 9;
- the identification, characterization and development of the partnership SoVs;
- the practical development of the value proposition and 'offers' associated with the SoVs.

Why 'offers'?

Let us begin with a simplified example of an intended partnership between two organizations. Organization A, driven by clear and deeply analysed motives – in our model, having completed Stages 1 and 2 – is determined to partner with organization B. But organization B will not yet have considered a strategic partnership with A. They might not even have envisaged a differentiated relationship. At some point in the dialogue, B will also run their own hard-edged testing of A's strategic and enduring worth to them, equivalent to that described in Chapter 8.

Organization A therefore needs to develop a 'value proposition' and identify the defining strategic 'hook(s)', ie the main driver(s) for both organizations, and particularly B to partner. These will of course arise from the mission, 'destination' and strategic framework defined earlier for the partnership, but we now need to deliver them, not simply design them. Multiple connected and surrounding 'offers' will also be developed to engage target partner B across the relevant parts of its organization in pursuit of credentials and value.

FIGURE 9.1 The partnership strategy: Key 'workstream' milestones

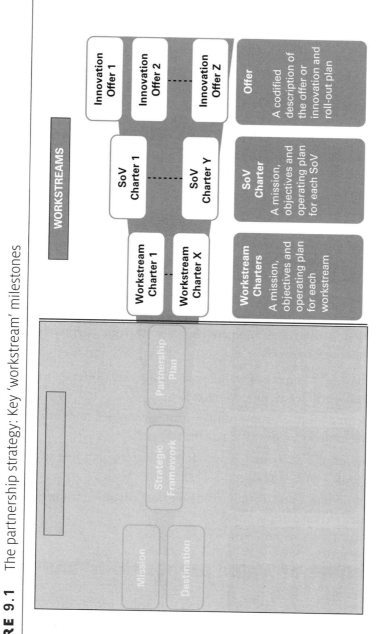

The 'value proposition' and 'offers' will make up the SoVs of the partnership throughout its lifetime. In practice, they will play a major role in convincing both organizations A and B to enter into a partnership, right up until Step 8 of the model. From Step 9, when the strategic partnership is declared, they will be about pure 'delivery'.

A challenging exercise ... again

The reality is that developing great 'offers' is universally recognized as one of the most difficult propositions facing a business. We meet organizations all the time that need and aspire to ramp up their 'offer-development' capability, otherwise they feel restricted in their options. Anecdotally, and as we were writing these lines, we reviewed the strategy of a world-class business who felt severely constrained in their ambitions for growth in fast-developing giant economies by their inadequate 'offer-development' competencies.

The secret to success lies in a rigorous 'offer' development process, often resulting in industry firsts, generated from the perspective of the target partner (B in our earlier example). This chapter will describe how to approach 'offer' development to make strategic partnerships successful, with a key focus on:

- sharing examples of 'value proposition' and 'offers', brought by our world leader interviewees;
- defining 'value propositions', strategic 'hooks' and 'offers' in the context of strategic partnerships;
- adopting a systematic approach to developing these strategic 'hooks' and 'offers';
- providing a set of rules to ensure the failings of traditional methods are not repeated.

Examples of 'value propositions' and 'offers'

There are of course infinite examples of value propositions and 'offers' between two or more organizations. Here, our interviewees share some examples and reflect on what they mean to them and their organizations with regard to the strategic partnership model. These mini-cases cover co-operations in the business-to-government (B2G), business-to-business (B2B) and business-to-consumer (B2C) spaces.

Model: B2B
Brought by: Andrew Mackenzie
Offer: Advanced products or process solutions provided to an operation
Sector: Mining industry

I think the partnership level, perhaps the strategic partnership level, is where there is a commitment to improve the business with a product or a solution which we are working on together, where there may be a degree of experimentation that sometimes works out and sometimes doesn't work and where there is a desire of a shared agenda of innovation. And that shared agenda of innovation is of course reinforced by more short-term operational or commercial work where we help each other out. You can only have a few relationships like that, but we should work those we choose and they should be as important to the Chief Executive as their relationships with their shareholders, with their employees, with politicians and the media.

Model: B2B2B
Brought by: Gerard Vittecoq, Former Group President, Caterpillar Inc
Offer: Marketing and servicing
Sector: Construction, mining, transportation, agriculture and defence

At Caterpillar, partnering with our dealers is an enterprise philosophy, a mindset. We believe in win–win and always ask ourselves how to make them as well as us successful and profitable. Mutual straight and honest communication finds its source in a deep culture of respect, integrity and standing behind our names. And multi-billion dollar relationships are on three months' notice contracts, so we all keep performance in front of us. Actually, the word 'CAT Dealer' stands for a full definition of what to expect from these partnerships and the joint offering it represents.

Model: B2B2C, B2B2B
Brought by: Michel Taride
Offer: Co-design and co-marketing of services to consumers and businesses
Sector: Travel chain: car rental, airlines and hotels

The Hertz–Air France strategic partnership started in 1988 through Air Inter, the domestic French airline later acquired by Air France. Twenty-five years later, we are proud to have just renewed the partnership for another five years. From the very start, this has been about developing joint offers to differentiate them and us markedly from the competition. We are both part of the 'travel chain' and our early joint promise was 'one-stop fly and drive'. We then created co-branded products and services. We continue to permanently innovate together. For example, we co-run call-centres, web transfers, micro-sites and loyalty cross-benefits, just to name a few offers. Recently, we developed and launched the Air France Abonnés Plus 'frequent flyer' card, which is uniquely capable of providing access to Hertz rental cars, through our latest 24/7 Hertz-on-Demand technology-based offer.

Model: B2B, B2G
Brought by: Tom Albanese
Offer: Integrated infrastructure and co-operative project management
Sector: Mining, infrastructure, energy industries

If we ever build a mine, let me use a fuel supplier as an example. Supply will be about who delivers the diesel to the site. Partnership is going to be who actually helps the mine company, being Rio Tinto, meet its own commercial objectives. So can that fuel infrastructure also help with the regional economic development? And if it is a place with challenges, for example with the government, can they help to reinforce commercial impacts, absolute transparency, etc …? In an emerging new location, can community specialists from both companies work together to say, 'Okay, what can we do with that local community that frankly is desperate for electrification and help them?', just as an example.

Model: B2B2C
Brought by: Wolfgang Reitzle
Offer: Joint process innovation, resulting in new consumer offering
Sector: Industrial gas and restaurant industries

We have this kind of partnership with a few companies around the world. One of these is McDonald's. In fact, their crispy chicken is only possible thanks to the new process we invented in collaboration with the McDonald's team. Our engineers worked not in our labs, but in McDonald's R&D department to develop the burger and its entire manufacturing line, where our gas is used to shock-freeze the ingredient. The chicken that comes out at the other end is crispy and succulent rather than dry and chewy.

This is one example of a typical win–win outcome. We are selling our gas to one of the most interesting food-processing customers in the world and they have exclusivity and the assurance that we won't supply our machines and our processes to another company. This is a good deal for us and is something we are doing in certain other areas as well.

Model: B2B
Brought by: Jeff Immelt
Offer: Advanced technology with transfer from one industry to another
Sector: Oil and gas, healthcare

We develop technologies in many areas. One of our offers is to combine technologies from various areas or leverage technology developed in one area into another. Take the example of an advanced system for pipe inspection used deep-sea. The user business is 'oil and gas'; the inventing business is 'healthcare'. And GE worked together with BP to transfer, adapt and tailor the healthcare expertise into deep-sea and pipeline inspection conditions.

Model: B2B2C
Brought by: Ian Robertson
Offer: Advanced technology under cost constraint
Sector: Auto and component industries

In the car business, customers have ever-increasing expectations. This means that the specification of our cars is rising constantly, but customers are often not able or willing to pay extra for these advances. Therefore, our challenge is constantly to search for innovative technologies, both within the company's own resources and through our component suppliers, which can meet our customers' needs and desires, but without increasing costs – or even at lower cost. We live in a competitive world and customers have a very clear idea about what represents good value. These expectations have got much higher in the last 10 or 15 years.

Model: B2G, B2B, B2B2C
Brought by: Shelly Lazarus
Offer: Integrated solutions
Sector: Professional services, communications, advertising

Clients today want integrated solutions. They don't want answers in pieces. They don't want one guy to come in, do an audit and leave and someone else comes in and assesses the IT program and a third person gives advice on tax and so on. They want one of the big firms to come in and give them a full assessment of how they manage risk in their company. These firms though are organized in silos. There's audit, IT consulting, insurance, whatever and this means a big challenge to ensure proper service and risk management. So there need to be strategic partnerships to fully deliver what a client needs today. And there needs to be one person who delivers all the services of the firm, in an integrated fashion, to the client.

I am thinking of a particular engagement. The goal was to 'transform' a company, it was to 'transform' a brand, it was not about 'give me a bunch of posters and write a speech for me'. It was, 'could we think together about how to take this brand that stood for X and get it to a point where it now stands for something much more meaningful, important, and exciting'. It was always about the big mission. And we were always invited to everything, to the launches, to the celebrations, to the important meetings. We were invited to share not just the effort, but share the moments of glory, share the moments of completion so that again your partners feel like real partners and not like suppliers who are brought in when needed.

Model:	B2B
Brought by:	Tom Albanese
Offer:	Strategic supply, including knowledge and training
Sector:	Mining and equipment industries

If you reach this level of partnership, you can deeply improve the connectivity. Leaders may not see important stuff or assess it as important, but the guys with the walkie-talkies do see important stuff. So you continuously improve at all levels, you build joint training programmes, you set up some workshops when there is a new piece of delivery that is coming in. So, six months before it is actually installed, you are not surprising those people on the ground with that new equipment or process.

Model:	B2B, B2G
Brought by:	Viren Doshi
Offer:	Strategic differentiation, knowledge
Sector:	Management consulting

Strategic partners are where you would invest your time to learn their direction and what they are doing. You would be looking at the investor reports, speeches and videos and preparing relevant competitive benchmarking when you have a spare moment. You would be looking at relevant regulatory trends or market dynamics that could identify the next set of icebergs coming to hit them, or something interesting or exciting we have seen that would be valuable to them. This is how we become relevant and add value.

Model: B2B, B2C
Brought by: Alan MacDonald
Offer: Best services with an integrated approach
Sector: Banking

Our 'institutional' clients have a wide array of needs – treasury, financing, processing – and usually globally. We have a very broad product offer covering all financial services. The strategic partnership will put this under an umbrella where the partner receives the best of these services tailored to their needs and we hopefully deserve to become the most important provider of financial services for them.

Model: B2G
Brought by: Andrew Mackenzie
Offer: Economic activity to a community
Sector: Mining industry

In mining, the reality is that as resources come as options, our licence to operate depends fundamentally on people's consent. It doesn't matter if we can get the capital, if the people who live around the resource say 'you can't develop that resource', because then, you can't do the business. So the first premise you have to start from is that there are two views that need to be taken into account: one, the people who live and work around the resource and own it; then us, who need to develop the terms and humbly seek the licence to develop that resource on their behalf. It will take time on their side, to get a sense of the benefits our development could bring and how we will handle ourselves; and on ours, an appropriate return for the risks that we take and to have some sense of constancy about how that contract will work.

Model: B2G
Brought by: Paul Deighton
Offer: Public–private co-operation
Sector: Government, infrastructure and utility industries

If I just stick to public infrastructure, more and more of it has shifted from being what I would call taxpayer-funded to ultimately being consumer-funded. This means it is financed and built by the private sector and then paid for by the prices set for the commodity in the offer. So it is all about regulating a market. Water is now operated on that model, energy is operated on that model, and others are as well.

> *Most of the private-sector companies involved with governments understand that because they can't succeed without government support in such projects and because changes in government policy can raise or ruin their business, there is no substitute to spending a lot of time working this through for themselves and also with the government. And to being extremely patient in building the partnership and even constantly rebuilding the partnership.*

In our experience, while the values, scales, scopes and stakeholderships may be different, the principles and practices underpinning these cases of joint-value proposition and 'offer' design can be calibrated and re-calibrated between most combinations of business, government, institution and consumer groupings.

What are winning 'value propositions' and 'offers'?

'Offers' provide access to invaluable capability

As represented on Figure 9.1, 'offers' are a vital component of the value-creation cycle, alongside the partnership workstreams and SoVs. The notion of 'offers' and their function are epitomized in the examples offered by our interviewees. Indeed, each of the examples refers to:

- Focused single or multiple 'areas of co-operation' (AoCs) or workstreams between partners, for example, Tom Albanese's co-design of a supply infrastructure extending to joint support to local economic development or community programmes.

- Within AoCs and workstreams, particular SoVs are highlighted as bringing different but mutual benefit to the partners; for example, McDonald's gets the ideal level of crispiness for their chicken 'offer' and Linde sells the gas that can do this.

- The unique respective 'offer' is what each partner brings to the joint 'destination', for example GE 'offers' its unique expertise in healthcare and BP its distinctive expertise in deep-water oil and gas production.

- The partnership develops and delivers strategic value through the mutual commitment behind the joint 'destination': in the example of BMW and their component partners, to lead on 'providing premium products and services for individual mobility'.

Often the 'offer' will consist of providing the partner(s) with access to knowledge, resources and capabilities, which they need to build their value and which are tailored to their circumstances. This cannot be done randomly or lightly, as 'chance' would lose most of the opportunity and mutual value. Instead, the 'offer' development process will consider and work hard the interface areas between the partners. By linking the partners' objectives and our own capability, we will design or invent a new combination, a renewed and richer form of interface, resulting in fully-fledged mutual SoVs.

The outcome of deep 'offer' development may be a new solution, product, equipment, relationship or model, inventing or 'transforming':

- consumer offering – as in the examples brought by Wolfgang Reitzle, Michel Taride and Ian Robertson;
- manufacturing processes – Jeff Immelt, Andrew Mackenzie;
- marketing and servicing – Gerard Vittecoq;
- new supply chain management – Tom Albanese;
- strategic 'transformation' and corporate simplification – Shelly Lazarus, Viren Doshi, Alan MacDonald;
- resource and cost efficiency – Ian Robertson, Andrew Mackenzie;
- human capital – Tom Albanese;
- quality of relationships and enhanced licences to operate – Andrew Mackenzie;
- new business models – Paul Deighton.

'Offers' developed in the context of, and as the substance of, strategic partnerships will indeed deliver the key motives for partnering, their 'destination' and ultimately the 'transformational' value they aspire to.

Strategic partnership 'value propositions' and 'offers' are uniquely powerful

The qualifier used above is 'offer development in the context of strategic partnerships'. It is a critical qualification, which our interviewees make explicit.

Andrew Mackenzie

" You can only have a few relationships like that, but we should work those we choose and they should be important to the Chief Executive.

Viren Doshi

" Strategic partners are the places where you would invest.

Alan MacDonald

" The strategic partnership will put this under an umbrella where the partner receives the best.

Tom Albanese

" If you reach this level of partnership, you can deeply improve the connectivity.

As clearly shown in the examples and experienced consistently, there is a great distinction in importance and impact between 'offers' developed in the general context and those engineered within strategic partnerships. The former will be largely developed internally, without benefiting from the full understanding of other parties. They will result in an arms-length rather than an integrated solution and offering. The depth of work, research and resource commitment will be of a different scale and quality. And ultimately, value will be at an 'improve' level, at best 'enhance'.

Instead, partnerial 'offer' development will bring 'transformational' reality and value to the involved parties. Based on deep mutual understanding and co-design, a strategic partnership 'offer' will procure partners to gain access to and leverage invaluable capabilities in a fully integrated and functional manner. 'Offers' will be provided in a form that cannot be bought or brought in otherwise.

Only strategic partnerships can deliver this!

Strategic 'hooks'

Target partner B might not be spontaneously inclined to enter a deep and differentiated co-operation with organization A, despite all the 'courting'.

Triggering the start of a strategic partnership may be incredibly challenging: getting the first dance is sometimes the hardest, isn't it?

After completing Stages 1 and 2 of the partnership model, organization A has become convinced of the joint mission of a potential partnership with B, its latent 'destination' and the required activity threads in the strategic framework. This gives A an unwearied determination to convince B, as the attraction of and the message about the inherent value of the potential partnership are clear and unambiguous.

In practice, experience suggests that among the SoVs and associated 'offers' identified in Stages 1 and 2, one will prove to be the persuader because the partner will want this high-quality, high-value proposition. This or these will be the strategic 'hook(s)' for the partnership. Identifying and leveraging this compelling contribution to B will be a key aspect of the partnership 'navigation', as discussed in Chapter 10. If they like to samba more than waltz, then samba for all you're worth because you can always come back and waltz later!

Systematic approach for developing winning 'value propositions' and 'offers'

As suggested earlier, 'offer' development is a challenging discipline and very hard to do well. But it is also the life blood of value creation in any business and integral to the opportunity in strategic partnering. Making the approach easier by progressing through successive steps provides the greatest opportunity of developing remarkable 'offers'. Figure 9.2 represents a method for achieving this in a fully intertwined manner with the partnership development model.

The internal steps of developing extraordinary 'offers'

Organization A has to convince target B to partner! Not simply with words, but with evidence of the material value that will arise from acting together and the uniqueness of what organization A has to offer. Stages 1 and 2 of the partnership development model are about deep internal preparation and the left-hand side of Figure 9.2 represents what we will do during these intimate stages to progress value proposition and 'offer' development.

FIGURE 9.2 Seven steps of value proposition and offer development

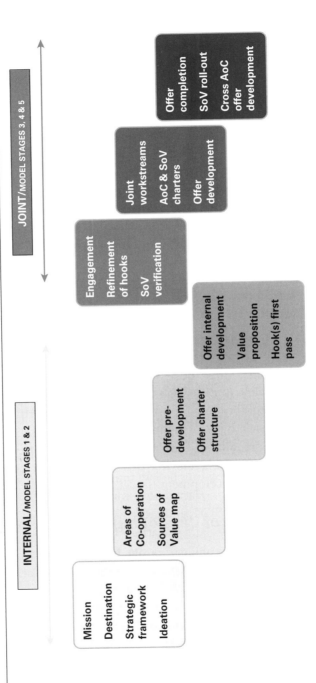

INTERNAL/MODEL STAGES 1 & 2

JOINT/MODEL STAGES 3, 4 & 5

Mission
Destination
Strategic framework
Ideation

Areas of Co-operation
Sources of Value map

Offer pre-development
Offer charter structure

Offer internal development
Value proposition
Hook(s) first pass

Engagement
Refinement of hooks
SoV verification

Joint workstreams
AoC & SoV charters
Offer development

Offer completion
SoV roll-out
Cross AoC offer development

Ideation

The intended AoCs and workstreams have emerged from establishing the partnership mission, 'destination' and strategic framework. It is now important to identify the possible SoVs associated with each workstream. This will occur in Stage 1/Steps 1–2 of the partnership development model, will be led by the central partnering team and result into a robust first-pass inventory of SoVs.

'Area of co-operation' (AoC) and 'sources of value' (SoV) map

In Stage 1/Step 3 of the model, the opportunity presented by the internal partner selection workshops (see Chapter 4) is used to test the AoCs with the involved area leaders and validate the SoVs, to firm them up from this point. A workstream and SoV map (see Figure 4.4) will emerge from this deep enquiry and provide considerable clarity both at enterprise level for the selection of partners and at workstream level for setting up the development activities. The enquiry will be led by the central team and accomplished together with the leaders of the organization's involved entities.

'Offer' pre-development and charter structure

Entering Stage 2 is a crucial time in the whole partnership development model. From Stage 1, we have decided on a strong target partner and developed an SoV map. We now need to assemble, improve and 'package' our capability into 'offers' which can deliver the deep and multiple SoVs. These 'offers' will then be combined into a full 'value proposition'.

Framing the 'offers' requires deeply founded expert contribution from the involved areas in the organization, which will not necessarily see the value at first. Hence the SPM, and more likely the specialized VOMs, will develop first-pass SoV and 'offer charters' themselves. This upfront clarity will help the workstream and AoC experts to gain a better perspective of the path forward, appreciate the uplift for their area and, by engaging with the joint task of improving the charter, eventually adhere to it.

Internal 'offer' development, value proposition and 'hooks' first-pass

Pure 'offer' development work will now be possible and start to kick in. The central partnership team will support the involved workstream and area leaders' effort and ensure that progress is made. Stage 2/Step 6 in particular may take weeks or even months to complete, so that the strategic partnership 'destination' gets strongly underpinned by a compelling value proposition and its related SoVs and powerful 'offers' to partners. One or more of these will hopefully prove irresistible and have the power of 'hooks'. As mentioned in Chapter 3, this whole approach is rather unusual, due to the depth of the 'offer' preparation and the absence of interaction with the desired partner … but a winner.

The joint steps of developing extraordinary SoVs

With the completion of a thorough 'offer' development internal process and a well-prepared 'story' in hand, it is time to move from 'I' to 'we', as represented on the right-hand side of Figure 9.2.

Engagement, refinement of the 'hook(s)' and SoV verification

The long-awaited engagement with the target partner can now be progressed resolutely. The earlier thorough preparation and strong 'offers' developed will nearly always trigger their interest. The carefully planned 'navigation' across the relevant entities and people of the target organization – discussed in Chapter 10 – will provide us with invaluable feedback on the power of the 'hooks' and the relevance of the 'offers'.

Two parallel tracks will run throughout Stage 3/Steps 8–9 of the model. Working together with the partner, the AoCs and SoVs will be fine-tuned and become definitive. Internally, continuous improvement of the 'offers', building on the partner's guidance will keep us in a position to constantly bring improved value propositions in the dialogue.

This will eventually result in a joint Strategic Co-operation Framework – Step 9 – reflecting each partner's understanding and agreement with the partnership's SoVs, respective 'offers' and ultimate mutual value proposition.

Joint workstreams, AoC and SoV charters and joint 'offer' development

Stage 4/Step 12 of the model is another critical time for the partnership, moving focus from internal and individual to common and shared practice. The quality of set-up of the joint workstreams will be crucial, so the right leaders and experts from each partners' organizations join forces to develop extraordinary substance for the strategic partnership. With the firm assistance, support, and guidance of the SPMs, RPMs or VOMs, these leaders will 'slice the elephant' by defining their joint workstream and SoV charters and engage in joint development, leveraging each other's capabilities, strengths and human capital.

The joint SoV development will result peculiarly in a new customer offering, a more efficient manufacturing or logistical process, an integrated value chain, a new access to market or a better regulation, to name but a few of our interviewees' examples. These will have scale and importance and deliver material 'enhance' value, and aim to deliver 'transform' value.

Alan MacDonald

The way we create substance and offers to our clients is firstly by using their feedback on a continuous basis. The products we offer can be mature, in which case our differentiation comes from the way we roll them out consistently across complex organizations, as well as their overall costs and efficiency. For new products, we certainly do R&D for and with clients and bring in our Citi product experts, who work with our relationship team, to develop and roll them out.

Even if much of the activity becomes common to both partners from now on, it is important to maintain a disciplined inner-organization approach. In practice, this means the internal work continues and will shadow the joint developments. These shadow endeavours strive to continuously simplify and therefore smooth and enable the joint development steps to be progressed. This will also firmly ensure the retention of a mindset of excellence in 'offers' within the organization and keep everyone on their toes at all times. The parallel approach will aim at consistently optimizing the partners' perception of the value we bring to the AoCs and keeping competition at a distance.

'Offer' completion and SoV roll-out: cross-AoC and SoV 'offer' development

This is when true magic happens! As the partnership teams know and trust each other more, they now move from 'need' to 'want'. In Stage 5/ Steps 14–15, they spread their wings to possibilities and value zones which could not be seen or accessed before.

There is a point when most members of each group see that the relationship is beneficial to both companies. What you then get is leverage that the folks at the top never thought they would ever get. That is the best thing for me, that we now have got people going away and working on it and bringing up much better solutions than frankly I would have hoped for. And that they are not talking because the bosses are asking them to, they are talking because they see the benefits.

And it is another reason why you should get more members around a table than you think you really need for a discussion. It is amazing sometimes where the help comes from because you just never quite think that this person would have input to it, or that company would have input to it.

So, often at the start of partnerships, you need to interface because there is a mutual requirement and that is okay. But when that starts to move from a need to a want, that is when I think the magic potentially can happen.

Supported by the SPM and his/her team, they now reach out to other workstreams and capabilities beyond their area, to develop cross-organization integrated innovations and solutions. In other words, the partnership becomes truly strategic and attains 'transformational' value across the enterprises, as breakthrough value propositions and strategic 'offers' continuously develop.

Zero compromise on key 'offer-development' principles

Beyond the disciplined use of the seven-step 'offer' development process presented in Figure 9.2, success also requires the strict application of a few principles and core practices, despite some perhaps runing counter to received wisdom.

Don't ask a partner what they want or need

If you simply go and ask your prospective or existing partner 'what do you need?' you will get an answer you may not want!

The situation this creates can destroy partnerships before they have any chance of success. Firstly, their answer will mostly be given from the biased perspective of the individual or the group asked. It will often be about an immediate issue rather than a strategic and long-lasting one.

It will most often integrate one perspective – theirs – and rarely yours. Ironically, it will double-guess how your expertise and experience should be used, removing your ability to bring the absolute best of it into the revisited interface. And finally, because you asked, a positive response will be expected and you may always say no, but then ...?!

Prepare, prepare and prepare

The meticulous cycle of internal preparation through the steps of the model will place you in an ideal position to deeply understand your partner's strategic and enduring needs and how you can play into those for mutual 'transformational' value. This will occur at enterprise level, through forming the mission, 'destination' and strategic framework; and at individual workstream and SoV level, through the diligence of the value proposition and 'offer' development approach discussed in this chapter.

This deep preparation will enable you to know what you want to offer to your partner. It will equip you to guide and focus your organization's capability and resources to develop the right value proposition and 'offers'. You will also be well placed to format these in a way that your partner can best see and appreciate their contribution. Because you so deeply understand your partner's business, specifics and issues, you will apply and bring the best of your organization into a truly strategic response. And the question to your partner will therefore evolve from 'what do you want or need?' into 'as we jointly understand and share the real issue and objective, here is a potential solution. Could we work to improve it together?'

Test and challenge yourself again and again

The 'offers' have to be right for the partners to be interested and to enter the partnership. They have to be right for you, ie beneficial strategically and 'performance-wise', as well as worth the complexity of a sophisticated co-operation. As challenging as it can be to identify and define 'transformational' SoVs and 'offers', the most impactful ones ultimately turn into very simple and compelling stories. The key is to identify and boil everything down to the most powerful and simplest 'mechanism to value' possible.

One of the strengths of the model is the shared practice of people in the partnering team and the ability to continually test their findings and 'offers' with close leaders and colleagues. We call this practice 'support and challenge'. When the SPM, the RPM, the VOM, the AoC or SoV leader have progressed the 'offer' development to an advanced point, they share and test it with a selected group of peers in a role-playing game as if they were the target for the 'offer'. Held with expert 'supporters and challengers', these are tough but invaluable sessions and usually provide defining guidance. The slogan we use for these sessions is 'wrong with support and challenge; right on the day': fairly similar to the US Olympic Committee rule of 'train like you compete; compete like you train'.

Always think as if you were the partner

This is perhaps the most needed muscle to develop extraordinary governmental or business strategic partnerships. Listening rather than simply hearing, embracing their 'story' rather than telling yours, giving rather than taking, epitomizing generosity and humility rather than self-centeredness are among the most indispensable and arguably least frequent traits held by enterprises or individuals.

Frankly, how often have you seen organizations entirely geared towards you? Or starting their interaction journey from your standpoint? Rarely, haven't you?!

Stephen Odell

One of the best business lessons I ever learned is to listen aggressively to what someone else or another company is saying. It doesn't mean you have to agree with it, but to listen and understand it rather than wait to speak – and most of the world waits to speak. A very small part of the world actually listens aggressively, whether to their own people, other companies, etc. True listening is the strength of a good partnership, because someone is going to give you a different perspective.

How often do we see organizations engage with others from more than one perspective? How many times do we come out of meetings to discover that we apparently attended two different discussions – one from the other party's angle and one from ours? Similarly, you see leaders who can be excellent listeners inside the organization and dangerously not at ease outside it – and others who are not as astute internally but in their element when dealing with external audiences, challenges and opportunities.

You cannot afford self-centred approaches in strategic partnering. As noted in Chapter 6, the capability and inclination towards others will be a main selection 'lens' and a critical area of professional and personal transformation for our SPMs, VOMs, etc. As they increasingly grow into mastery of their role, they will naturally 'give more to receive more'.

Create familiarity in your 'offers'

Because we are applying the strategic partnership model, let's assume that we have become able to think like our partners, that we deeply understand their objectives and issues in the area of the 'offers' being developed, and that we have prepared the value proposition and 'offers' accordingly. As tremendous as this is, we still have to succeed with our 'offer' placement and will apply a structured 'navigation', the subject of Chapter 10 of this book. Because as compelling as the 'offer' may be, the partner might simply not see it that way.

David Marley

We do indeed find it often challenging to be heard and get traction on issues and solutions that seem very obvious to us. In the majority of cases, I would say that smart people initially don't welcome input from outside.

There is of course one possible approach to fix this: go through the boss and simply have everything imposed downwards. Not an advisable course though, as the subsequent roll-out and the next opportunity might both prove 'interesting'. As mentioned earlier, the winning alternative is to create 'day-after-day' familiarity with the concept, the idea and the 'offer', which will then sound the natural solution when introduced more formally. And when doing so, the art will be to aim to improve the 'offer' jointly, so it truly feels like 'invented here'.

Enrol your organization, as the main limitations might come from inside

For people inside the organization, true 'offer' development in partnership can easily become the enemy: it is ambiguous, new and uncertain; they might be held accountable for something they can't see at first; it is hard, demands the highest quality knowledge, requires resilience; and the partnership 'offers' can mean extra work now, but only bring return in the mid- to long-term. So, it is not easy to activate and may encounter strong resistance.

To avoid missing the required people's commitment and expertise, it is crucial to act to eliminate these impediments. And it comes down to method again. It starts with reducing colleagues' anxiety by bringing clarity and simplicity to the 'offer' objective. Instead of coming with questions, SPMs and VOMs progress deep up-front pre-work themselves and then engage on the basis of clear targets, pragmatic 'offer' components and a first-pass 'offer' charter. People will usually react well to such teamwork and a sense of shared accountabilities. The VOMs will then stay very close, notably in the beginning of the 'offer' development process, adding a human aspect to the process and keeping the team focused. Finally, the 'biased towards inputs' partnering 'performance' management system presented in Chapter 11 will set intermediate measures of success, encouraging momentum and incentivizing teams and individuals by reflecting continuous progress.

Recognition of the internal human challenge and pragmatic handling by the partnership team will usually result in a positive enrolment and mobilization of the experts instrumental to winning 'offers'.

Make strategic 'offer' development the key measure of 'performance' of your partnering team

Once a strong, mutually beneficial 'offer' has been developed and vetted by the partners, it will almost unavoidably be rolled out and lead to on-target or above-target strategic or financial performance for the partners.

As we will discuss in Chapter 11 on partnering 'performance', the milestone of developing and placing a new 'offer' is therefore the most critical performance indicator for any person involved in strategic co-operations. The authors have often used this measure to account for 50 per cent of any year's assessment of SPMs, and even above this level for VOMs. And if on average you manage to achieve one 'transformational', world-class strategic 'offer' each year for any partnership across the portfolio, your next year can be banked!

Conclusion: Developing compelling partnership 'value propositions' and 'offers'

Strategic co-operations are justified and defined by their SoVs and 'offers' to the partners. Clarifying this hard substance, turning it into compelling 'offers' and agreeing on them, is a long road paved with obstacles and challenges. But it is a road to 'transformational' value, a road to heaven.

SPMs and their teams will play a major role in success. Their specific experience and resilience will see them accept and take on all that others would not do in normal business: boil down complexity into achievable tasks, unlock obstacles on the way, be more dedicated about precise codifications than others and keep at it whatever the challenge. They will complement and support their internal – and then external – workstream colleagues, those who make 'real stuff' and true innovation happen. And the secret of extraordinary 'offers' is in the intimate 'day-after-day' combination of partnering experts and substance experts. Get this to work and your 'offer', your value, your enterprise will never be the same again!

Over the last 30 years, the authors have been privileged to oversee, lead or be party to the development of more than 300 world-class 'offers', either geared to partners, or assembled together with partners to their stakeholders' benefit, such as governments, customers and consumers or providers. Almost all have been tough jobs but have also offered the most valuable and rewarding business experiences.

The applicability of these approaches is similar or the same for large corporations and institutions as for smaller and medium-sized enterprises. Strategic partnering can translate across boundaries and 'offers' are about depth, durability and something new forged through a unique relationship. The scale of the entities is irrelevant to the power of the process.

There is indeed magic in creating strategic and material value to others, and be well rewarded for it in return, often just by adding up collective or individual ingenuity, a disciplined model and a fierce determination. There is magic in deeply 'transforming' the quality and 'performance' of an existing and therefore only partly fructified business base. There is magic in seeing these 'offers' continue delivering millions and sometimes even billions of dollars of value or margin after years. So, let's share this amazing model and the excitement of winning together!

Here is a summary of the guidelines from this chapter, detailing how to design a partnership value proposition and develop component 'offers', resulting in 'transformational' substance and extraordinary 'performance'.

Summary: Developing compelling partnership value propositions and 'offers'

- Substance, SoVs, value proposition and 'offers' are at the heart of successful strategic partnerships.

- Once the mission, 'destination' and strategic framework have been established, we are all set to develop the partnership SoVs and their component 'offers'. Some will be compelling to the partners and will act as the strategic 'hooks' for the co-operation.

- Succeeding at 'offer' development is a true challenge and is enabled by a systematic approach, intertwined with the partnership model. We use a seven-step 'offer' development process.

- Strictly apply the following key principles to succeed: do not ask partners what they need or want; prepare 'offers' deeply; test 'offers' thoroughly; think as if you were the partner; enrol your internal organization; and measure your partnering team's performance primarily on the number and quality of strategic 'offers' developed over a given period of time.

In no other chapter was it as important to be a true 'cook book' as in this one. So close your eyes, and let yourself be guided by the model and process and their iterative, interactive and guiding nature. Then what at first seems impossible will happen ... almost to your surprise. In the automobiles of the future, this is called 'automation technology'. The principle is that you always have the leading hand, but if you let it go, the vehicle will drive you.

We now have what it takes to win again and again and create value with a near 100 per cent success rate. Let's not lose it with a failing partnership 'navigation' or a poor 'offer' placement. Hence defining a winning 'navigation' is the subject of the next chapter of *Strategic Partnering*.

10
Navigating towards a successful strategic partnership

The Strategic Partnership Model

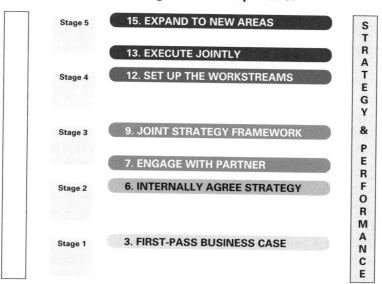

> *The winds and waves are always on the side of the ablest navigators.*
>
> EDWARD GIBBON

> *Train like you compete; compete like you train.*
>
> US OLYMPIC COMMITTEE

The most apparent, natural and well-planned partnerships can fail from the very first steps simply through poor 'navigation'. In our case, we mean by 'navigation' the process of managing and monitoring the steps of positioning, and developing the strategic partnership idea with the partner's multiple stakeholders.

Strategic partnerships are like the best stories: they need the right beginning and an orderly and continuous narrative to ensure they reach a fantastic ending. Often much less science and focus is applied to thinking through and preparing a partnership's 'navigation' than to other aspects of the co-operation. Furthermore, and because it is mainly a human activity, 'navigation' is most often left to individuals and their best intuition. Instead, we believe that 'navigation' is key to successful partnerships and this chapter helps bring clarity to the essential 'navigation' process.

The watershed moment where 'navigation' planning is most crucial is Stage 3/Step 7 of the model, the time of first engagement with the target partner. By this point, considerable preparation will have gone into selecting the partner, designing a clear mission, 'destination' and plan for the potential relationship, developing a set of integrated value propositions and 'offers', and assembling contact maps and a great partnering team. It is therefore vital not to put all the hard work in jeopardy because of a few badly planned 'navigation' steps.

As crucial as the 'engage' Step 7 is, however, 'navigation' is vital not only at this point but should be a continuously evolving strategic foundation in the building of extraordinary partnerships. Some people would even say that 'navigation is everything in strategic partnerships'. Although we don't subscribe to this fully, if only because 'navigating' well in the wrong direction would do no good, it is indeed absolutely critical to success. As noted in Chapter 8, 'navigation' planning needs to attract the same attention and discipline as other areas of the partnership and to be fully integrated into the co-operation's strategy and plan.

This chapter provides the route to successful 'navigation' and ways to consider several of its facets and angles. It will offer methods not only to avoid failure through poor progression, but to take full advantage of the opportunity latent in brilliantly executed 'navigation' to enhance and accelerate the partnership development. It includes:

- six key areas of 'navigation' in strategic partnering, pitfalls and opportunities;
- the two main 'navigation' strategies at enterprise level;
- planning for a phased management of content;
- ensuring the right 'people navigation';

- maximizing 'navigation' benefits by leveraging the successive phases of value creation;
- being equally thoughtful on internal and external 'navigation';
- handling the specificities of governments.

Six key 'navigation' areas in strategic partnering; pitfalls and opportunities

This chapter will unpick, examine and discuss the six key areas of 'navigation' in strategic partnering shown in Figure 10.1, analysing their respective importance, as well as their inherent risk and opportunity potential.

FIGURE 10.1 Six navigation areas for strategic partnering

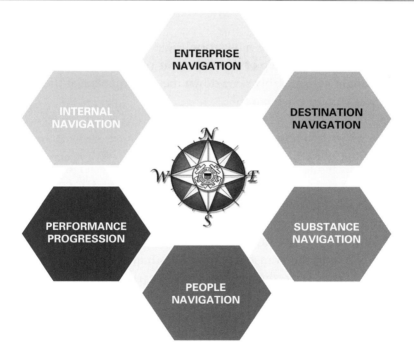

Enterprise 'navigation' of the partnership

This is the 'navigation' strategy for the entire partnership. It defines the base itinerary for the partnership and encompasses all areas of 'navigation'. It is fully integrated into the partnership development model and is a core component of the partnership plan introduced in Chapter 8.

Ian Davis shares insightful views on the progression towards reaching strategic importance for the partnership:

Ian Davis

> Some strategic partnerships can be defined retrospectively, not prospectively. You can have a partnership and then it becomes strategic, because it is so important or it clearly drives strategy for both companies, and sometimes you don't know that at the start. So the natural evolution of strategic partnerships is partnership first, strategic second. You should still have the strong idea of a strategic partnership, but you wouldn't reach this level of commitment until after some years, when you have huge confidence in the relationship. So sometimes, strategic partnering is retrospective and sometimes it is prospective.

Getting the enterprise-level 'navigation' right will ensure a smooth progression through every step of the multi-year partnering journey. Getting it wrong might considerably slow down the development of the partnership, if not damage it irreparably.

Partnership 'destination navigation'

As progress is made through Stages 1 and 2 of the model and described in Chapters 8 and 9, the central partnership team will develop clarity on the mission and 'destination' of the partnership, and underpin its deliverability through relevant 'areas of co-operation' (AoCs), 'sources of value' (SoVs) and 'offers'. The model's unique focus and intensity of inquiry will help highlight the 'transformational destination' at an early stage.

It can be a mistake to share this vision too early in dialogue, both with partners and internally. In general, people do not like and will oppose change. 'Why would good organizations need to "transform" themselves?' And, by the way, 'Who are you to come, suggest or request that we "transform"?'

Timely unveiling of the partnership mission and 'destination' is crucial to keep organizations and people onside and avoid the creation of barriers to the partnership. And also patiently progressing the discovery of the objective through successive 'performance' peaks, as suggested by Ian Robertson.

Ian Robertson

Of course, we have to keep raising the bar. It's like the old adage that when you finally attain the summit of the most challenging mountain, the view is of an even higher peak. So we have to challenge ourselves constantly and also challenge the partner companies we work with, because otherwise, we won't be successful. This attitude and approach of constant challenge is a vital behaviour and mindset for all our people. Without it, we won't continue to be successful.

Substance 'navigation'

The same logic applies to value propositions, SoVs and 'offers'. Being too broad too early with the number of SoVs, or getting too deep too soon about strategic and 'transformational' SoVs, carry the same risk of overwhelming people and generating 'fear-driven' opposition to the nascent or growing partnership.

Instead, and as suggested in Chapter 9, a path of selective 'offers', starting with one or a couple of 'hook' SoVs and building credentials through delivery, might be ideally suited to underpin a successful spreading and deepening of the co-operation later on, as noted by Wolfgang Reitzle.

Wolfgang Reitzle

It is crucial to be careful when selecting the first topic area. A winning project right at the beginning can become a positive story that attracts the attention and sponsorship of line managers and even top management. Such successes will often open the door to the next project. It is important, though, never to overstretch and to stay focused on making every aspect of the partnership a success.

People 'navigation'

This is the area where mistakes are most commonly made in partnership 'navigation'. This issue is explored in greater detail later in the chapter, but here are a few simple examples of people-led risks:

- start the engagement journey with 'a brilliant idea' submitted directly to the 'hands-off' CEO of a potential partner;
- start the engagement of a value-added strategic 'offer' with traditional procurement;
- start the engagement with people you know – or the opposite, forget or don't respect them enough;
- go directly to the boss of your main contact in the partner's organization.

We absolutely need to get this right, or risk becoming bogged down in unproductive processes, sucked into limiting relationships or worse, creating barricades and enemies.

'Performance' progression

There is a huge opportunity in projecting and leveraging the progression of value creation, in particular in the early phases of the partnership, to 'convince' the target organization to partner, expand or deepen the relationship.

John Seifert

When we consider the factors to winning a prestigious client's business globally last year, we focused most of our efforts on what would create enduring value for the client's business. We looked across our entire client portfolio to isolate those value drivers that we thought would be most valued by this particular new client opportunity. We then combined and customized these value drivers into an integrated value proposition that exceeded their expectations of our offer.

Internal 'navigation'

Throughout *Strategic Partnering*, we have stressed the critical importance of enrolling and aligning the organization. Because strategic alignment and freedom to act are required from the top. Because active leadership and commitment are also needed from the AoC and SoV leaders and more generally from the 'informal' team. Because a consistent partnering tone is important across the enterprise.

Internal 'navigation' could in theory absorb all the time and energy of the partnership team and many others beyond them. It is important to be selective in this effort and we will discuss good practice in more depth later in this chapter.

Each and all of these specialized 'navigations' are of course fully embedded in the steps of the partnership development model. Let's consider successively how they play out in practice.

'Navigating' the strategic partnership at enterprise level

There are two main alternative paths for the development of a strategic partnership. A lot of activities and milestones will be common to both of course, but different starting points will trigger alternative itineraries, as represented on Figure 10.2.

FIGURE 10.2 Enterprise navigation options for strategic partnership

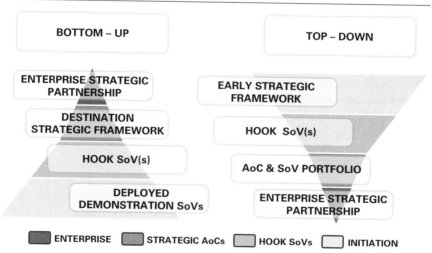

| BOTTOM – UP | | TOP – DOWN |

ENTERPRISE STRATEGIC PARTNERSHIP

DESTINATION STRATEGIC FRAMEWORK

HOOK SoV(s)

DEPLOYED DEMONSTRATION SoVs

EARLY STRATEGIC FRAMEWORK

HOOK SoV(s)

AoC & SoV PORTFOLIO

ENTERPRISE STRATEGIC PARTNERSHIP

■ ENTERPRISE ■ STRATEGIC AoCs ■ HOOK SoVs □ INITIATION

The top-down enterprise 'navigation' path

Any 'navigation' path option will be largely dependent on the starting point. The 'top-down' path represented on the right-hand side of Figure 10.2 may occur in any of the following circumstances:

- An enterprise's strategically important 'needs-based' initiative requires deep expertise, capability or resources from other entities. There is therefore obvious mutual interest. Those organizations able to bring in the needed assets or competencies are natural candidates, hence the partner selection looks simpler.

- A government, company, university or NGO CEO creates an executive intent or imperative, by which deep relationships will be the way to go forward in certain areas or for certain critical developments of their institution. This can arise from deep strategic resolution or from pleasant dinner conversations!

In such cases, partnering-savvy organizations should still run a robust Stage 1 selection process, such as that defined in Chapter 4, although it might be simplified and fast-tracked appropriately. We remain boringly insistent that this stage should still be performed conscientiously, even if an area of mutual interest is identified from the start, to ensure an early attractive fit does not obscure other indispensable characteristics to success.

From completion of the selection phase, the rest of the partnership model unfolds as expected: a dedicated team would be set up, a strategic framework would be jointly agreed, with a particular focus on the starting strategic initiative as the 'hook' for the co-operation. All other mechanisms in the model would apply, and hopefully materialize more easily than when starting from little or nothing, as discussed later in the 'bottom-up' scenario.

Building on the success of the early 'hook' strategic initiative, the teams, and notably our partnership team, would actively search for and consider other AoCs and SoVs and eventually elevate the relationship to an enterprise strategic partnership level.

The bottom-up enterprise 'navigation' path

This is the path we have been considering and describing throughout this book, because arguably it represents the most challenging and comprehensive case. Here, the partnership starts from little or nothing, perhaps an idea only, and goes through the full journey of the partnership development model: firstly, the internal steps of selection, business case formulation, value proposition and 'offer' design. Then, the now familiar engagement and joint growth phases with the partner.

As suggested earlier by Wolfgang Reitzle and represented on the left-hand side of Figure 10.2, the winning progression will often depend on the success of one or two early 'hook' SoVs, delivering mutual value and positive familiarity between the organizations. Alternatively, the same credentials might arise from a set of already existing and disjointed but productive activities between some of the organizations' verticals. As described in Chapter 9, these might expand into AoCs and SoVs, firstly growing value for their own sake and then cross-fertilizing to reach enterprise 'transformational' value. Tom Albanese talks about this steady navigation:

Tom Albanese

I think the best strategic relationship should not need regular breakthroughs. It should require continuity and stability. They are actually built on the avoidance of surprise, the avoidance of shock and recognizing that each layer of the organization has a different role and a different timeline on their hands, so we focus on what can be done to improve the connectivities. If there is important stuff going on between the two organizations, the guys at each level, including those with the walkie-talkies, will see the important stuff and work at it together.

The main differences with the earlier top-down path is the challenge associated with starting the journey from very little and not playing into an early 'demand' or a recognized need. This will be an almost pure start-up, with all the challenges and glory it can entail ... and with the key advice to base success on following the strategic partnership development model throughout, in a highly disciplined manner.

Leveraging the partnership 'performance' progression

The 'performance' of the partnership, in creating increased value, accompanies and supports partnership development, and contributes to and influences strongly and consistently the enterprise 'navigation'. As we will see in Chapter 11, 'performance' is both an outcome and a cause. It is obviously an outcome, being the result of the value-added activities in a successful partnership. But it is also a cause, as creating acknowledged value helps to convince, legitimize and reward the joint efforts and most often enables the next commitments to be supported and undertaken.

It is this role of 'performance' as an important input and stimulus that is being stressed here. And, as shown on Figure 10.3, we are encouraging the discipline of building and leveraging credentials along each and all successive steps of the partnership model. So in essence, deliver throughout and get the message out to everyone involved as consistently as possible!

Wolfgang Reitzle

A winning project right at the beginning will be a door opener for the next project.

Figure 10.3 represents the value-creation phases in the partnership's bottom-up path and how to leverage them as we develop the co-operation.

FIGURE 10.3   Leveraging the performance progression

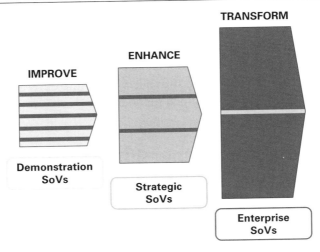

- In the early days, a series of 'improve'-level SoV activities and 'performance' delivery should be pursued consciously across the portfolio verticals or functions. They are the multiple layers on the left-hand side of Figure 10.3. These 'demonstration' activities might often be an improvement on already existing links between the organizations. Experience tells us that verticals will help, as they naturally strive to 'improve' their existing business, once an organization is declared a strategic partner target. If not, the central team will intervene and ensure that this is the case.

- The areas of 'improve performance' and demonstration activities will be leveraged as evidence of the quality and value-added nature of 'what we already do together'. These demonstrators will therefore become strong contributors to accessing a focused selection of significantly more strategically important and material AoCs or SoVs, for example the three in the middle box of Figure 10.3. Hence we will reach the 'enhance' value zone, a level which only few partnerships ever attain and get to perform at.

- Continuing on our partnering journey, the visible, material and evidenced excellence from existing 'enhance performance' will build the incentive and confidence in the organizations to strive to the enterprise strategic level and with it, 'transformational' value. One or two cross-enterprise SoVs (eg the two in the right-hand side box of Figure 10.3) will then be built with boldness on the earlier foundations of value. As described in Chapter 11, 'transformational' value will range from 8 to 20 times more than 'improved' value.

A 2011 IBM study conducted with more than 1,700 CMOs globally, shares the same views. As shown on Figure 10.4, it actually identified three priority areas of focused improvement: 'deliver value to empowered customers'; 'foster lasting connections'; and 'capture value, measure results'.

All three priorities are absolutely relevant to this book and to the considerable role of 'performance' in progressively building strong relationships. And, to this point, one of the tough questions asked by the study is: 'How well are you measuring the results of your initiatives and communicating them to advance your credibility and accountability?'

FIGURE 10.4   Chief marketing officers' three priorities

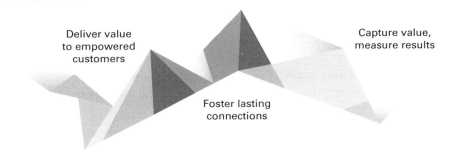

Deliver value
to empowered
customers

Capture value,
measure results

Foster lasting
connections

SOURCE: IBM Institute for Business Value, *Global CMO Study*, 2011

'Navigating' the partners' people skilfully

The area of people 'navigation' should receive the greatest attention when planning your partnership development. Because this is all about people, their territories, successes or failures, facts and emotions, careers and egos, it is vital not to make mistakes in this space! On the opposite side, considerable opportunities exist with engaging and developing strong connections with the right people at the right time.

Chapter 7 of *Strategic Partnering* has stressed the importance of both corporate and individual relationships in building successful partnerships. It has defined what these interactions look like, how to develop them and the structures and processes associated with making them enduring and productive. But we still have to define the right succession of relationship construction, so this practical people 'navigation' delivers the powerful picture of Chapter 7.

A mixture of principles and judgement

The right people 'navigation' should be led primarily by principles, with a significant overlay of experience and judgement. On the principles side:

- Prepare and apply the contact map presented in Chapter 7 diligently. Partnerships are hardly ever successful in the absence of a good quality map, because otherwise, some important decision makers are likely to be missed, powerful silent objectors forgotten, etc.

Peter Foss

You should know companies well enough, understand their decision-making process, who the people are, what they do and their decision rights, and of course what is important to them. Otherwise many times, what you may try to do will miss the target.

- Don't be led by familiarity ('I know X and he/she will help'); nor by the apparently natural functional route ('Procurement is accountable, so let's go to them'); nor by the tempting path through the boss ('Their CEO has shown great interest, so let's talk to him directly'). Any or all of these might appear exactly the right thing to do in the circumstances, but often they are not. They have the sense of a tactical approach. Effective 'navigation' needs an active decision and should be a well-thought-out and deliberate act. Only ever go when strategically prepared to do so.

- Be disciplined in sticking to the designated tags in the contact map when initiating new engagements. In practice, this means not going for tempting short wins, sometimes with people offering easier access or spontaneous help. Executive Champions should engage with Executive Champions, AoC leaders together, VOMs with expert leaders, etc. Otherwise, expectations, loyalties and obligations might be wrongly created and weigh on the future.

Good and best practice of enterprise partnership 'navigation', AoC set-up and 'offer' placement all include deep consideration of the people 'navigation'. Each planning or 'support and challenge' session should give as much consideration to the proposed 'navigation' with our partner's people as it does to progressing and testing the substance of the 'story' with them.

Prime 'navigations' for the bottom-up and the top-down paths

The people 'navigations' will be somewhat different in the bottom-up and top-down paths presented in Figure 10.2, as their respective starting points will also be different. Here are the related people 'navigation' profiles as illustrations:

Top-down path

In the top-down 'navigation' path, a strategic mutual interest has been expressed by the parties, usually at executive level. It is opportune to capitalize on the personal involvement of the executive and establish this level of connection and relationship early, while the matter is 'hot' (upper circle 1 on Figure 10.5). An early objective for the SPM will be to also identify his or her main enterprise counterpart, so this level is operative and can support the partnership effectively almost from the start (lower circle 1).

Then, a defining priority will be to identify and engage the relevant AoC leaders, those whose area is central or involved in the early 'hook' initiative (circle 2). They will need to be committed to and own the solution and value development as soon as possible. The central team and AoC leaders will then deploy VOMs and experts from both sides (circle 3), so the desired development work is progressed in a determined and ambitious manner. The outcome and solution will then be rolled out and implemented by the verticals or businesses, to realize the now available value potential (circle 4).

Building on their achievements, both organizations will explore other possible AoCs and cross-AoC 'transformations' and eventually progress further towards extraordinary value.

Bottom-up path

This is the path directly reflected in the strategic partnership development model. As shown on Figure 10.6, the central partnership team has the first hand in leading the partner selection process (circle 1 and Steps 1–2 of the model), with no interaction with the partner at this stage. The SPM involves internal vertical and functional leaders to validate the SoVs and early business case (circle 2 and Step 3) and to progress the internal strategic framework (Stage 2).

First interactions with the target partner occur in Step 7 and usually involve AoC leaders and selected experts (circles 3 and 4). This will provide immediate focus on value creation, building credentials and progressing towards 'transformation'. Verticals and benefiting units will then be mobilized again, this time for the roll-out and implementation of the SoVs (circle 5). From Step 9, the governance and Executive Champion processes and engagement are triggered, leaning on the early positive achievements of the partnership, and providing support and the organization's mobilization to progress the co-operation to the next levels.

FIGURE 10.5 People navigation: Top-down

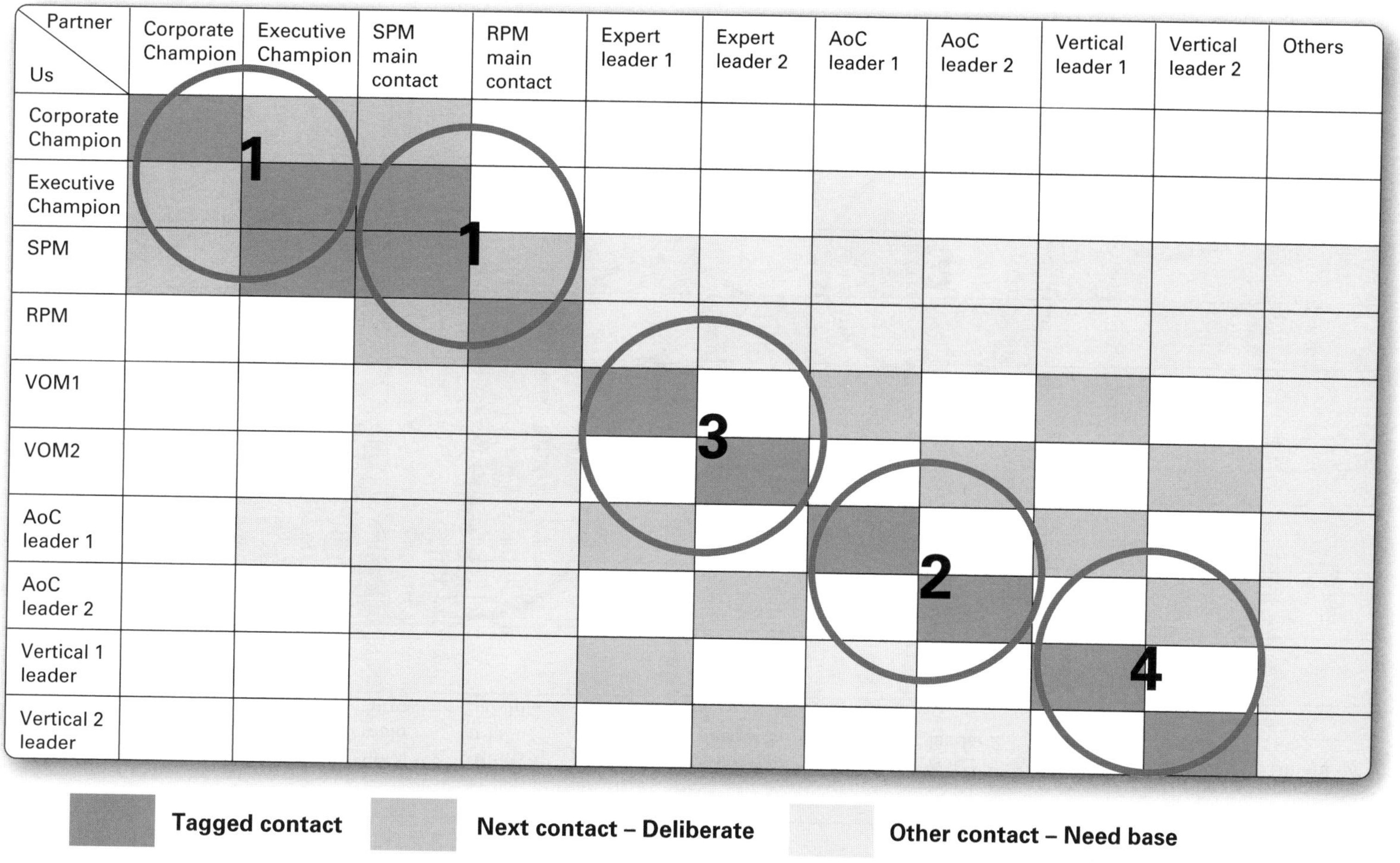

Partner / Us	Corporate Champion	Executive Champion	SPM main contact	RPM main contact	Expert leader 1	Expert leader 2	AoC leader 1	AoC leader 2	Vertical leader 1	Vertical leader 2	Others
Corporate Champion	1										
Executive Champion	1										
SPM		1									
RPM			1								
VOM1					3						
VOM2											
AoC leader 1							2				
AoC leader 2							2				
Vertical 1 leader									4		
Vertical 2 leader									4		

Tagged contact   **Next contact – Deliberate**   **Other contact – Need base**

FIGURE 10.6 People navigation: Bottom-up

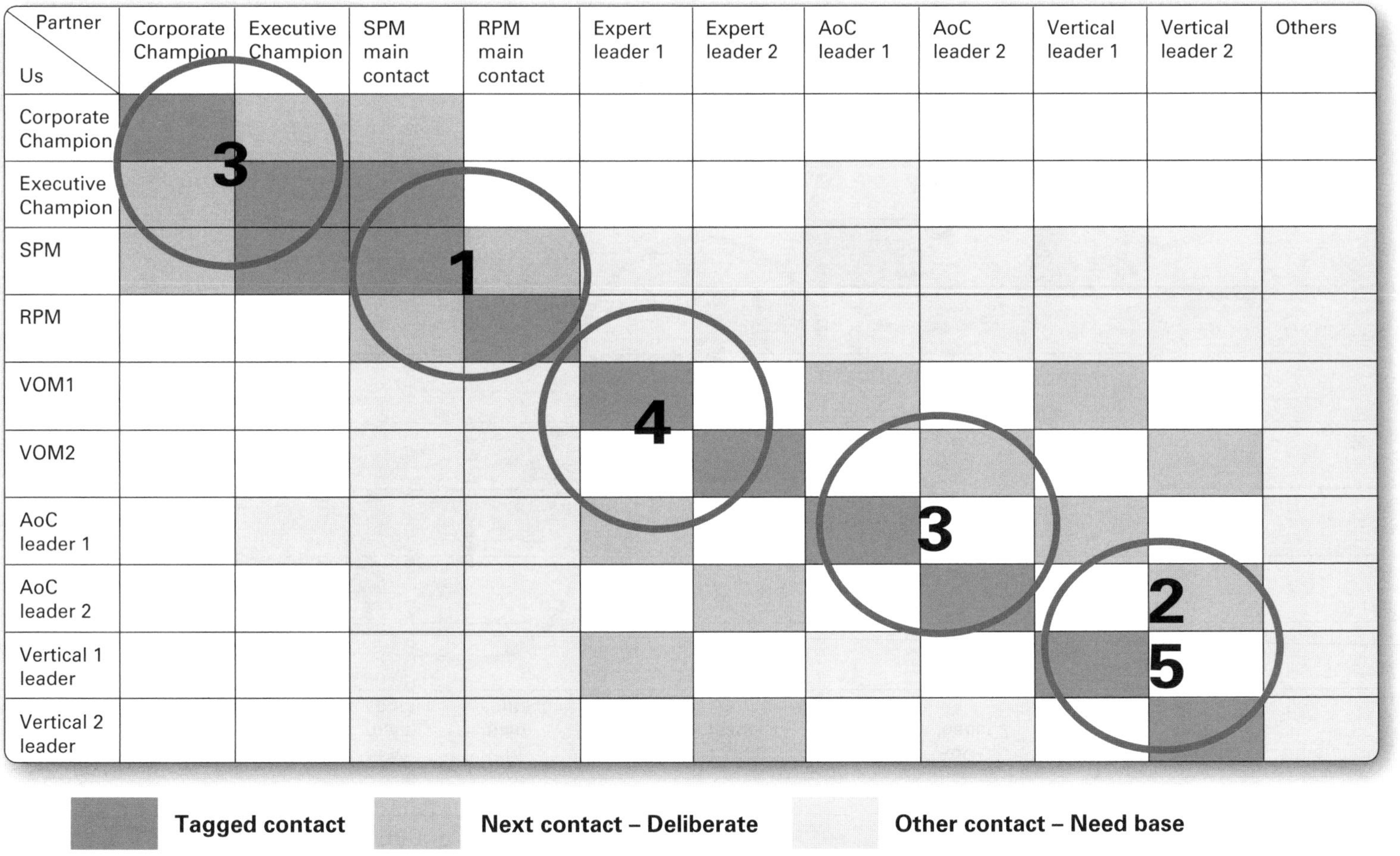

Partner / Us	Corporate Champion	Executive Champion	SPM main contact	RPM main contact	Expert leader 1	Expert leader 2	AoC leader 1	AoC leader 2	Vertical leader 1	Vertical leader 2	Others
Corporate Champion	3										
Executive Champion											
SPM											
RPM			1								
VOM1					4						
VOM2											
AoC leader 1							3				
AoC leader 2										2	
Vertical 1 leader										5	
Vertical 2 leader											

Tagged contact   Next contact – Deliberate   Other contact – Need base

Quite obviously, neither of these two 'typical' paths will ever occur exactly as described. But these two indicative people 'navigation' profiles will hopefully illustrate the point of needing a thoughtful approach to the engagement steps and provide some sense of effective engagement sequences, a number of which might feel counter-intuitive.

'Navigating' well internally to rally support

Throughout *Strategic Partnering*, we have stressed the vital importance of taking our own organization and colleagues on the journey.

The importance and challenges of enrolling the organization

There is much to say around this challenge and certainly in the authors' experience, there is often evidence of organizational hostility and a need to fight hard throughout ... until 'transformational' value is achieved. As people say: 'Victory has many fathers'. But let's be clear, the early stages of a partnership are not good times for those who like to be loved!

Viren Doshi

"You can't serve your client without mobilizing the rest of the organization – but they don't all have the same motives as you have. So, for example, right now, one of our teams in a country is very busy as there is also a mega-merger going on in that country. They are not bothered too much serving a new client for them from another country. At one extreme, they don't want to waste one second on something which is not relevant to them. This is understandable but may be short-sighted from a global perspective. So, we have to find ways to work together to serve our partners globally, irrespective.

This resistance is particularly strong in the early days of introducing strategic partnering into an organization, or when starting a new complex partnership. And there are understandable reasons for this push back, which we have explored earlier in *Strategic Partnering*: a new partnership goes across and into established territories and accountabilities; it is uncertain and hard to do; it requires effort and attention now, with payback later; it does not live well with egos or 'we can do it better'. The partnership team will have to walk steadily and with considerable resilience through hurricanes, thunderstorms and heavy hail, and may have to do so for a number of years of the partnership.

Peter Foss

"The people running the individual businesses have their own agendas and it is sometimes very difficult to work your way across the multiple verticals. So, as you are trying to work across a boundaryless organization, you have to knock down functional barriers, get rid of separate agendas and be a stand-breaker. To do this, you need to build great credibility and this can only come through results and trust. In turn, these arise from being very clear, from driving well-defined goals and measurements that are mutually agreed upon and, in the end, getting tangible results.

Tom Albanese

"We need to recognize that people and their own attitudes and their biases create a constraint on contestability. It is just the nature of the beast. So there are these inherent biases that need to be overcome. And it just takes time. And sometimes it takes some brute force at a higher level for that to happen. So, decisions often reflect biases and this is what needs to be overcome.

Gaining the critical internal supports

In addition to being deliberate about a positive enrolment, other key principles for succeeding with internal 'navigation' are pragmatism, being value- and fact-based, and humility in terms of your ambition. Pragmatism will manifest itself in identifying those who will support the partnership, and those who will not, enabling you to manage around them.

Humility will translate into setting the 'convince and enrol' milestones at the minimal threshold required to avoid hindering the development of the partnership, with every additional supporter a plus. The sequence of winning these indispensable levels of support is illustrated in Figure 10.7.

FIGURE 10.7 Internal navigation: Typical sequence

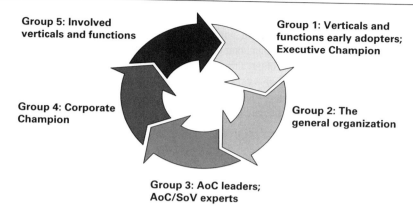

Group 5: Involved
verticals and functions

Group 1: Verticals and
functions early adopters;
Executive Champion

Group 4: Corporate
Champion

Group 2: The
general organization

Group 3: AoC leaders;
AoC/SoV experts

- Early adopters and supporters usually exist across the organization. We should identify them and ask for their help right from the beginning. We will add other important voices early to this base from the verticals and functions (Group 1 on Figure 10.7) as we complete the partner selection process (Stage 1/Step 3). Some of these leaders might initially be objectors and a focused effort will be made to win them over, based on the potential prize, the positive developments brought by the target partner to their unit and the kudos for them of being associated with the partnership and therefore in control.

- The Executive Champion should also be involved in the first wave of supporters, by giving his or her approval to the target partnership. He/she might play an important role as the central team moves through 'the swamps', engaging, pacifying, managing, overcoming, and if necessary leaving behind the continuous 'nay-sayer' and toughest critic or blocker.

- The general organization (Group 2 on Figure 10.7) will be expected to provide a consistency of tone from Stage 2 onwards, when the target is managed as a strategic partner, especially those people likely to appear at the interface. Quality communication and targeted follow-up will usually secure this need, as no real action is requested from most people, except to project a positive inclination to the partnership when interacting with the partner.

> ### Ian Davis
>
> It is no good just the board knowing why an organization is strategically partnering with another. It needs to be communicated and even engrained across the ranks. So, time spent on alignment of the different levels of an organization and letting people get to know each other is very, very important. There needs to be the human dimension, the review process while really making it clear that you are separate, you are different but you are together focused on a unified purpose.

- The positive enrolment of AoC and SoV leaders and experts (Group 3) will be defining to the success of the evolving partnership. They will be the human cornerstones behind the development of value for the partners. Considerable consideration, attention and then support will be provided to this small but essential group. When they exist, their motives of objection might range from hard considerations, such as work overload or limited availability of resource or funding, to softer ones like 'not invented here' or 'couldn't we do this well by ourselves?' They will be won over using a combination of personal attention and support, the clarity of the case, the prize resulting from the co-operation and sometimes the 'gentle' help of the Executive Champion. At no other time and with no other group will it be as important for the partnership team to adopt a 'servant–leader' posture. By 'servant–leader', we mean an individual or organization that leads by serving a cause and strongly influences and motivates others through a supportive, skilled, emphatic, humble but firm, determined and clear attitude in service of the 'greater good'.

- The executives' engagement, including that with the Corporate Champion (Group 4), is being progressively established as value and the strategic importance of the co-operation are being evidenced. Challenges will mainly come in two forms: their time and capacity; and their inclination, or lack of it, to practise the inversed hierarchy. Experience suggests that these engagements usually work, as executives bring their weight to the governance process and to the peer relationship, but are hardly ever perfect, given the natural limitations arising from their busy roles.

Peter Foss

CEOs are the great public faces for the company and you have got to have them with you – and ask for their help. But you should tell them what you need because otherwise, they may go in a direction the organization will not want to go in. And too often, they would have a great meeting, good discussions, some ideas would be exchanged and then they leave and nothing happens. They go on to do whatever they were doing and things don't get followed up on because people in the organization didn't really want to do it or didn't think it was important.

Frankly, many times I would not take my CEO to a big customer for an initial meeting. Before you took them in to help with a partnership, you would first have a good idea of where you want to go and you should have done a lot of pre-work, already developing some strong bonds with the different layers where the work gets done in the organization.

- The verticals and functions (Group 5) will come in strongly to roll out and implement the innovation and advanced solutions from the partnership. Their main challenge will usually be around resources, conflict of priorities, management of change and practice, and the need for clear standards. Such debates will be held in a pragmatic manner at various levels of the involved verticals and across the entire organization, as is practical and useful. At this stage, it will be about immediate value and 'performance' delivery, which should make the case straightforward in most instances, as long as focused attention and support is provided by the RPMs and VOMs.

Well done! You have now gone through the cycle of internal 'navigation' and rallied core support behind action. But the cycle never stops and the time has come to start again with new AoCs and SoVs. There is good news though, as those in the organization who have 'lived it' will already be converts, advocates and willing practitioners of the model. It should be getting easier!

How many times have you heard: 'it is so hard internally and so rewarding externally'. Sounds familiar? Well, firstly this is not always the case. Some organizations were born with partnership at the heart of their business model and quickly become fluent with the model. Others get through the agony of the early phases of strategic partnering, but then adopt the model as an integral way of doing business. And in the majority of circumstances, when you meet obstructions, put your head down, deploy the model consistently, keep at it ... and endure. The light of success shines at the other end of this long and demanding tunnel.

Some specifics on 'navigating' governments

Governments and public agencies increasingly participate in some of the most material and complex partnerships.

The 'why' they do so is rather straightforward. It includes the build and management of schools and academies, hospital facilities and healthcare services, major highways and roads, water and waste, energy and defence projects, the exploitation of national natural resources, etc. Partnerships can accelerate and dramatically improve the delivery of public services, while reducing demand on taxpayers' money. Partnerships can be grown across a number of governmental departments, involve national companies and the private sector.

The 'what' is also well established. Public–public and public–private partnerships can follow formalized and sophisticated practices, notably under the form of so-called Public–Private Partnerships (PPPs). These PPPs are either a government service or a private business, resulting from the partnership of government and private companies. They deliver a public infrastructure or a service, for which the private parties provide access to and delivery of financial resources, technical expertise or management capability. Activities are usually performed within special companies formed with this intent, called a Special Purpose Vehicle (SPV). These or similar approaches are practised in most countries around the world and their scale is considerable. For example, over the last 20 years, more than 1,400 PPPs were signed in the European Union, representing a value of approximately €260 billion.

As often with co-operations, it is the 'how' which raises most questions and is the predominant source of improvement. These arrangements are highly formalized (in the United Kingdom, HM Treasury holds responsibility for setting PPP policy) and contracts can be extremely sophisticated, requiring extensive co-operation between government, agencies and the involved private companies. But the nature and mechanics of politics being different to those of business, we need to interrogate the extent to which it is possible to go beyond transactional practice, albeit complex, towards true strategic partnerships with governments. And if it is possible, find out if and how the co-operation approach and 'navigation' differ from the private–private methodology.

Is true partnering with governments possible?

Co-operating with governments in one way or another is a must for all organizations in the private sector. The scale and extent of the interface might range from minor contacts, mainly to do with compliance, taxes, etc, to major connections, involving mutually important joint contracts. In the latter case, the question revolves around the meaning and practice of the relationship and how far down the road of strategic partnering it might be taken.

Stephen Odell

I think partnerships with governments are time-bound, which means they are probably not a full partnership. Governments, or members of governments, come and go and policies can change dramatically as governments change. This goes against the need for consistency in strategic partnerships. And changes of policies will definitely change the way that they interface.

I think it is very easy to be a good partner with a government at the time that you are investing. It can be possible to have a good partnership with a government through tough times when you are staying. But this latest recession and the dramatic need for the car industry to restructure has also proved that it can be difficult on occasions to have good ongoing partnerships with governments.

Tom Albanese

It is hard because, in reality, you cannot force a government to do anything beyond their term. It is really hard because you can have long-term contracts and it has got to be in the best interest of that future government to stay with it, rather than being opposed to it. Because you are in with the sovereign right of nations.

The regimen and accountabilities of governments create different dynamics to those of the private sector. Governments change and so do their objectives, policies, what they value and their leaders. The electoral nature of the system builds a constant tension and trade-off between real and political value, short and longer term perspectives. Extraordinary scrutiny imposes considerable limitations to what can be done before reaching the zone of political risk.

The terms of engagement with politicians and senior officials are also bound by strict compliance rules. With the introduction of global laws and compliance requirements covering bribery and corruption, export controls, conflicts of interests, competition laws, etc, deepened relationships with strategic partners, particularly those that are government bodies, need to be handled with much care. Hence, within organizations, the relationship between leadership, marketers and compliance officers is almost becoming an internal strategic partnership. Training in these areas is increasingly important in large global organizations, to learn how not to be fully prevented from offering your key contacts ... even a cup of coffee! A recent example was the London 2012 Olympics which demonstrated how such large-scale sport sponsorships are now subject to greatly increased scrutiny. Risk-based and proportionate compliance processes are a must-have and require working closely with legal and compliance colleagues and encouraging them to understand the strategic objectives and business intent, so that sponsors can obtain a return on their investment, leverage the benefits and so forth.

But are the public and private sectors so deeply different or are there more similarities than might appear at first sight? The average tenure of CEOs of the top global companies is around five years, not too dissimilar to that of many government heads. As new incumbents come in, enterprise strategies are often re-evaluated and leadership changed. Companies have their 'voters' with their key stakeholders, be they shareholders, partners, customers or employees, and need to manage tensions, trade-offs and time horizons accordingly. And compliance and ethics rules create strict boundaries around the forms of engagement.

This is no attempt to pretend that public and private sectors are so similar that the rules of the game or practices are applicable like for like. Instead, recognizing similarities and differences helps to adapt the partnering idea and methodologies to the specifics of states and their agencies. John Browne offers a view on the steps available to governments and companies to get closer and partner better.

John Browne

I would think of governments in a different category. Because there is no choice here and when you go into a nation, there is a whole set of laws, tax regulations and this, that and the other, all of which are subject to change. You either accept them or you don't, so you can't call it a partnership. The state is up here at the top and you are at the bottom and you submit. Then they might change and the new leaders say, 'I need to change something'. So, corporations are in a far weaker position than most people realize.

That said, they are much more accepting of this as a real issue and I even see it in some of the work that I am doing with the government. They have some of the elements of a strategic partnership, like long-term procurement activity with account managers on top of them, where the rough and the smooth can be taken together, even in the face of political scrutiny. It is very tentative because if you slice a small piece of a relationship out, you can always find something wrong with it. But they are beginning to try and build more.

Best-in-class 'navigation' with governments

The authors' experience includes developing and overseeing remarkable long-term working relationships with states and governmental departments. It also involves multiple cases of passionate debates with public leaders on how to improve partnering and relationship practices. In some ways, and as our interviewees determine, these relationships might not present each and every aspect of strategic partnerships. But applying most of the partnering system will greatly benefit the establishment of quality and enduring relationships with governments.

Having led major private and public institutions, Paul Deighton shares his unique perspective, including the considerable merits of applying 'organization and system' to the relationships with governments.

Paul Deighton

Organization and system are important with governments. Interacting with government is hard work, because you have constantly to repeat yourself across all the different interfaces you have with them. Government doesn't lend itself to managing relationships through a single channel, so you have to be across it everywhere. It is of course time-consuming and inefficient in a sense, but each part of the interaction will have a slightly different perspective on what you are trying to accomplish. You can't rely on a system to channel you in and through but you have to have multiple interfaces, so you can put your position forward and develop your own understanding based on all the nuances that come out of these interactions. This puts the onus on the private sector to organize itself to be unified and yet diffuse throughout the finest parts of government.

I think this way works better even if the government is actually trying to improve its partnership practice. Some time back, the UK government established a strategic relationship management function, which is jointly owned by UKTI and the Foreign Office, where there are designated government relationship managers so companies have someone to go to if they need some help. So, we do have a way of trying to help companies do what is of common interest and it can actually be quite helpful.

Pursuing the objective to develop mutually beneficial public–public or public–private relationships, there are consequently significant positive effects in:

- Being clear on a mission and 'destination', in the context of the specific risks associated with electoral cycles. Both usually surface quite naturally, as governments decide a public policy or objective.

- Developing compelling 'offers', well thought-through and codified within the PPP rules or other public procurement procedures and processes.

- Designing and managing a comprehensive relationship map, to exchange, inform and learn from each relevant and involved group in government. The people 'navigation' will mainly be of the top-down type, given that explicit needs and SoVs often initiate and drive the relationship.

- Creating focused teams to run the partnerships and embed deep expertise in public logic and rules. The authors have established and overseen a number of such teams with great admiration for their distinctive approach and capability.

Here again, there is no real reason to feel somehow intimidated or constricted by the ambitious and comprehensive language of *Strategic Partnering*; on the contrary, let's apply the partnering system diligently, to improve the practice and effectiveness of public–public or public–private co-operations.

Conclusion: 'Navigating' towards a successful strategic partnership

If there is one message to take away from this chapter, it is be very strategic and deliberate with the 'navigation' of the varied aspects of your partnership; work at it and apply best practice to planning for each of them in order to ensure a determined and staged progression both of content and relationships. 'Navigation' is too often left to last-minute individual improvisation which results in slower-moving, under-performing or even lost partnerships.

To return to our cooking metaphor, we have been carefully 'peeling the onion', with the many layers, textures and opportunities it presents. This hopefully reveals something of why it is important to go step by step and ensure we follow not only the recipe, but also each of the individual tasks. Because every onion layer matters!

Here is a summary of the key components of successful 'navigation':

Summary: Navigating towards a successful strategic partnership

- 'Navigation' is often poorly considered in the portfolio of partnering good practice. However, experience suggests that success or failure to 'navigate' well through the partnership model is often the make or break factor.

- Think through and actively manage the various areas of content and relationship progression to your advantage.

- 'Navigation' is not singular but multiple: engineer the enterprise partnership itinerary; phase how you unveil the co-operation 'destination' and substance; leverage the growing value as it occurs; be deliberate in phasing the engagement with the partners' people and colleagues within the organization.

- A winning 'navigation' with governments relies broadly on similar mechanisms as with the private sector, although it has its specifics related to a potentially higher politically-driven volatility. So keep calm, be astute and apply the model!

- Deliberate and successful 'navigation' requires deep strategic skills and strong determination and resilience. Keep at it until you reach the end of the long tunnel.

In cooking terms, we have just figured out in which sequence to introduce the ingredients of the aspired-for dish. Using the right order optimizes their effect and minimizes the risks associated with their addition.

This concludes a series of three Chapters – 8, 9 and 10 – where we have unpicked the components of value creation and reflected on the system and terms by which extraordinary value will be identified, accessed and successfully delivered. But what exactly is this value which we are spending so much effort creating? Chapter 11 of *Strategic Partnering* will now attempt to provide insights to this central question for successful strategic co-operations.

11
Boosting performance with strategic partnerships

The Strategic Partnership Model

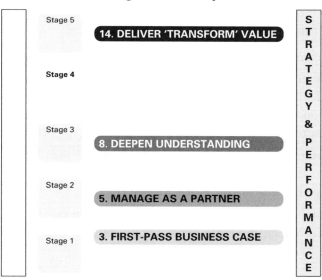

Stage 5

14. DELIVER 'TRANSFORM' VALUE

Stage 4

Stage 3

8. DEEPEN UNDERSTANDING

Stage 2

5. MANAGE AS A PARTNER

Stage 1

3. FIRST-PASS BUSINESS CASE

STRATEGY & PERFORMANCE

Don't lower your expectations to meet your performance.
Raise your level of performance to meet your expectations.
Expect the best of yourself, and then do what is necessary to
make it a reality.

RALPH MARSTON

The more I practise, the luckier I get.

GARY PLAYER AND ARNOLD PALMER

'**P**erformance', extraordinary 'transformational performance', is the name of the game in successful strategic partnerships. We have now presented the partnering system, but what is the true purpose of the model, what are the tangible goals and what is the reward?

Unlike the majority of corporate actions that are measured with quarterly financial performance targets, strategic partnerships can take years to formulate, execute and evaluate. And most of its essential value cannot always be measured with traditional metrics. Being clear on the precise type of 'performance' to be achieved and representing it with the most useful measures and KPIs are critical aspects of the strategic partnering system. These measures require mutual recognition and consent, both internally and with the partner. They also need to relate to the overall value proposition inherent in the partnership mission, 'destination' and goals, reflect its individual components and also show progress made.

In this chapter, we explore how such measures are defined and established. We then analyse the partnering 'performance' management approach under four main themes:

- 'Performance' defines and is at the centre of strategic partnering.

- How to characterize 'performance' in strategic partnerships, and particularly how to prioritize inputs versus outputs, express outcomes in quantifiable terms and identify the non-financial measures that are pivotal to 'transformational' performance.

- What are the principles and mechanics recommended for successful corporate 'performance' management, in order to succeed with strategic partnering?

- What are the principles and practices of team members' 'performance' management in successful strategic partnering?

'Performance' is at the heart of strategic partnering

Consistently capture and communicate 'performance', with the partner and internally

'Performance' evaluation and continuous communication of it are absolutely necessary to the survival and the sustainable running of strategic partnering. Value creation provides the indispensible and unchallengeable legitimacy to the whole programme and to the individual strategic partnerships. It also removes the perception often held within organizations of partnering being a 'soft' discipline built on relationships, rather than its reality of 'hard' facts and strong delivery.

Indeed, the whole rationale of engaging in progressive partnerships is to deliver value. At enterprise level, the partnering organizations' commitment will only be justified and sustained if strategic and 'transformational' value is accessed through the partnership. At the level of the participating vertical units, resources will be provided and activities kick-started only if they produce returns. And finally, individuals and teams will only be drawn into a determined and focused participation if it offers significant value to their careers and scorecards. Dr Wolfgang Reitzle sets some principles for strategic partnering value management.

Wolfgang Reitzle

It's a great idea for companies to pool their respective competencies in order to achieve more together. In essence, 1 plus 1 should no longer make 2, but 3 or 4. Strategic partnerships prove themselves to be successful when, in the long run, there is mutual benefit. This cannot only be measured in profit, but also in motivation, satisfaction and sustainable success. True strategic partnership is dependent on both sides gaining something that they could not have achieved alone.

Is the partner's value greater than ours?

Real or perceived lack of equity in the distribution of the partnership's value among the participating parties is often a risk to extraordinary co-operations. We advise a good balance of the following:

- Organizations should not consider or enter into strategic partnering with a 'one dollar for them, one dollar for us' mentality. The whole focus should be to grow the joint value, rather than to focus on its distribution. As long as each party reaches its expected benefit thresholds, what others get from it should be celebrated and seen as an opportunity to do more rather than provoke jealousy.

- Of course an excessive and enduring bias in the distribution to one party would not be sustainable, probably more for psychological reasons than any other. The equity principle should be given sufficient attention that one party doesn't turn negative to the partnership simply from a perception of being treated unfairly.

Bringing these two principles together, the priority will be to always maximize the overall partnership value with little or no compromise on the grounds of equity and then, as benefits become material, ensure that mutual value meets each party's expectations. Dr Wolfgang Reitzle reflects on value distribution.

Wolfgang Reitzle

"You can see that strategic partnering is successful when there is, at least in the long run, a certain balance of advantage for each partner – and it is really win–win. I have no problem at all when a new application leads a partner to a billion euro advantage and we get only a hundred million. This is normal because they can be 10 times bigger than us. So it is a win–win when you derive an advantage comparable to your size and input as an organization, but not necessarily expressed in equivalent financial terms. In these circumstances, we would be very happy because the more you have, the more motivated you are of course. But, when we have nothing or only a little advantage and this means almost losing to others, then we have an excessive imbalance.

This is what I mean by balance. I don't mean that it has to be one for one or even close to this. But when it is one billion for your partner, it could be a hundred or fifty million for us, and that would already be credible and big enough, because it is an advantage you wouldn't have had otherwise.

So, the balance I am talking about is more about both sides having an advantage and, bottom line, it is an advantage neither could achieve on their own. To me, this is the criterion.

Use 'performance' as a primary input to partnership strategy

Our partnering system structures our strategic planning process in such a way that we can learn and be informed continuously about the health and progress of the partnership's core activities from their 'performance':

- In the initial Stage 1 scoping, clear and best estimates of the benefits from all possible joint activities will guide our strategy and choices.

- As we define and progress the individual 'sources of value' (SoVs), we strive to develop a crystal clear understanding of the value drivers and mechanisms linking activities to benefits.

- As the SoVs deliver and yield grows, we permanently test and learn if their value mechanisms work and rectify and improve as required.

This continuous usage of 'performance' to inform strategy makes the partnership and its component parts stronger. It enables the identification of potentially greater benefits, allows the realization of increased value and provides access to new connected ideas. Very often, areas of co-operation whose value drivers are unclear or don't remunerate from the start don't do well later. Conversely, those who perform early will perform even better over time. Use 'performance' as the barometer to inform choices throughout the partnership process. Sir Frank Williams shares how 'performance' continuously guides strategy.

Frank Williams

Formula One is an amazingly competitive business. It is also seen as a business which is very dynamic but sometimes unstable. We have entered significant partnerships with external companies who are fundamental to our ability to compete. Our performance on the track at each race is of great importance to us and to our partners and their ability to derive their own commercial benefit by being associated with success on the track.

There are two types of partnership: one is where a company comes in and says, 'we want to stick a badge on your car and give you some money for this'. The second, the real partnership, says, 'we want to help you to win races and be an important "component" of your team' and then, it is always about performance and winning and about giving total commitment to excellence at all times.

It is possible that our competition occasionally possesses a second-a-lap advantage. It becomes imperative that we make every possible effort immediately to remove this advantage by finding more performance from our car. It is today's performance versus the competition that is our guide and we build on it for the future.

Defining 'performance' in strategic partnering

As we embrace the importance of measuring and communicating value, how will we achieve this? From the very start of defining and creating a critical-to-success 'performance' system, it is vital to stress the clear distinction between outputs and inputs.

Win with prioritizing inputs over outputs

Outputs from strategic partnerships are what organizations usually recognize as and call 'performance'. They are the traditional financial metrics, or a joint patent, a market share or other standard KPIs and we will come back to these in the next paragraph. Inputs are the resources, activities and milestones which pave the way and mark the progression of the partnership and its SoVs to ultimately deliver the outputs.

Often organizations only celebrate and reward the former. Using an over-simplified example: if two organizations, after months of joint work, agree a mutual supply contract with $100m thresholds, would they celebrate the contract and the quality of its provisions now – the input – or the profitable growth from the additional sales when it occurs later – the output?

In strategic partnering, the former is the critical win, as experience shows that delivering the right inputs almost inevitably leads to the right outputs, which incidentally exceed the expected value in the majority of cases. Hence, focus on and celebrate inputs, which can be as different as, for example, selecting a great new strategic partnership manager, a contract signed, a new 'offer' vetted, or a first appointment with a key decision maker.

In practice, 'performance' management in strategic partnering is about talking to the organization primarily through output measures and metrics, and to the strategic partnering teams mainly through input measures and milestones. Exploring and applying this duality successfully is central to success and discussed in the following sections.

'Performance' outputs are not only financial

Our first challenge is to define the relevant output 'performance' measures, so they represent the value created and talk clearly and powerfully to each partners' organizations. Although some measures may be different to the metrics and KPIs generally used, they will need to be expressed in the organization's language to ensure value is recognized.

In Chapter 2 and as represented in Figure 2.3, we outlined six main sources of 'transformational' value: advanced technologies, integrated supply chains, new markets, licence to operate, new solution offering and new business models. The strategic partnering teams and their corporate or vertical unit colleagues will need to identify and agree relevant, recognizable and enduring measures and KPIs, such as the examples below and shown in Figure 11.1:

- advanced technologies: net present value (NPV) from innovation, technology competitiveness, time to market, R&D cost savings;
- integrated supply: risk reduction, time to market, costs and cost benchmarks, avoidance of capital spending;
- new markets: genuine access, time to project, avoidance of capital spending, cost savings;

FIGURE 11.1   Outputs from six sources of transformational value: Examples

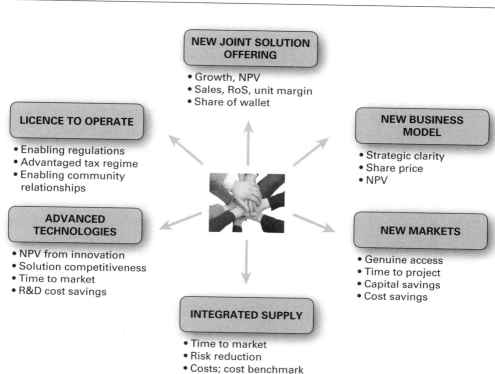

- licence to operate: obtain enabling regulations, obtain a stable tax regime, steps towards enabling community relationships;
- new solution offering: growth, NPV, sales, return on sales (RoS), unit margin, share of wallet;
- new business model: share price, strategic clarity enabling the right choices, NPV.

When developing their own strategic partnership model, organizations will need to diligently set their enduring 'performance' measurement system.

It is about our 'performance', our partner's 'performance' and – primarily – our joint 'performance'

Capturing, quantifying and communicating 'performance' within our own organization is vital to the programme. Equally critical is to understand in depth our partner's value and be able to talk confidently about it. This will enable us to know where the partner stands strategically, focus on the right areas, create authority and leverage points from rigorous delivery and ultimately support the partnership's momentum. This might appear to be good '101' practice in B2G and B2B relationships, but unfortunately it is easier to discuss than achieve and is more often talked about than done well.

A challenge lies in that the benefits from the same SoV, and therefore measures for this SoV, are often different for each partner. Take a specialized equipment company and the users' industry leader. They would enter into a strategic partnership grounded in technology, to combine their respective best hardware and application knowledge and 'transform' the equipment's 'performance'. The equipment company would ultimately measure 'performance' as enhanced sales and margins; and the user as enhanced operating 'performance' from the improved equipment, eg production output, costs, etc. These are extremely different assessments and, without a strong mutual understanding, the parties would likely risk missing 'transformational' value by pursuing sub-optimal solutions, being too self-focused, short-term and under-committing.

Another frequent issue in many strategic partnerships relates to the lack of leverage across its SoV portfolio. If and as partners continue to increase the co-operation's depth, quality and value, the work on single SoVs evolves into a systematic exploration of a full portfolio of SoVs, as shown in Chapter 4 and as illustrated in Figure 11.2.

FIGURE 11.2   Value importance of the SoVs: Illustrative example

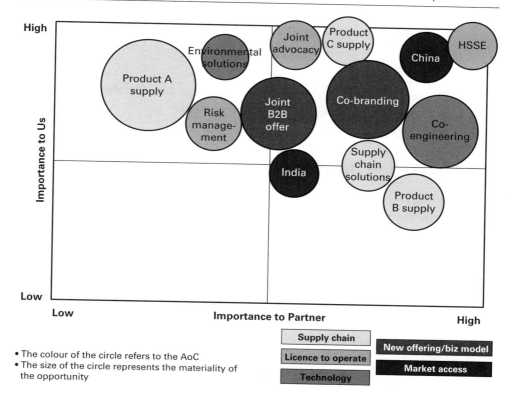

Looking at the figure, some SoVs are clear joint priorities to the partnership (top right-hand corner). Others can offer considerable value but at very different levels to each partner (top left- and bottom right-hand corners). 'Transformational' value is reached when these different perspectives are recognized and each partner supports the other's critical priorities to obtain a similar commitment to their own.

Andrew Mackenzie

"The happy thing about the very diverse way that most portfolios are put together and the way the world revolves, is that it is very rare that both counterparts have the same objectives, by this I mean the same commercial objectives. So there is a way of finding a set of high-level outcomes which they can share, and a part of the co-operation will deliver the strong commercial objectives that one side wants, while another part will deliver more strongly for the other side, and that's the essence of a good partnership.

Hence, be absolutely clear what success looks like and the key 'performance' measures for both partners!

'Transformational' value is not the enemy of immediate delivery. Deliver all along or quit!

Often there is a concern that fighting for the short term may risk jeopardizing the longer game. But the strategic partnering model should aim at delivering value at all stages and times to both partners. And the benefits should be quantified as much as possible.

FIGURE 11.3   Steps and scale of value creation

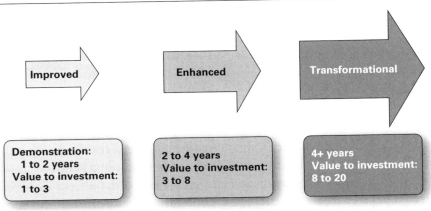

At every stage of the partnership's development towards and consistent with the 'transformational' value 'destination', there is more value delivery available from the stronger relationship. As shown in Figure 11.3, a rule of thumb is to return one to three times the specific inputs in the first two years; three to eight times in Years 3 and 4; and of course reach unparalleled returns thereafter.

Successful corporate 'performance' management in strategic partnering

'Performance' evaluation from strategic partnerships can be controversial and complex. Controversial, as vertical units of the organizations will often be tempted to claim having been at the origin of value generation: it is often said 'success has many fathers'. Complex, because some of the most relevant value measures differ from the metrics and KPIs traditionally used by organizations, notably as partnering timelines can be very different to those of established businesses. And it is not about one single organization talking to and about itself, but two partners or more, with different objectives and methods. When facing these challenges, one direction is key: simplicity.

Use your organization's existing management processes and measures as much as possible

Yes, strategic partnering is different. But let's ensure it is not different for the sake of being different and also not too different to avoid the risk of rejection. This balancing act can be classed as 'different but compatible', and can be applied accurately to the 'performance' management of strategic partnering.

For the compatibility part, we advise leaning on the organization's existing processes as much as possible, up to the point where using more of them would put the strategic partnering at risk. Master processes like strategy reviews, planning cycles, reporting cycles, financial metrics, non-financial KPIs and people reward cycles are usually appropriate as such, with little risk or compromise in using them.

Experience shows that success does not stem from differentiation from these wider organization's processes, nor in most of the output KPIs. Instead, it is generated from:

- how they are applied effectively to the strategic partnering practice;
- the additional specific processes and tools used by the strategic partnering teams, mainly focused on inputs.

With regard to the latter point, our partnering 'performance' model requires two particular types of additional measures, which are important enough for us to insist on defining and including:

- Adding specific measures and KPIs, which reflect material strands of value and are not usually tracked by the organization. For example, using 'equivalent media value' to reflect the contribution from brand projection through the partners' channels; or 'avoidance of technology investments' to reflect the cost savings coming from the activities organized by our partner rather than us for our benefit.

- Specific input-focused measures used to performance manage the teams associated with strategic partnering. Usually these additional KPIs can be largely confined within and managed by the strategic partnering teams themselves.

Viren Doshi shares a few aspects of Booz & Co's partnering 'performance' system:

Viren Doshi

We engage in client clinics where we develop campaigns. We have a map of the stakeholders who make decisions; we have issues that we need to be working on where we are distinctive and advantaged; and we have a history of where and how things work in the partner organization. All this is how you define the goals that you want to achieve, which are not only financial and can include specifics such as: have five meetings at the partner's senior level; or, have these meetings been a success or a failure? We define success as 'advances' and measure these as outcomes that we can track.

So, why not make everybody's life simple and easy by using our organization's processes and talking its language as much as possible and appropriate? And then adding to it what best-in-class partnering practice requires!

Establish a shared functional 'value and performance' expert team within the central strategic partnering unit

A small expert team will be accountable to capture value where and when it is created. As represented in Chapter 5 and Figure 5.4, it sits within the central strategic partnering unit (SPU) and is shared across all partnerships, with its key roles being:

- Internally: capture value where, when and in the form it is created (ie using the right measurements); lead the planning and reporting processes; manage the interfaces in these functional areas with the rest of the organization in the name of the SPMs; provide support and challenge to the individual partnership teams on assessing SoVs and complex contracts.

- Externally, ie with and about the partners: provide scorecards to represent and demonstrate the mutual value creation; capture and provide any KPI or measure jointly agreed, as well as data on any of our organization's obligation to the partner.

Each member of the shared 'performance' team could support a few partnerships globally, a rule of thumb being one manager for four partnerships, though this number can vary considerably subject to the scale and complexity of each co-operation. In a matrix sense, each 'performance' manager would also become the tagged expert for designated business verticals in the organization.

Senior and experienced people will be required in these roles, given the need for personal impact, interactions with leaderships both internally and with the partner, and extensive dealings with many parts of the organization. Actually, their profiles and attributes will look very similar to those of the SPMs or VOMs.

Don't centralize value; leave it in the organization's verticals

This is probably the most critical principle of all. Intuitively, the organization's verticals do not like a structured strategic partnering practice intervening in their space from outside and, on top of this, dealing with a fairly glamorous part of their agenda. They will sometimes question the strategic fit and certainly wonder, if not complain about, the deployment of an operating model that is different to theirs. On top of this, try to take away from them the value that this produces and you may create some fierce unwanted opposition!

The solution to the challenge is rather straightforward. Let's just create value – a lot of value – and then keep it within and to the advantage of the vertical units and their people. In practice, operational activities are run within and by the verticals, as execution of the strategic and contractual agreements set by the central partnership teams. Naturally, the verticals report measures and KPIs as part of their own system. The central SPU 'performance' team collates these performance measures and KPIs for each partnership across all verticals involved. They build a consolidated dashboard – as represented on a simple illustrative example in Figure 11.4 – and a memo-accounted balance sheet, cashflow and P&L for each partnership, which are represented and managed as a complete business.

The early days of setting up this system can be challenging and success will rely on the clarity of the approach and the quality of people in the shared 'performance' team. Once it is established, our experience is that it works. And not only does it work, but it does so very successfully! Verticals and their people can see and own their value; the strategic partnership teams and our senior SPMs have a full balance sheet, cashflow, P&L and 'performance' management system; the agenda is shared by the verticals and the central partnership team through joint and commonly represented 'performance' objectives, meaning that everybody increasingly works as One Team.

We have seen verticals and their people far exceed their targets only from reaching a single strategic partnership's 'transformational' SoV. After this, not only do they become fully converted, but passionate advocates and friends!

Agree value measures with the organizational verticals and businesses

A few conditions are required to make the 'don't centralize value' principle work well. The key ones are:

- The same joint measures and KPIs are used by the verticals and the partnering team.
- There is a strict discipline in planning for and reporting only the same data and numbers for a given SoV in the verticals and the partnering team.
- Individual yearly 'performance' contracts of people in the verticals and in the partnership teams use the same data and numbers for a given SoV.

It will be a continuous task to build up and agree these joint measures or KPIs. But it is of great benefit when all parts of the organization think, act on and talk about the partnerships with the same mind. Actually, this is invaluable!

FIGURE 11.4 Consolidated performance across business verticals and markets: Illustrative example

Areas of Co-operation	Sources of Value (SoV)	SoV potential (net margin)	SoV specifics	Value by geography – 2013 ($m)								Growth yoy	Share Wallet
				USA	South America	GY	Rest Europe	Japan	Rest Asia	Aus/NZ	Total		
New Offering	Branded solution selling	120	Net margin: 4/unit	16	4	8	4	16	16	4	68	25%	55%
	Unbranded solution selling	120	Net margin: 2/unit	16	10	8	10		20		64	12%	53%
	Solution royalties	60	Net margin: 1/unit pa			8	10	10	16	10	54	0%	90%
	Year service	300	Net margin: 2/unit pa	40	16	26	10	40	20	10	162	20%	54%
	Licensing margin	70	Net margin: 1/unit pa	4		4			10	30	48	8%	69%
	AoC 1 Total	670		76	30	54	34	66	82	54	396		59%
Technology	Application value vs base	300		40		40		20	30	40	170	8%	57%
	Raw material cost savings	100	Based on 2013 costs	10	10	6	8	10	15	10	69	12%	69%
	R&D revex avoidance	150	70% one off 2013 + 50% each year	60				45			105	25%	70%
	Licencing fees	150			20		20		40		80	20%	53%
	AoC 2 Total	700		110	30	46	28	75	85	50	424		61%
Partnership Total		1,370									820		

Define and use a simple historical base

In effect, the strategic partnering management system can usually and for the most part fit naturally into the organization's core systems and become an inner part of it.

Let's even go further and do all we can to keep the 'performance' management principles and processes as simple as possible. Remember that we are looking for 'transformational' value. Therefore, 'performance' management to the exact cent or penny is not the point. Also remember that our mission is strategic, about new value propositions and extra-ordinary relationships. Let's focus most of our energy on these priorities rather than complex measurements of value.

One of the simplifying principles relates to how the value base is established. Indeed, as partnerships develop, it is important to report 'performance' against a base line. This reference base should be established in Stages 1 and 2 of the partnership model. From then, we advise that all value, gains or losses captured in relation to the partner should be attributed to the partnering effort, wherever it happens. This simple rule prevents complexity and debates and actually provides for what is important and guiding, a simple clear assessment of the value delivered and created from the relationship.

Financialize outputs value and delivery as much as possible and where appropriate

Numbers are neither always possible nor the most appropriate way to report value. But numbers are simple and memorable, arguably more than any other measures. It is therefore convenient, helpful and adequate to talk the language of numbers as often as possible, notably when tracking outputs.

In many cases, SoV outputs are or can be reflected in straight numbers, in which case this guideline is simple to apply. Examples are growth, sales, margins, cost savings, technical benefits, etc.

For other SoVs, the outputs are not numbers and the question is to identify a fair quantitative proxy for the value created. When one is available and appropriate, the proxy should only be used if and when: the value is real and the proxy is an equally robust and justifiable number as the other data reported within the organization; external sources have already validated, or can validate, the methodology used; the involved internal verticals accept the methodology and the resulting numbers.

Building on an example used earlier: the value of the endorsement of our organization's brand and its projection across a partner's channel might be measured as the 'equivalent media value' for this exposure, assessed by using standard industry methods and validated by experts. When it is worth the effort, expertise in 'SoV financialization' can be brought in by audit or marketing communication firms, or specialized boutique companies such as Brand Finance in the United Kingdom. In other words, we try where possible to ascribe authentic financial values to areas of benefit whatever they are, such as brand value, synergies, the impact of being first to market and the like.

A critical and necessary thread of value is efficiency

Value creation will be a strong answer to any critics of strategic partnering and the more is generated, the less the opposition. The Holy Grail is efficient value creation, so consider making efficiency a central objective and component of your 'performance' system.

When financials are a good representation of the value created, efficiency is the ratio of net value created to the capital or cost used to do so:

$$\text{Efficiency} = \Delta \text{ Net Margin} / \Delta \text{ Cost or } \Delta \text{ Capital}$$

This ratio can reach extraordinary levels through strategic partnerships, well above norms usually seen in the organization, owing to the combination of: reaching 'transformational' value; sharing costs with the partner(s); and tapping into intelligence and knowledge as main inputs to value, rather than expensive assets.

By focusing on and tracking the efficiency of value creation, the strategic partnering team is often able to offer a better use of resources than traditional business verticals. Professional vertical organizations might actually recognize this, use and exploit it!

Successful individual 'performance' management in strategic partnering

Together with selecting the right team members, almost nothing is more important to the success of strategic partnering than a thorough 'performance' management system applied to each individual directly involved. This is an area where significant additions and specifics will complement the enterprise's processes, methods and measurements, in order to support the partnering model effectively.

Run a comprehensive people 'performance' cycle

As noted earlier, there is usually no need to materially alter the organization's existing 'performance' cycle in this area, but instead play into it and use it as a base for development, especially in the following dimensions:

Planning

The primary component is to set a high-quality individual 'performance' contract or score card. Indeed, success requires full clarity on the output objectives and each team member will need to articulate their goals during the planning phase of their 'performance' cycle. Full clarity will also be required on how they will achieve their targets. Like a student who needs to resolve a maths problem, he or she will find it helpful if intermediate steps – or questions – are set clearly, rather than only having the ultimate goal or final question as the marker. Hence and as we will discuss later in more detail, this 'performance' contract also needs to include significant intermediate steps towards the ultimate objective, as indicators of progress.

Self-assessing

A second essential component is to create the conditions for continuous 'day-after-day' self-assessment by each individual involved. Because our partnering individual 'performance' contract is more detailed than usual and therefore very transparent, the individual will be ideally placed to self-assess him- or herself continuously, build on progress made or intervene on issues that surface. As some colleagues used to say: 'there is no place to hide in strategic partnering'!

Improving through others, with the leader acting as a coach

A third component is deep dialogue with others, notably with the team leader positioned and utilized as a coach. In the same way that strategies, 'navigations' and value propositions are deeply 'supported and challenged', the ability to reach clarity and quality in setting the ultimate and intermediate markers for success and progress will benefit considerably from this dialogue. Here is Michael Johnson on 'performance' and the critical role of the coach to the SPMs or VOMs 'athletes'.

Michael Johnson

Performance definitely comes step by step and by this, I mean producing optimal performance is certainly a process. It is one that requires very hard work and a tremendous amount of patience. You have to be prepared to be constantly monitoring your performance and your level of success – or lack of success – and make the required adjustments. You have to plan opportunities to understand where you stand in your process, whether it is the world championships or different competitions that you schedule. And then you have goals, short-term goals feeding into the longer-term objective for success. They help you to understand that maybe that wasn't the right direction and an adjustment is needed to the strategy. So it is constantly evolving in terms of what you have to be learning and for me this is, both in business and as an athlete, what I have found to be the most beneficial in terms of achieving optimal performance.

I had the same coach for 4 years of university and 11 years as a professional, so 15 years. With my coach, we were absolutely partners and I think that's what helped me to achieve the success I did. Because in that type of relationship, the coach cannot feel what the athlete feels and it is up to the athlete to relay that information accurately to him. When the coach prescribes a training programme or a session, he relies heavily on the athlete and needs to understand the effect of that training session, so he can make decisions as to what the next part of the cycle will be. So the coach needs to feel that he can trust the feedback that the athlete is giving him. The athlete also needs to feel confident that the coach is listening, that the information is helpful and that the coach trusts the athlete's feedback to then be better at his job. So it is absolutely a partnership where both are relying on one another heavily for ultimate success.

A good coach, an effective coach, will understand that he is never going to be the athlete. He is never going to be the one getting the accolades. But, as a coach who is passionate about his profession and his job, helping athletes to reach their full potential will be his reward. And it will be seen as such by everyone who knows that athletes don't get there and achieve success by themselves, but they need the support of a team – and most of the time the coach is the one who is leading that team. And the coach is also the one behind the scenes and helping the athletes to be successful. The more success the coach has with the different athletes that he is in charge of, the more respect he will have in that profession.

Inputs, inputs and inputs! A priority for the team members' 'performance'

As established earlier, the strategic partnering teams will identify the critical inputs required to drive the desired outcomes. These will need to be relevant and recognizable to the team's activities, be enduring measures

FIGURE 11.5   Input 'performance' of the 5 +1 missions of the partnering teams: Examples

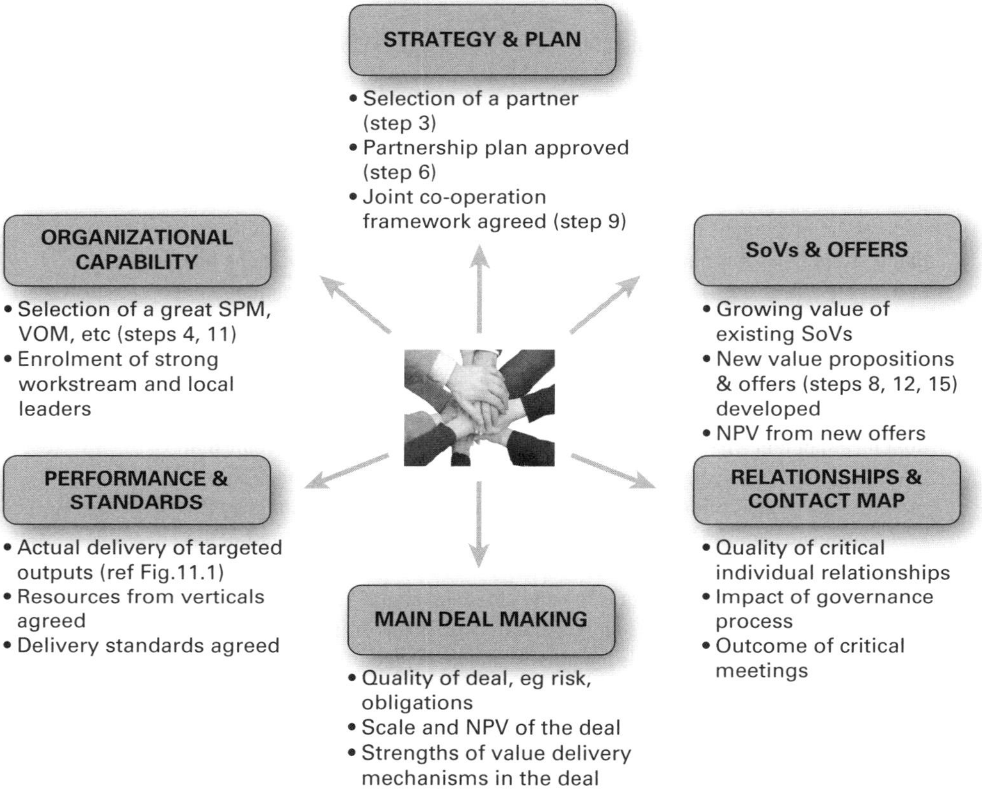

STRATEGY & PLAN

- Selection of a partner (step 3)
- Partnership plan approved (step 6)
- Joint co-operation framework agreed (step 9)

ORGANIZATIONAL CAPABILITY

- Selection of a great SPM, VOM, etc (steps 4, 11)
- Enrolment of strong workstream and local leaders

SoVs & OFFERS

- Growing value of existing SoVs
- New value propositions & offers (steps 8, 12, 15) developed
- NPV from new offers

PERFORMANCE & STANDARDS

- Actual delivery of targeted outputs (ref Fig.11.1)
- Resources from verticals agreed
- Delivery standards agreed

RELATIONSHIPS & CONTACT MAP

- Quality of critical individual relationships
- Impact of governance process
- Outcome of critical meetings

MAIN DEAL MAKING

- Quality of deal, eg risk, obligations
- Scale and NPV of the deal
- Strengths of value delivery mechanisms in the deal

and KPIs, to provide a stable 'performance' framework. Figure 11.5 shows some examples of such critical inputs (mirroring Figure 11.1 on outputs), and also how they relate to the strategic partnership development framework steps:

- **strategy and plan:** selection of a partner (Step 3), partnership plan approved (Step 6), joint co-operation framework agreed (Step 9);

- **SoVs and 'offers':** growing value of existing SoVs, new value propositions and 'offers' developed (Steps 8, 12, 15), NPVs from new 'offers';

- **relationships and contact map:** quality of critical individual relationships, impact of governance process, outcome of critical meetings;

- **main deal making:** quality of deal, eg risk and obligations, scale and NPV of the deal, strengths of value delivery mechanisms in the deal;
- **'performance' and standards:** actual delivery of targeted outputs, resource allocation from verticals agreed, delivery standards agreed;
- **organizational capability:** selection of a great SPM, VOM, etc (Steps 4, 11), enrolment of strong workstream and local leaders.

Focus on setting individual 'performance' criteria, objectives and measures

As discussed earlier, this is mainly about identifying and setting the right inputs to command success. This may be unusual within the organizations and may often be an addition to their core systems. When setting your partnering system, it is important to give thought to what these inputs should be and how to bring them to life on a systematic basis. A powerful 'performance' contract for partnering team members should combine four main threads:

- adherence to the core expectations, rules and values of the organization (input and output);
- strategic value and milestone achievements (input);
- 'navigation' and tactical milestones passed (input);
- outputs and metrics (output).

Viren Doshi reflects on the 'performance' of strategic partnering teams.

Viren Doshi

The professional selling cycle can take two, three years or even more. You need to measure your progress towards the 'big contract' – to come home every day and feel like you've won. We have a number of techniques to be able to declare success – or to identify blockages – along the long selling cycle. This is how we plan for, and celebrate, the mini-successes along the way. We do training on that and the clarity this provides keeps the team energized along the long journey.

Outcome is less relevant because if you do the right things, outcomes happen. It's around making your luck and all the techniques around how you make luck happen. 'How to be lucky' is the title I have given to my training session on building strategic partnerships.

How to compensate strategic partnering team members

This is often discussed and considered a genuine challenge. The main questions usually gravitate around the following themes:

- How to compensate and incentivize SPMs, VOMs and other involved colleagues during the partnership development phases, when very little seems to happen despite their deep commitment and ingenuity?

- How to reward team members when 'transformational' value is attained, in ways that are commensurate with the scale of success and usually out of the organization's norms?

- To what extent should the reward system therefore differ from the one used with the rest of the organization?

Many organizations set up separate schemes for their partnership teams. We do not necessarily advise this, and rather prefer to leverage the organization's existing compensation schemes, as long as they offer the space for a few important mechanisms required by our practice, such as: meaningful yearly incentive variable pay; qualitative flexibility to link reward closely to the 'performance' contract and the inputs (as much as outputs); off-cycle exceptional awards for extraordinary, long-pursued achievements.

As for the vast majority of people, financial incentives are of course important to the partnering team members. But we have also found that most of our partnering team members are at least equally motivated with building their own skill set and developing distinctive experience as career accelerators. The time and support provided to help team members with their own development will generally have a greater impact than most financial incentives during their years in strategic partnering.

Conclusion: Boosting 'performance' with strategic partnerships

'Transformational performance' is the name of the game in strategic partnering. Managing 'performance' well and being clear about how this is done systematically is an integral and critical part to any strategic partnering system. Here is a summary of the guidelines from this chapter:

Summary: Boosting 'performance' with strategic partnerships

- Reaching 'transformational' value is the name of the game of strategic partnering; use 'performance' as a primary input to partnership strategy.
- It is our own 'performance', our partner's 'performance' and, primarily, our joint 'performance'. Consistently capture and communicate 'performance', with the partner and internally.
- Our partner's benefits may be greater than ours and this is ok as long as we get a fair share.
- Win by prioritizing inputs over outputs; inputs are the priority in your team members' 'performance' assessment.
- 'Performance' outputs are not only financial – define clearly what they are; but when you can and where appropriate, strive to financialize output value and delivery.
- Strategic 'transformational' value is not the enemy of immediate delivery. Deliver throughout or quit!
- Use your organization's existing core management processes and measures as much as possible.
- Build a small shared functional 'value and performance' expert team within the central strategic partnering unit, to act as a critical measurement authority and provide vital insights on developing SoVs.
- Don't centralize value; leave it in the organization's verticals and businesses and agree joint value measures with them.
- Simplify 'performance' management as much as possible and use a simple and enduring historical base.
- A critical thread of value is efficiency.
- Run an in-depth, comprehensive people 'performance' cycle; bring great focus and quality to setting individual 'performance' criteria, objectives and measures.
- Compensate strategic partnering team members mainly using the organization's core schemes, but define and apply judicious adjustments.

So, putting method, edge and some intensity into this area will be defining to success. Good luck with developing your own partnering 'performance' system!

12
Conclusion: Is your culture ready to drive strategic partnering success?

The Strategic Partnership Model

Culture eats strategy for breakfast.

PETER DRUCKER

The road to success is dotted with many tempting parking places.

WILL ROGERS

As *Strategic Partnering: Remove chance and deliver consistent success* comes to its conclusion, let's reflect on the key themes critical to strategic partnering success.

Although the strategic partnership model and processes may appear to be more inspired by common sense and thorough diligence than pure innovation, in reality they are quite the opposite. Many assumptions are commonly made about partnering and that is where partnerships don't succeed. And it is often when people believe they know 'how' to do partnering that they risk failing.

In fact, adopting the overall system approach and being disciplined in applying its detail can prove 'transformational'. Many leaders or practitioners who have rigorously used these frameworks and methodologies have commented that it has not only helped them to deliver successful high value partnerships time after time, but also 'transformed' their approach to business altogether. Some have even shifted from using the strategic partnering approach as 'a' strategy to making it 'the' strategy.

Other people might comment that the model appears rather demanding, with its multiple steps and apparent significant intellectual and resource mobilization. But for strategic partnering to function and succeed as a comprehensive business model and a fully-fledged operation, it needs the basis of a deliberate enterprise decision in its favour and the right level of attention and inputs.

Actually, when comparing the new resources required for building and managing successful strategic partnerships with those already residing in the business – be they capital, people or processes – this model will prove extremely, if not uniquely efficient. People are simply intuitively not used to bringing the same science and discipline to such 'soft' techniques, as when they run 'bricks and mortar' operations such as public services, manufacturing or even sales.

An absolutely valid question should be: is it all worth it? Let's be unambiguous on the 'yes' answer and even amplify our Chapter 11 narrative on 'performance'. Evidence from experience repeatedly reinforces how succeeding with strategic partnering can bring a 'transformational' prize to any organization. Not only because successful partnerships can deliver material value very efficiently, but strategic partnering is also deeply important strategically, as it takes the whole organization's licence to operate, technology, 'offers', access to market or channels and capabilities to very different levels of ability than before.

If the rewards of strategic partnering are so defining, what does it fundamentally take for the approach to succeed? No surprise that we strongly advocate that organizations should define their own partnership model and apply it consistently and diligently over long periods of time. Yet it is also essential to get the culture right. Indeed, culture has been obsessively present in this book, overarching and underpinning every aspect of success or failure with strategic partnering. And our world leader interviewees all epitomize cultural leadership by emphasizing the essential values and behaviours required for success. Andrew Bester summarizes it all in just one sentence:

Andrew Bester, Group Director, Chief Executive Commercial Banking, Lloyds Banking Group

I strongly believe that we, in Lloyds TSB, have the essential raw material to succeed: because our people care deeply about the company – and they care deeply about the clients.

So in preparation for success, this final chapter centres on the four themes of: the strategic partnering system; how to think about it; its defining prize; and organizational culture. It summarizes the overall approach to strategic partnering and provides a simple question-based method recap, to help launch or 'enhance' your strategic partnerships under the prescribed principles of this book. The subheadings include:

- Which culture leads to success with strategic partnering?
- How the strategic partnering system generates deeply 'transformational' prizes, even greater than those described so far.
- Overview of key methods and principles for winning with strategic partnerships.
- Are you ready to succeed with strategic partnering?

Organizational culture and character to win with strategic partnering

'Culture eats strategy for breakfast' said Peter Drucker. And the simple picture on Figure 12.1 neatly represents how core strategies may aim

FIGURE 12.1   Culture eats strategy for breakfast

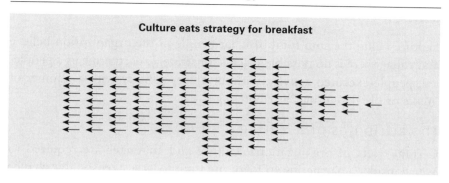

in one direction but may meet an invincible resistance if that direction is counter-cultural.

Before even starting on the journey, it is vital to assess the organizational culture and character and its fit with strategic partnering. And actually, it is not through one lens only that you might want to enquire about culture, but through at least three:

- your partner's culture;

- your own organization's character, both collective and that of key individuals;

- the ability of both cultures to combine for success.

Stephen Odell

The DNAs of the companies have to make sense and normally, they don't have to be the same, but they have to be able to blend and make sense with each other.

Andrew Mackenzie

You need to have an ethos of that sort of relationship which goes right through the company. I mean, it starts with value sets and integrity, it does mean that you hold people to what they've said as well as hold yourself to what you say. And in this case, I do think that there are strategic relationships that have worked.

Strategic partnering: a culture and character on its own

Culture being the sum total of what people in the organization believe and value, there is no possible success for strategic partnering as a people-led, people-executed activity, without a deep affinity with a number of 'make or break' cultural attributes.

The attributes of a 'caring' culture

Certain traits of organizational culture and character are required to even consider a partnering strategy and for it to have a reasonable chance of succeeding. Some of these qualities have been covered in Chapter 4, on 'Selecting the best strategic partners' (page 86) and in Chapter 6, on 'Developing world-class strategic partnering human capital' (page 120), where we analysed the strong commonality of attributes shared by those organizations or people who are best at strategic co-operations. Figure 12.2 captures six cultural traits which our interviewees have reflected on and which we equally regard as critical to strategic partnering success.

FIGURE 12.2 Six cultural traits indispensable to strategic partnering

Giving

This is the ability to always think and act as if the partnership were made of one single entity and therefore look for mutual advantage. The way the prize is shared is rather secondary, as long as value is created, it reaches a sufficient threshold for each partner, and any imbalance of benefits is acceptable.

Andrew Mackenzie

It is so rare these days to have genuine organizations and people who are ready to give. We have been conditioned to be different and through narrow training, we've made the assumption that it is possible to win whilst someone else loses. But that only happens for a short period of time until they realize that they've been silly. So the next discussion they're having with you is to make you lose, so that they can win, and that's no way to build a strategic relationship.

Mike Glenn

The main thing is whether the organizations are truly committed to those areas of common interest or whether there is less commitment and one organization puts their individual interest above the relationship. In this case, the relationship couldn't last several years.

John Browne

The view of some organizations is 'get the best deal and then we'll live to fight another day'. Some would still talk about strategic partnerships but it doesn't actually make sense. So, it has to provide something which is a mutual benefit to both parties and for the long term.

Shelly Lazarus

I think there is inherent generosity in people who are good at forming strategic relationships, because in the end it is all about giving and sharing.

Trusting

The involved parties and their people are able and willing to trust the partners and the extent of their listening, generosity, judgement and capabilities. Trust is absolutely crucial to strategic partnerships and requires openness, frankness and the highest level of authenticity and transparency. It will initiate unique access to knowledge, capabilities and resources.

Tom Albanese

We are in a world of distrust. Post global financial crisis, institutions are not trusted, banks are not trusted, governments are not trusted, corporate CEOs are not trusted. There is a higher element of distrust of anyone in any kind of position of power now. In such an environment of distrust, you will have to be very transparent.

Shelly Lazarus

You have to start with trust. If two parties don't trust each other, it doesn't matter how mutually in sync they are or how much their capabilities complement each other. You have to basically trust the other person! And so you'd better be careful who you pick to partner with.

Kevin Murray

When it comes to partnering, you need to trust and be clear about the elements of trust that you need in the relationship. Clearly, competence is one of the areas that you need to trust: is this person or organization capable of delivering what you need? The second area is: do they make the right judgements and have a track record of making the right calls? Because competence without judgement can lead to some real problems. And then the final element is about integrity: do you trust the integrity of the people that you're dealing with? So when you start breaking trust down into those areas, do you feel comfortable in each of those dimensions with this organization you are working with?

Respectful

Deep respect will be expected whatever the circumstances and will impact on everyone associated with the relationship. Respect, honesty and integrity are keystones to any strategic partnership and failing in any of these inevitably risks major limitations to the relationship.

Shelly Lazarus

In all great relationships, there is mutual respect and when there is mutual respect, you can disagree with someone for whom you have great respect because it is not personal. The worst relationship to me of all is where you can smell that there is disrespect, where people are going through the motions, but they really don't respect the view, the brain, the heart of the other person who is in that purported relationship.

Kevin Murray

It is about authenticity and honesty and that means that you are sometimes saying things that are unpalatable but which you truly believe so that people know where you are coming from. And people don't actually agree but they trust and respect each other because they know what their partner stand for.

Committed

The whole thrust of strategic partnering is to bring important capabilities to and from other parties, so 'transformational' value is created over and for a significant period of time. It requires a mutual commitment that endures through the highs and lows of the partners' fortunes, to provide genuine support to each other and never to be closed to their evolving situations.

Martin Sorrell

Most of our client relationships have been very long-term, and we have built them together over time, as those companies and we have expanded. If the companies that you're dealing with fail, then you fail with them. I therefore think critical factors are loyalty and commitment to the companies that we have relationships with.

Michael Johnson

One of Nike's founder's famous quotes to all Nike employees which remains deeply held within the organization is to 'always listen to the voice of the athlete'. So obviously, when I was an athlete, having that company supporting me from the standpoint of Michael, looking at what type of product would help me to be more confident, to perform at the level that I felt capable of performing, was genuine and integral to that relationship thriving from the very beginning. And this partnership is still lasting many years later.

Humble

There is no place for ego in strategic partnerships, neither from the organization nor from individuals. Pursuing 'transformation' and excellence means there cannot be any complacency at any time, anywhere. And because strategic partnering is about leadership of 'offers', of relationships, of performance, these are approached and delivered with empathy to the needs and requirements of others. But don't get us wrong: humility is not a sign of softness but rather an expression of serene confidence towards others.

Ian Robertson

We as a senior team and as a company are never complacent. We would rather look at what else we could have done rather than congratulate ourselves with 'wasn't that a fantastic outcome'. I believe that one of the things which can go wrong with partnerships is when complacency creeps in.

Shelly Lazarus

I actually think you need humility to be successful in strategic partnerships because you have to believe from the start that we are going to be better together than any one of us would be alone. And we will land on something that is more inventive, productive, and smarter by coming together rather than being apart. If you are self-absorbed, self-congratulatory or you have got to be the smartest person in the room, it is really hard to have this kind of relationship.

Learning

The learning quality takes its source from the other five and is a core component of success. It has major effects on the whole enterprise. Many institutions claim to be learning organizations, but this is seldom really the case and an open-minded disposition and determination to deeply listen and understand others will make a huge difference to any partnership. Learning goes hand-in-hand with taking a long-term view – reaching 'transformational' value by using everything grasped on the journey. Ultimately, learning gives the confidence to act with the determination, edge and strength of will required in any successful partnership.

Stephen Odell

" A strong DNA, I think, is a learning culture that is not afraid to change. Actually, nobody really likes change and at a certain point either in your life or in your job, it gets comfortable and it would be nice, just for a couple of months for it to stay like this. But, the world is moving so quickly that unless you are at the forefront of change, not just change for change sake, but looking what the future is and understanding that the future isn't the same as today then, you know, the company won't survive for the future anyway.

Ian Robertson

" As a company, we think long term. That's easy to say, but I do believe that we are able to be more consistent in our thinking compared to many companies around the world. We tend to make decisions for long-term prosperity, not short-term gain. That comes from our structure and from the way we do business.

Cultural gates

In addition to 'hard' competencies required to succeed, any institution keen to partner will need a good blend of these six cultural traits, making up a deeply caring culture. This is about:

- caring about our organization's qualities and effectiveness as a partner;
- caring about our associates and their people to achieve mutual value;
- caring about doing the right thing in and as a partnership relative to its targeted stakeholders.

It should be checked these values are present in both partners' DNA, at least to some extent. Not that there is a need for a 10/10 mark on each individual trait, but these attributes all have to be part of the mix to some extent, to build and improve on existing levels. Jeff Immelt offers a powerful summary of critical cultural traits required to succeed with advanced partnerships.

Jeff Immelt

" The company and the partner are on the same side. You need personal trust. You need to understand each other's culture and what is important to the partner. You need a strong commercial culture, one that has respect for partners and customers. No one has to lose to have someone win! Inside the company, the brand comes first; so protect and grow it through partnerships, as you want people to trust your company, you want people to feel we will stand behind them and help them solve problems.

Get impressed by deep partnering cultures!

Over the years, we have met many great enterprises whose cultures were an extraordinarily natural fit for strategic partnering; and others who were not at all. Not to say that the latter organizations are bad, but partnering is simply not who they are, as also observed by our interviewees.

Mike Glenn

"We do try to make sure that we apply a reasonable filter to the partnering opportunities. And if there is an opportunity for both organizations to benefit, it is largely based upon 'is the culture of the other organization such that they would be willing; and is there trust in the relationship?' And we find terrific customers of ours with whom it would be difficult to enter into this type of relationship, because the conversation, and this is largely a cultural issue, would be very much one-sided.

Shelly Lazarus

"There are great enterprises and also people who are not good at partnerships. And there are lots of them, because they don't have inherent respect, because they believe that they are smarter than anyone else and therefore can't really be respectful to somebody else's opinion.

The automotive sector case

As mentioned before, some organizations are culturally fit to partner, and the automotive industry is rich in a number of such strong practitioners. Over the last 35 years, the authors have been privileged to work continuously with many of the leading light and commercial vehicle global companies, their parts suppliers and distributors. It is a fascinating and extremely complex industry, facing extreme pressures from regulators, competitors and customers. The participating companies have to excel in a great variety of capability domains, including fashion – for vehicle design, multiple advanced technologies, complex integration of external parties, advanced lean manufacturing, sophisticated marketing and global integration.

It is a tough task to provide quality mobility and the related freedom to the world. And one that makes the sector participants predicated to strategic partnerships, so critical to their business is their long-term interfacing with governments, competitors, technology partners and universities, suppliers, distributors, dealers and customer groups. In fact, a Booz & Co study reports that automotive is the single sector with the highest proportion of cross-border strategic alliances, ahead of aerospace, transportation, energy and natural resources and industrial. So what is there to learn from these role models?

DNA and cultural fit

There is a considerable diversity of approaches and practices to relationships in the automotive sector. On the one hand, some of the companies' DNAs simply do not have long-term mutual partnerships on the map. Others hold dear the type of values that make partnerships very natural to them, as well as strive to become ever better at it. We feel privileged in *Strategic Partnering* to benefit from some of their top leaders' insights.

Shoichiro Toyoda

One year, when I was at the Davos Forum and attended a panel, a question was raised to me: 'What's the most important thing to you?' and my answer was 'Building good relationships based on mutual trust.'

To determine to what extent we should co-operate and complement each other, and to facilitate decision making in respect to strategic partnering, it is essential to nurture smooth face-to-face communications with our partners. Moreover, we must work to foster trust on an individual basis and build person-to-person relations, as well as between and across organizations.

Francisco Garcia Sanz

Organizations that are engaged in good partnering need to 'live up' to values such as co-operative behaviour, long-term orientation, reliability, flexibility, and operational excellence. They need to be open to information sharing and joint planning processes. Additionally, they should commit to mutual resource investments, be proactive on 'issue spotting' and welcome a shared problem-solving approach.

Certain organizational cultures enable such strong partnership values by establishing a co-operative working environment and setting up a strong motivation for collaboration. Company leaders have to strive to generate this motivation every day and with each employee.

Stephen Odell

We are going to have to be good partners everywhere. A strong DNA is a learning culture. So, we are learning to be good partners and it starts within One Ford and with our joint venture partners, who are very important to the growth of our business.

Ian Robertson

"Yes of course, partnerships are important to us. We have a number of long-term partnerships in the component area for example, in which we invest a great deal of time and attention. It is only by doing so that we can find vital competitive advantages. Do we share goals? Certainly. But do we agree how we are going to get there? Probably not. That is where we look to our partners to bring their specialist expertise to bear. These relationships are certainly challenging for both parties, but the power of working jointly to meet a shared goal is prodigious.

In the automotive sector, some global leaders truly stand out for their extraordinary culture, values and ability to engage and rally partners behind their long-term aspirations and objectives. Naming a few, at the risk of missing others:

- Ford Motor Company's 'Go Further' is guided and inspired by Henry Ford's pioneering and still absolutely modern philosophy for mobility, as well as its 'One Ford, One Team, One Plan, One Goal' unifying cry.

- The Volkswagen Group's 'Driving Ideas' represents an impressive and relentless dedication to and focus on technological excellence and innovative advancements across every aspect of what they do, including the selection of their senior leadership.

- The BMW Group's 'Ultimate Driving Machine' stands for, epitomizes and projects a universal passion for the group's iconic brands, ensuring they live and blossom in everything they do at all times and globally.

For these three leaders their absolute search for excellence and globalism does translate into the critical cultural traits required for successful partnering and makes them remarkable partners – although, admittedly, demanding and not always easy ones. But is this a negative? Not if the tension is held as a mark of mutual respect, understanding and aspiration.

A cultural leader

Toyota is also famous for its vision and dedication to a set of common principles captured in the 'Toyota Way'. And an important component of its approach relates to how Toyota works with others in partnership. Said with all humility, we have always been inspired with how Toyota's long-term philosophy and system's principles are aligned with and similar to those of our strategic partnering approach. We have also been privileged to participate first-hand and see Toyota's values in action over many years and in significant depth.

FIGURE 12.3   The Toyota Way and the six cultural traits for successful strategic partnering

Figure 12.3 reflects the strong correlation between the Toyota Way and its five core values, with our six partnering cultural traits and the partnership development model:

- manage with a long-term view rather than for short-term gain;

- pursue continuous improvement – *Kaisen* – towards a quality outcome;

- use principle-led processes – the Toyota production system three Ms (*Muda, Muri, Mura*) and five Ss (*Seiri, Seiton, Seiso, Seiketu* and *Shitsuke*);

- deeply respect people, focus on team achievements and treat business partners as your own employees, so they become better and stronger;

- *Genchi genbutsu* – humbly 'go and see' for yourself the real place, to solve issues at the source;

- examine options thoroughly and implement rapidly – *Nemawashi* – while continually being a learning organization by critiquing every aspect of what you do.

Let's hear the perspectives of Uchiyamada-san, Chairman of the Board of Toyota.

Takeshi Uchiyamada

"I have been with Toyota for 40 years and in that time, I have discovered that the way Toyota thinks is really related to how Toyota was founded and started. And this was Mr Kiichiro Toyoda wanting to make a contribution to society by inventing something new like the automobile in Japan. So I think that the overwhelming culture within Toyota is to challenge to make something new. And also, as an organization, to support people willing to take a risk and take on a new challenge.

Without this overwhelming corporate culture, we would not have been able to come up with the catalysts invented during the '80s, with the Lexus through the study of deep engineering capabilities, with the Hybrid system invented in the late '90s, etc. In the Toyota Way, you will find very important keywords such as 'teamwork' and also 'respect' for people. But personally, my favourite word in the Toyota Way is 'challenge'.

According to my experience in developing the Prius, I think trust in relationships is the most important element for success. When organizations are looking at the mid- and long-term perspective and building respect and a trusting relationship, we are able to show our strategies to each other and we are able to disclose data to each other in a very open manner. And you know, this couldn't happen without aiming at the mid- and long-term relationship.

We have just started an alliance with other automotive OEMs such as Ford and BMW on important developments and when we form alliances with companies like this, we always think about whether we are able to establish mid- and long-term trusting relationships with those organizations. We just don't look at the short-term economic advantages.

Our experience has allowed us to get to know and develop partnerships with multiple organizations, whose enviable cultures and values are a strong fit for partnering. Although this quality is not a core component of a strong majority of organizations, it is clearly part of the fabric of a very material and important group of leading institutions, often their sector's leaders.

But even when a strong partnering culture exists in an institution, many of the fantastic organizational traits and capabilities are not fully leveraged and exploited in the arena of partnerships, not because of a lack of willingness but more often because of gaps in the methodology. Indeed, what is the equivalent of the Toyota production system, its *Kaisen*, Ms and Ss guidelines, for partnerships? They are almost universally missing, a gap we hope *Strategic Partnering* will help to fill to some extent, by enabling everyone to approach alliances in a more programmatic, systematic and disciplined way.

Overview of key methods for winning with strategic partnerships

Rather than repeating or paraphrasing the earlier chapters, let's now use the following questions as a basis for considering your readiness and capability to succeed with strategic partnering, having gone through the system.

Testing your readiness for successful strategic partnering, through 12 questions

1 Does your enterprise hold major interfaces with other parties?

2 Do you see natural 'missions' for possible deep relationships with other organizations:
   - from your stand point?
   - from the stand point of other institutions which you already impact materially or could impact more?

3 Do you need a step change for one of or a combination of the following: advanced technologies, integrated supply chains, new geographies, enhanced licence to operate, new solution offering or new business ventures?

4 Is the culture of your organization in the zone of 'relationships', 'mutual advantage', 'caring'?

5 Do you believe your organization is able to operate as 'One Team'?

6 Do you believe your organization – and you personally – can genuinely practise the inverted hierarchical pyramid?

7 Do you already have a cross-organization model or a programme for managing key relationships, accounts, suppliers, universities, NGOs?

8 Is your organization good at designing an operating model and standing behind it, including providing enduring executive support?

9 Is your organization patient, resilient and does it run things from A to Z in a methodical way?

10 Do you believe you have or can build a talent pipeline able to generate leading Strategic Partnership Managers (SPMs)?

11 Is your organization good at business innovation, substance and 'offer' development?

12 As a leader, do you deeply believe in partnering, its potential to deliver strategic 'transformation' and the 'make or break' importance of a thorough system?

Score your answer to each question from 1 to 10, 10 being best-in-class. If, before or after reading this book, your score is over 60 and no single mark gets under 3 (except Q7), your assessment of these key methods is mainly positive – congratulations! And time for you to move towards the 'transformational' prize.

An enterprise-wide 'transformational' prize from strategic partnering

The multiple motives and incentives for developing strategic partnerships have been analysed throughout this book. The main prize is 'transformational' value. Let's take a summary 360-degree perspective of the true strategic importance and unparalleled legacy that can be derived from a determined and successful partnering business model.

The deeply strategic impacts of the partnering model are represented in the six areas of 'transformational' prize shown in Figure 12.4. Their existence has been evidenced through repeated experience and transcends 'value' as described in Chapter 11, to reflect deep strategic 'transformation' accessible through or by applying a thorough strategic partnering system.

FIGURE 12.4   Six areas of transformational prize from strategic partnering

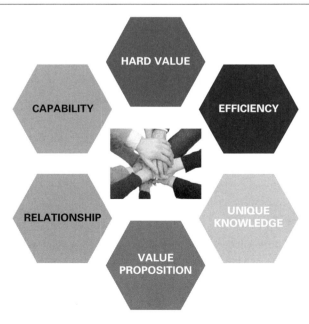

Deliver material direct 'hard' value

This is the straight value delivered from deeper relationships – 'improve' and 'enhance' – or the enterprise value generated from strategic partnerships – 'transform'. As discussed in Chapters 2, 8 and 11, it usually arises from advanced technologies, integrating supply chains, new geographies, a 'transformed' licence to operate, new solution offering or new business models. This is value that can and should be measured (and quantified if possible), is commonly and mutually recognized, and will reach significant enterprise materiality.

Access unparalleled efficiency of value generation

Though it might sometimes run counter to people's intuition, there is not a more efficient and productive model to generate value:

- Firstly, new inputs into strategic partnering are usually limited in scale and scope, in terms of people, research and technology or marketing investments.

- With strategic partnering, organizations can optimize their existing high-capital/high-cost infrastructure – products, plants, marketing, etc. There is nothing more rewarding to businesses and people than to develop massive and often under-fructified existing business bases, bringing them to very different levels of performance – which quite often the strategic partnering business model is ideally suited to achieve.

- Due to its discipline, the model achieves close to 100 per cent partnership conversion rates and an almost equal success rate with its value propositions and new 'offers'. This is better by a long way than the performance of average business development, where considerable resources are often absorbed in failed attempts.

It is not unusual for strategic partnerships to produce ratios of 20 units of value for one unit of new input. Also, a number of studies have shown that the sum of resources used across the distributed entities of an organization to manage their individual relationships with a complex third-party counterpart are two to three times higher than through a central partnership team, and produce significantly lower performance.

Redefine critical interfaces through unique knowledge and 'seeing what you couldn't see'

Transactional or non-strategic relationships leave the interface or complementary areas between organizations largely unexplored. This is the syndrome of the 'unknown unknowns'. As Donald Rumsfeld famously said in 2002:

> There are known knowns; there are things we know we know. We also know there are known unknowns; that is to say, we know there are some things we do not know. But there are also unknown unknowns – the ones we don't know we don't know.

And as we probably only possess 1 per cent of all possible knowledge and know that we do not know perhaps another 2 per cent, this leaves 97 per cent of knowledge as the unknown unknowns! As represented by the arrows of Figure 12.5, the opportunity for deep partnerships is to uncover the relevant 'unknown unknowns' through our partners' knowledge and jointly explore fruitful 'unknown unknowns', to access and deliver the considerable related value.

FIGURE 12.5 Seeing what you couldn't see without partnering

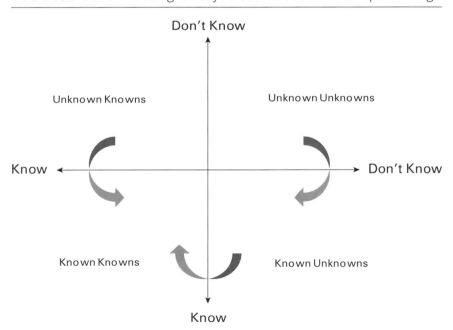

Strategically 'transform' the organization's value proposition

Another factor of experience is the extent to which the advanced work and development with partners can impact their respective overall value proposition. The mechanisms of this happening are rather straightforward: best-in-class organizations enter into strategic partnerships and develop deep substance and advanced knowledge and 'offers'. This comprehends the deepest level of mutual understanding of their real strategic needs and expanding the consequent ability to truly respond to these. After a time, aspects of these advancements permeate into the organizations and are brought into 'offers' to other stakeholder groups. The pull effect of strategic partnering elevates the whole enterprise value proposition and is of major benefit across the vertical entities of the partner organizations.

For example, some technology companies have, in just a few years of true strategic partnering, moved and focused 80 per cent of their whole R&D effort into their partnerships' workstreams and activities.

Strategically 'transform' the organization's relationship

As is the case for value propositions and 'offers', the search for excellence and thoroughness required in the relationship area of strategic partnering has the potential to create a mindset, a benchmark and an expectation for the entire organization in this space. The cultural traits and practical methods required for success, as shown in Chapter 7, permeate across institutions and entities and are amplified and practised increasingly widely. This builds a new relationship model and a distinctive strategic advantage for the whole organization. It also establishes a powerful ecosystem for the organization to base its success upon.

We have witnessed the mindset of organizations shift from being internally to externally focused, owing to the impact of a strategic partnering programme. Often companies can use the impact of a few iconic partnerships to 'bring the customer back in'. We have also seen organizations 'transform' their segmentation approach – as referred to in Chapter 4 – as they sought clarity on who was at the 'top of their relationship pyramid'. By doing so, they redefined the relationships with the 'lower' levels of the relationship pyramid and the model to serve them (or to be served by them).

Andrew Bester

❝Our strategy is to create a clear, balanced and productive relationship of equals with each level of customer groups ... regardless of the size of the customer. A real relationship of equals at all levels from the smallest to the biggest customer. That is customer partnership nirvana.

Strategically 'transform' the organizational and human capability

The prize and impact from strategic partnering will be extremely 'transformational' to organizational and human capability:

- on culture, acting as a strong guide to the disciplines, attributes and traits for success, such as excellence and caring;

- on people, developing the unique talents of expert leaders, through the demanding school of strategic value development at pace and the deep practice of a widely applicable business model;

- on capability, providing a comprehensive best-in-class relationship management model, which permeates throughout the organization, as partnering people move in and out the central partnering team, and the informal teams are fully involved;

- on organization cohesiveness, in enhancing internal co-operations into One Team and One Approach across the globe, such as for the 'Toyota Way' or 'One Ford', irrespective of what people's diverse origins might be.

'A' or 'the' model?

So, there is extraordinary strategic 'transformation' and value latent in the strategic partnering system, which raises the question: should strategic partnership be 'a' component model of the way we run businesses; or be adopted as 'the' prevailing model for the organization?

Indeed, shouldn't we relate consistently to each other internally through the 'lenses' of this model and culture, as well as externally? And, as the strategic partnership development model becomes an embedded way of working, shouldn't we take full advantage of the related 'transformations' to redefine leadership across the enterprise, from rules-based to values-based?

A '100 per cent success' rate with strategic partnerships

This is a cook book. We started with cooking; we have cooked all along; and here are a few final 'make or break' dimensions of the winning recipe for strategic partnering.

Build a full model

The key to 100 per cent repeatable success with your dream strategic partnerships is in the 'how' you go after them. A full partnership model is arguably critical to consistent success, subject to it being designed with great attention and applied in a determined and disciplined way. Step back, develop your partnering model, roll it out and stick to it! As Will Rogers says: 'Don't duck the challenges by pausing in "tempting parking places"'. And not only are there many of these, but also many obstacles and oppositions along the way.

Don't do it half-way

Like a popular saying, 'let's not half-bake the cake', using the partnership system 'in part' does not work. So, do it in full to truly achieve 'transformational' value. Many times, people say, 'I love your model: it is unique and powerful; but it is hard, it is big, it is not the right time for us, my colleagues protect their patch. So could I use a little bit of this, a little bit of that?'

This does not work. Strategic partnering is not a training programme. It is about years of pursuing relationships and trust, innovation and 'offers' ... and absorbing deep learning through failures and successes. So, if you hit limitations, scale your participation down, select one or two partnerships only but apply the model in full to them and complete the development journey in its entirety and purity.

Viren Doshi

Strategic partnering is like this: you cannot be rich by talking about being rich, or you cannot be happy by talking about being happy. You cannot build a big account by talking about it – you have got to do the right things. And doing the right things requires patience.

It helps to take the focus off your own agenda, so that you can focus on your partner's agenda. That's where a lot of organizations make mistakes in building strategic partnerships – they front-load the initial interfaces with their own agenda.

Don't get us wrong. It is absolutely appropriate and valid to use some of the techniques of the model with the next groups down in the relationship pyramid, such as global or key accounts in the commercial world. We have seen this done with very positive effects, enhancing the organization's relationship practice and delivering 'improve' and even 'enhance' value with these groups. But it is extremely unlikely that such partial use of the model would lead to strategic partnerships and 'transform' value.

A few little secrets

There are lots of 'little' secrets of major importance to success in these pages. Let's bring up a few again:

- care deeply and give;
- them before you;
- the model first and in full;
- no compromise on quality;
- SPMs are like the priests in the army;
- VOMs and workstream leaders are key;
- relationships exist in support of substance;
- build authority from excellence;
- what is the simple clear 'story'?;
- don't ask your target partner what they want;
- prepare, prepare, prepare;
- support and challenge;
- mastermind your 'navigation';
- 'day-after-day'; no negotiation;
- inputs are the 'performance';
- 'transformational' value is the only 'destination';
- 365/24 personal attention;
- embrace ambiguity;
- absolute resilience and determination.

It is worth it every single day!

At the point of putting a full stop to *Strategic Partnering*, our ambition is to leave one single legacy from it, which is: the value case for strategic partnering done well is multi-dimensional and compelling. Accessing the 'transformational' prize is predicated on applying a complete system. Winning requires execution and operation of this model thoroughly and consistently. Your outcome with be magic and you will be unique!

Let's leave the final word to Kevin Murray, who was instrumental in inspiring this book.

Kevin Murray

In today's world of increasing uncertainty, volatility and change, the role of strategic partnerships can only increase because it is the only way that institutions and companies will be agile enough, flexible enough, adaptable enough to succeed in a context that is changing so fast. But they themselves couldn't adapt fast enough to meet those changing needs. So the more great partnerships you have, the more options you have got, the better you will be able to adapt to the changes at the record pace that is the feature of today's business world. So, I think it is all about agility, and by folding in more partnerships, you build in greater agility to meet changes in demand.

Best of luck with your strategic partnering-led 'transformation'. Let us know how it goes – or maybe we'll just look for you and your partners in the successful headlines of the business press!

MEET THE LEADERS INTERVIEWED FOR THIS BOOK

Jill Ader

Member of the Board, Egon Zehnder International

Jill Ader sits on the Board of Egon Zehnder International and focuses on board effectiveness and succession, including Chairmen, Non-Executive and CEO mandates. She spent her early career with NatWest Bank before moving into strategy consulting and then retail with Kingfisher. She joined Egon Zehnder, one of the largest search firms, in 1995 and has worked with board-level executives for the last decade.

Tom Albanese

Former Chief Executive Officer, Rio Tinto Group

Tom Albanese was the Chief Executive Officer and Board Member of the Rio Tinto Group from 2006 until he stepped down in January 2013. He joined Rio Tinto in 1993 on Rio Tinto's acquisition of Nerco and held a series of senior management positions before being appointed Chief Executive of the company's Industrial Minerals group in 2000. After this he became Chief Executive of the Copper group and Head of Exploration in 2004. He served as Director of Ivanhoe Mines from 2006 to 2007, Director of Palabora Mining from 2004 to 2006, and was a member of the Executive Committee of the International Copper Association from 2004 to 2006. He has been a member of the

Board of Visitors, Duke University, Fuqua School of Business, since 2009 and has recently joined the Board of Canada's Franco-Nevada.

Andrew Bester

Group Director, Chief Executive Officer, Commercial Banking – Lloyds Banking Group

Andrew Bester is Group Director and CEO Commercial Banking at Lloyds Banking Group, responsible for commercial banking for all Lloyds clients from the smallest business to the very largest global company. His focus is to build on the bank's 300 year heritage and create a truly client-centric commercial banking business that will help restore pride in banking in the UK. Andrew is a broad-based General Manager having worked across frontline client-facing roles, product management, finance and general management roles across three different continents. He has spent most of his senior career specializing in transforming businesses toward pure client-led business models. Prior to joining Lloyds, he was with Standard Chartered as Global COO and CFO of Consumer Banking and was a key member of the team that pivoted the business from being product-led to client-led. Prior to that, he led the Wholesale business for Standard Chartered in both Africa and then Greater China, driving a pure client-led banking business. Andrew qualified as a Chartered Accountant and is a keen sportsman. He enjoys skiing, cricket, cycling and golf and has completed 21 marathons.

Lord John Browne of Madingley

Former Group Chief Executive, BP

Lord Browne is a Partner at Riverstone Holdings LLC, a leading energy and power investment firm. Prior to this he spent 41 years at BP, serving as Group Chief Executive from 1995–2007. Highlighting his enduring passion for engineering and science, he was President of the Royal Academy of Engineering from 2006–2011, and is currently the Chairman of the Trustees of the Queen Elizabeth Prize for Engineering. He is a Fellow of the Royal Society and a foreign member of the US Academy of Arts and Sciences. He was appointed the UK Government's Lead Non-Executive Board member in 2010 and is Chairman of a variety of advisory boards, including the Chairman of the Trustees at Tate. He was knighted in 1998 and made a Life Peer in 2001. He holds degrees from Cambridge and Stanford. Lord Browne's memoirs, *Beyond Business*, were published in 2010 and his new book, *Seven Elements That Have Changed the World* (2013), blends science, history and reminiscence to tell the stories of the chemical elements that have had the biggest global impact.

Lord Sebastian Coe CH, KBE

Chairman, British Olympic Association and CSM Sports and Entertainment

Sebastian Coe is Executive Chairman of CSM Sport and Entertainment and was elected Chairman of the British Olympic Association. He was Chairman of the London Organising Committee for the Olympic Games and Paralympic Games (LOCOG), having previously been Chairman of the London 2012 bid company. Coe set 12 world records during his athletic career and at the Olympic Games in Moscow in 1980, he won Gold in the 1500m and Silver in the 800m, a feat which he repeated in Los Angeles in 1984. He retired from competitive athletics in 1990 and became a Conservative Member of Parliament. In 2002 he was made a Peer. He received a Knighthood in the 2006 New Year's Honours List. Coe is global adviser to Nike and works with Chelsea Football Club. He is Vice President of the International Association of Athletic Federations (IAAF) and Chairman of the Sports Honours Committee. He received a Companion of Honour in the 2013 New Year's Honours List.

Iain Conn

BP Group Managing Director and Chief Executive Refining & Marketing

Iain Conn is Group Managing Director and Chief Executive, Refining and Marketing at BP. In this role he is accountable for the Group's customer-facing businesses in fuels refining and marketing, petrochemicals and lubricants globally. He also has Group regional responsibility for Europe, Southern Africa and Asia Pacific. He is also responsible for Brand, Sales and Marketing and Strategic Accounts. He joined BP oil international in 1986, working in a variety of roles in commercial refining and oil trading and in corporate headquarters before moving to BP exploration in Colombia in 1996. At the end of 1997, he became Senior Vice President of BP oil in the US, responsible for retail and commercial marketing operations, refining and supply. On the merger between BP and Amoco, in 1999 he became Vice President of BP Amoco exploration's mid-continent business unit. At the end of 2000, he returned to London as Group Vice President and a member of the refining and marketing segment's executive committee, with responsibility for marketing in developing markets, and then Europe. From 2002 until 2004, he was Chief Executive of BP petrochemicals and led the strategy to divest of BP's European and US Olefins and Derivatives activities. On joining the BP Board in 2004 he had responsibility for many Group Functions and Regions, including Safety, Marketing, Human Resources, Technology, IT and Procurement. He took up his current role in 2007.

Ian Davis

Former Worldwide Managing Director, McKinsey & Company

Ian Davis is Chairman of Rolls Royce and a non-executive Director on the Boards of BP and Johnson & Johnson. He is a non-executive member of the UK Government's Cabinet Office Board. He spent more than thirty years with McKinsey & Company, including six as Chairman and Worldwide Managing Director. During his time with McKinsey, Ian served as a consultant to a range of global organizations across the private, public and not-for-profit sectors. He is also senior adviser to Apax Partners LLP.

Lord Paul Deighton

Commercial Secretary to HM Treasury

Lord Paul Deighton took up the post of Commercial Secretary to the Treasury in January 2013, having served as Chief Executive of the London Organising Committee of the Olympic and Paralympic Games (LOCOG), which was responsible for preparing and staging the London 2012 Games. Over six and a half years as CEO, he was in charge of day-to-day operations, overseeing recruitment of a workforce of around 6,000 paid staff, 70,000 volunteers and 100,000 contractor roles, as well as overseeing LOCOG's procurement programme. Over its eight year life, LOCOG achieved revenues of £2.41 billion generated through the private sector, while managing £2.38 billion of expenditure. Prior to joining London 2012, Lord Deighton was the Chief Operating Officer of Goldman Sachs in Europe, and a member of its European Management Committee.

Viren Doshi

Senior Partner at Booz & Company

Viren Doshi is a Senior Partner and Leader of the Energy practice at Booz & Company with 30 years of industry experience, primarily in the oil and gas sectors. Viren is recognized professionally for his insight and knowledge in delivering business transformation, business evaluation and strategy formulation, supply chain management, trading in volatile markets, and business models for market leadership. Prior to joining Booz & Company, Viren conducted operational reviews of Exxon affiliates in Europe and Africa for Esso Europe. He also worked in systems engineering at ICL.

Peter Foss

Former President, Corporate Accounts, General Electric

Peter Foss was President of the General Electric Company's Olympic Sponsorship and Corporate Accounts from 2003–2013. With GE for 35 years, he served in multiple diverse roles, including as General Manager for Enterprise Selling and as the President of GE Polymerland, a commercial organization representing GE Plastics in the global marketplace. Foss serves as a Director of CBF, Capital Bank, N.A., and Capital Bank Corporation and Green Bankshares, Inc., two subsidiary bank holding companies in which CBF has a majority interest.

Dr. rer. pol. h. c. Francisco Javier Garcia Sanz

Member of the Board of Management, Volkswagen AG

Since 2001, Francisco Javier Garcia Sanz has been a member of the Board of Management of Volkswagen AG with responsibility for Procurement. He performs these duties in addition to his tasks as member of the Board of Management of the Volkswagen Passenger Cars Brand responsible for Procurement, a function assigned to Francisco in 1996. In addition, he is Chairman of the Board of Directors of SEAT, S.A. (Barcelona). Before joining Volkswagen AG in 1993, Francisco was Executive Director Worldwide Purchasing at GM Corporation in Detroit (USA). He has an honorary doctorate from the Institute of Business Administration at the University of Stuttgart.

Mike Glenn

Executive Vice President, Market Development and Corporate Communications – FedEx Corporation

Mike Glenn is Executive Vice President of Market Development and Corporate Communications for FedEx Corporation. He also serves as President and Chief Executive Officer of FedEx Corporate Services, responsible for all marketing, sales, customer service and retail operations, for all FedEx companies. Before FedEx Corporation was formed in 1998, Glenn was Senior Vice President, Worldwide Marketing, Customer Service and Corporate Communications for FedEx Express. Glenn currently serves on the Board of Directors for Pentair, Inc. and Level (3) Communications.

Jeff Immelt

Chairman of the Board and Chief Executive Officer, General Electric

Jeff Immelt has been President and Chief Executive Officer of GE since 2000. During his thirty-year career at the company his global leadership positions have included roles in GE's Plastics, Appliances and Healthcare businesses. Immelt has been named one of the 'World's Best CEOs' three times by Barron's, and since he began serving as CEO, GE has been named 'America's Most Admired Company' in a poll conducted by Fortune magazine as well as one of 'The World's Most Respected Companies' in polls by Barron's and the Financial Times. Immelt was Chairman of President Obama's Council on Jobs and Competitiveness.

Michael Johnson

Four Times Olympic Gold Medallist; Founder of Michael Johnson Performance

Michael Johnson is a four-times Olympic track and field gold medallist, nine-times World Champion and world record holder. During his 11-year career, Johnson established a record of 13 Olympic and World Championship medals, all of them gold. Johnson represented the USA in the Olympics on three occasions. After his retirement in 2001, he founded Michael Johnson Performance with a mission to help athletes of all ages and all sports reach their full potential, using the same training philosophy and training techniques he used as an athlete. He has also gone on to establish himself as a leading corporate motivational speaker, and has achieved success as a television commentator and personality, working primarily for BBC in the UK. Johnson received his bachelor's degree in marketing from Baylor University.

Shelly Lazarus

Chairman Emeritus, Ogilvy & Mather

Shelly Lazarus is Chairman Emeritus of Ogilvy & Mather. Shelly has been working, as she would say it, 'in the business I love,' for more than four decades, almost all of that time at Ogilvy & Mather. Shelly rose through the ranks of Ogilvy & Mather assuming positions of increasing responsibility in the management of the company, including President of O&M Direct North America, Ogilvy & Mather New York and Ogilvy & Mather North America. She was named worldwide CEO of Ogilvy & Mather in 1996 and Chairman in 1997. She became Chairman Emeritus in July 2012. Shelly serves on the boards of several corporate, philanthropic and academic institutions: The Blackstone Group, General Electric, Merck, New York Presbyterian Hospital, Committee Encouraging Corporate Philanthropy, World Wildlife Fund, Partnership for New York City, Lincoln Center, and the Board of Overseers of Columbia Business School, where she received her MBA.

Alan MacDonald
Vice-Chairman, Citibank/Chief Client Officer

Alan MacDonald serves as Chief Client Officer of Citigroup. He is also Vice Chairman of Citibank. He has served as Chief Operating Officer of Global Banking and as Head of the Global Corporate Bank where his responsibilities covered teams of industry heads, market managers and relationship managers overseeing Citigroup's broad client base of multinational corporations and financial institutions based in North America, Europe and Japan. Prior to Citigroup, he was an economist with the United Nations Economic Commission for Europe.

Andrew Mackenzie
Chief Executive Officer, BHP Billiton

Andrew Mackenzie is Chief Executive Officer of the BHP Billiton Group, BHP Billiton plc and BHP Billiton Ltd. He joined BHP Billiton Group in 2008. Prior to this, he served as Chief Executive Officer, Diamonds & Minerals at Rio Tinto until 2007 and as Chief Executive of Industrial Minerals Division from 2004. His wide-ranging international experience includes 22 years with BP, primarily in the UK and North America in a range of senior positions, including Head of Capital Markets, Chief Reservoir Engineer with oversight of oil and gas reserves and production, Head of Government and Public Affairs worldwide, Group Vice

President Technology and Group Vice President of BP Petrochemicals. From 2005 to 2007, he served as Chairman of the Board of Trustees of the think tank, Demos. He was an Independent Non-Executive Director of Centrica Plc from 2005–2013.

David Marley
Managing Director IBM, BP

Dave is IBM's Managing Director responsible for all of IBM's business with BP. He has been a Managing Director for four strategic clients of IBM and is a recognized thought leader in the field of Information Technology. He is a member of IBM's Integration and Values Team which is comprised of the top three hundred executives responsible for leading IBM. Before joining IBM, he was the CIO of GPU Nuclear and his work was featured in CIO Magazine. He has a Masters in Management from Purdue University. Dave is married with three children and lives in London.

Kevin Murray
Chairman, The Good Relations Group; author of *The Language of Leaders*

Kevin Murray has 40 years of experience in communications, first as a journalist, then in corporate communications, and now consultancy as Chairman of The Good Relations Group, which is part of Chime Communications plc. For the past three decades, Murray has been advising global Chairmen and Chief Executives (and their leadership teams) from a wide range of organizations. He has provided personal coaching for many of these leaders, helping them to become more effective communicators. Previously Kevin was the Director of Communications for British Airways and, before that, Director of Corporate Affairs for the United Kingdom Atomic Energy Authority. He is a former national newspaper journalist and magazine publisher, having started his career as a crime reporter on *The Star* newspaper in Johannesburg. He is also author of a book entitled *The Language of Leaders* (2012), which examines how top CEOs communicate to inspire, influence and achieve results.

Stephen Odell
Executive Vice President, Ford Motor Company and President EMEA

Stephen Odell is a recognized leader in the global auto industry. He is Executive Vice President and President of Europe, Middle East and Africa, Ford Motor Company, where he is leading Ford's transformation in Europe to return to profitable growth through an unprecedented focus on new products, a strong brand and increased cost efficiency. Prior to this, Odell was Group Vice President, Chairman and CEO, Ford of Europe, and also has held other senior posts within Ford. Under Ford's ownership, he was President and CEO of Volvo Car Corporation. He has held a number of senior posts at Mazda Motor Corporation in Europe, the United States, and ultimately in Japan where he was Senior Managing Executive Officer in charge of Marketing, Sales and Customer Services. Odell was also Vice President, Marketing and Sales, Jaguar North America.

Professor Dr Wolfgang Reitzle

Chief Executive Officer, Linde AG

Professor Dr Wolfgang Reitzle is Chief Executive Officer of Linde AG (also known as The Linde Group). His career began in 1976 when he joined BMW AG. For 13 years, he was a member of the Executive Board of the automotive manufacturer, and was credited with bringing many of its most successful products to market. Between 1999 and 2002, Reitzle was Group Vice President at Ford Motor Company and Chairman and CEO of Ford's Premier Automotive Group, overseeing the Volvo, Jaguar, Lincoln, Land Rover and Aston Martin brands. When he left Ford in 2002, he joined Linde AG as Member of the Executive Board and became CEO of Linde AG in 2003. Today, Linde is the world's largest industrial gases company. Wolfgang Reitzle is an Honorary Professor at the Technical University of Munich, Germany. Furthermore, he is Chairman of the Supervisory Board of Continental AG, Hannover, Germany, and Member of the Board of Directors of Holcim Ltd., Jona, Switzerland.

Gerhard Resch-Fingerlos

Partner, Spencer Stuart

Gerhard Resch-Fingerlos leads Executive Assessment Services for Spencer Stuart in Europe, South Africa, the Middle East, India and Asia. In addition, he is a member of the firm's Technology, Communications & Media and Industrial practices. With more than 15 years of consulting experience, he concentrates on top-level search and assessment assignments for international clients.

Dr Ian Robertson (HonDSc)

Member of the Board of Management, BMW AG, Sales and Marketing

Ian Robertson has been a Member of the Board of Management of BMW AG since March 2008, strengthening some of the car industry's most renowned brands – BMW, MINI and Rolls-Royce Motor Cars. Previously, he served as Managing Director at BMW South Africa from 1999 to 2005 and was Chairman and Chief Executive for Rolls-Royce Motor Cars from 2005 to 2012. From 1979 to 1994, he held various management roles at the Rover Group, including Managing Director at Land Rover Vehicles and Group Purchasing Director. He started his career in the automotive industry with the Rover Group in the UK over thirty years ago and his passion for cars has been growing ever since.

John Seifert

Chairman and CEO, Ogilvy & Mather North America

John Seifert is Chairman and CEO of Ogilvy & Mather North America. For over 30 years he has traversed the Ogilvy worldwide network, in client service and agency general management roles in Los Angeles, Chicago, Bangkok, Singapore and New York. John has led branding and strategic communications work for global clients, including: American Express, BP, DuPont, Siemens, GE Capital and many more. He's a member of the O&M Worldwide Board and Executive Committee, and a frequent speaker on the subject of 'New Age' branding.

Sir Martin Sorrell

Chief Executive Officer, WPP

Sir Martin Sorrell is the entrepreneurial founder of WPP plc, the world's largest provider of advertising and marketing communications services. Collectively, WPP employs more than 165,000 people (including associates) in over 3,000 offices in 110 countries. The Group's worldwide companies include: JWT, Ogilvy & Mather Group, Y&R, Grey Group, Mindshare, MEC, MediaCom, Kantar, Wunderman, Burson-Marsteller, Hill+Knowlton Strategies, Cohn & Wolfe, Landor, The Brand Union, AKQA and WPP Digital. Sorrell actively supports the advancement of international business schools – advising Harvard, IESE, the London Business School, the Indian School of Business and the China Europe International Business School. He has been an Ambassador for British Business, and has been publicly recognised with a number of awards including the Harvard Business School Alumni Achievement Award. He received a knighthood in 2000.

Michel Taride

Group President, Hertz International

Michel Taride is Group President of Hertz International at The Hertz Corporation, responsible for the company's car rental and leasing businesses in Europe, the Middle East, Africa and Asia Pacific. The Hertz Corporation brands under his leadership in Hertz International include: Hertz, Dollar, Thrifty, Firefly and Ace Car Rental. Taride has served with Hertz for over 30 years. His industry contributions include advisory board member for The Global Travel & Tourism Partnership, a multi-country educational programme to introduce students in developing economies to career opportunities in travel and tourism. He is also a member of the World Economic Forum's SlimCity Initiative, an exchange between cities and the private sector to support action on resource efficiency in cities.

Dr Shoichiro Toyoda

Honorary Chairman, Toyota Motor Corporation

Shoichiro Toyoda was born 27 February 1925. He graduated from Nagoya University in September 1947 with a degree in engineering and joined Toyota Motor Corporation (TMC) in July 1952. He later earned an engineering doctorate, with the subject of his thesis centered on fuel injection. Automotive technology, quality control and factory management have been primary emphases for Dr Toyoda throughout his career. He became Managing Director in 1961, and after promotions to Senior Managing Director in 1967 and Executive Vice President in 1972, he was named President of Toyota's sales organization in 1981. Upon the merger of the sales and production organizations in 1982, he assumed the presidency of the newly integrated TMC, and later served as Chairman of the Board from 1992 to 1999. After serving on the Board for 57 years, Dr Toyoda now serves as Honorary Chairman, a position he has held since June 1999.

Takeshi Uchiyamada

Chairman of the Board, Toyota Motor Corporation

Takeshi Uchiyamada is Chairman of the Board of Toyota Motor Corporation (TMC). After joining TMC in 1969 and following a number of senior roles, he became Chief Engineer of Vehicle Development Center 2 in 1996, which developed the Prius – the world's first mass-produced gasoline-electric hybrid car. After being named to the Board of Directors in 1998, Uchiyamada became Chief Officer of Vehicle Development Center 2 and Managing Director and Chief Officer of the Overseas Customer Service Operations Center. He was made a Senior Managing Director and Chief Officer of the Vehicle Engineering Group in 2003. In 2004, he became Chief Officer of the Production Control & Logistics Group and in 2005, Executive Vice President and member of the Board. Uchiyamada was appointed Vice Chairman in June 2012 and Chairman of the Board of Toyota Motor Corporation in June 2013. He is also Vice Chairman, Nippon Keidanren (the Japan Business Federation).

Gerard Vittecoq

Former Group President, Caterpillar Inc.

Gerard Vittecoq served as a Group President of Caterpillar for 10 years and led the Energy & Power Systems Group from 2010 until June 2013. After joining Caterpillar in 1975, he held various accounting and finance positions, and served as a Vice President of Caterpillar Inc., Treasurer of Caterpillar Overseas S.A. and Managing Director of several Caterpillar manufacturing plants. Vittecoq is the President of the association of the multinational companies in Geneva (GEM). He is a member of the International Institute for Management Development (IMD) Foundation Board, the Evian Group: Free Trade Think Tank and the World Business Council for Sustainable Development. He is also a Director of Best Buy Co. Inc.

Sir Frank Williams

Founder and Team Principal, Williams

Sir Frank Williams CBE is Founder and Team Principal of the Williams F1 Team. Williams founded Frank Williams Racing Cars in 1966. In 1977, he established Williams Grand Prix Engineering Ltd alongside Patrick Head. The team's first win came in 1979 at the British Grand Prix, and since its foundation Williams has won seven drivers' championships, nine constructors' championships and a total of 114 races. A road accident in 1986 left Williams unable to walk. In 1987, the Queen awarded him the title of CBE, and he was knighted in the 1999 New Year's Honours List. He is also one of only a few non-Frenchmen to have been made a Chevalier of France's Légion d'Honneur, for his work with Renault engines. In 2008, Williams was awarded the Wheatcroft trophy for his contribution to motor sports. In 2010, he received the Helen Rollason Award for 'outstanding achievement in the face of adversity' at the BBC Sports Personality of The Year Awards.

CONTENTS IN FULL

LIST OF FIGURES

INDEX